T0373587

Pursuing Excellence in Healthcare

Preserving America's Academic Medical Centers

Endorsements

"This is a terrific resource for anyone interested in understanding the indispensable role of the academic health center. But this is not an apologia. Dr. Feldman identifies the key problems we need to solve and the kinds of solutions we must adopt to ensure the excellence of our essential missions in research, training, and health care going forward. A book all health care leaders should read and then read again."

Michael M.E. Johns, MD
Chancellor, Emory University

"You will not agree with everything that Dr. Feldman writes in Pursuing Excellence: Preserving America's Academic Medical Centers, which is precisely why you should read and debate it. Scientist, scholar, educator, entrepreneur, and, especially, clinician, Dr. Feldman has given us a provocative and passionate insider's view. It arrives just in time to stimulate our thinking at this moment of great opportunity."

Andrew L. Epstein, MD
Managing Director, Navigant Consulting, Inc.

"This is a splendid book that explores the unique role and contributions of academic medical centers in society. Enhanced by the author's intimate knowledge of the subject matter, it is well structured, easy to read and thought provoking. It details the evolution of academic medical centers from their origins as small, simple enclaves for medical scholars with altruistic motivations to their current form as large, complex enterprises that serve as a home for cutting edge health care, biomedical research and health professional education, and as an economic engine for the communities they serve.

The author underscores the essential importance of excellence in health care as a cornerstone for most successful academic medical centers and explores the synergistic roles of four elements that he proposes as components or spheres of action of a model for a successful academic medical center: structure, research, education and business. Each is explored in some detail, often benefiting from the author's knowledge and personal experience. Always based on fact, the author's passion for the subject matter is ever present and makes this a very interesting book to read. I recommend it for anyone who wants to know about the elements that have shaped and continue to influence the structure and functioning of academic medical centers in the United States. Dr. Feldman is to be congratulated on writing a very important, timely and remarkably entertaining book."

Paul K. Whelton, MB, MD, MSc
President and Chief Executive Officer
Loyola University Health System, Loyola University Medical Center

"This comprehensive overview of the academic medical center enterprise brings together, in a remarkably coherent fashion, history, economics, and politics as they intersect with the traditional academic missions of education, patient care, and research. It is informative and perceptive, with substantive insights and recommendations. The book is a welcome addition to the growing literature in this area."

Steven A. Wartman, MD, PhD, MACP
President/CEO, Association of Academic Health Centers

"Dr. Feldman has done all of us who care deeply about the future of academic medical centers a service in presenting the wealth of facts and thoughtful analysis that he provides in *Pursuing Excellence in Health Care: Preserving America's Academic Medical Centers.* Whether one agrees with his final recommendations or not, his arguments are well developed and persuasive, and the important issues are delineated comprehensively and fairly. I was particularly struck by his introductory comment that the four C's that ought to provide the foundation of our work as physicians—compassion, confidence, commitment and competence—are in danger of being replaced by the four A's that define success in the modern healthcare marketplace—affability, availability, affordability and accessibility. I would take this one step further to say that the greatest value of the academic medical center to society likely resides lies within the four I's: imagination, intellect, innovation and idealism. Reading this book may help us to keep it so."

R. Sanders Williams, MD
Senior Vice Chancellor for Academic Affairs
Duke University School of Medicine

"Arthur Feldman, MD, PhD, has produced a landmark work, documenting the plight of the U.S. academic medical center (AMC), highlighting its importance, and charting a course for securing its successful future. Dr. Feldman appropriately places clinical care at the center or the AMC's mission and insightfully guides the reader through the labyrinth of interdependencies among the AMC's essential clinical, teaching, and research missions. He hones in on the complexities of structure and business operations, exquisitely describing how we got where we are, and providing a clear vision for surviving and thriving in the upcoming challenging era. Dr. Feldman's book is a must-read for all stakeholders in the mission of preserving what is good about US healthcare and fixing all that is broken about it."

Marvin A. Konstam, MD
Chief Physician Executive
The CardioVascular Center, Tufts Medical Center
Professor of Medicine, Tufts University School of Medicine

"Art Feldman has done a great service to the world of academic medicine by conceptually redesigning the "three legged stool" academic medical center architecture into a thoroughly modern pyramid with academics, business, structure, and research as its base and outstanding clinical care as the apex. The ramifications for AMC leadership effectiveness of acknowledging and embracing this bold revision are profound—as are the accompanying challenges of identifying, preparing, and sustaining such leaders. Dr. Feldman's comprehensive and insightful perspective on the AMC's dilemma in our time not only validates and informs the struggle AMC leaders face but illuminates potential strategies for their success going forward. Kudos!"

Stephen Blattner, MD, MBA
Founding Principal of exägoMD, LLC
Sponsor of the Health Care Leadership Blog
(www.healthcareleadershipblog.com)

Pursuing Excellence in Healthcare

Preserving America's Academic Medical Centers

Arthur M. Feldman, MD, PhD

Foreword by Edward J. Benz, Jr., MD

CRC Press
Taylor & Francis Group
Boca Raton London New York

CRC Press is an imprint of the
Taylor & Francis Group, an **informa** business

A PRODUCTIVITY PRESS BOOK

Productivity Press
Taylor & Francis Group
270 Madison Avenue
New York, NY 10016

International Standard Book Number: 978-1-4398-1657-8 (Hardback)

Library of Congress Cataloging-in-Publication Data

Feldman, Arthur M. (Arthur Michael), 1949-
   Pursuing excellence in healthcare : preserving America's academic medical centers
/ Arthur M. Feldman.
      p. ; cm.
   Includes bibliographical references and index.
   ISBN 978-1-4398-1657-8 (hardcover : alk. paper)
   1. Academic medical centers--United States. I. Title.
   [DNLM: 1. Academic Medical Centers--United States. WX 27 AA1 F312p 2010]

RA981.A2F45 2010
362.12--dc22   2009026677

Visit the Taylor & Francis Web site at
http://www.taylorandfrancis.com

and the Productivity Press Web site at
http://www.productivitypress.com

To my mentors, who passed on to me the traditions of excellence

Kenneth L. Baughman, MD

Michael R. Bristow, MD, PhD

Saul W. Brusilow, MD

Myron L. Weisfeldt, MD

Foreword

Academic medical centers (AMCs) have served a unique and vital role in the advancement of health both nationally and worldwide. Their uniqueness arises from the special way that they combine biomedical research, clinical research, high-quality professional education, and a full array of cutting-edge clinical services within one entity. During the roughly 100 years of their existence, they have become worldwide models for the kind of organizational framework that best promotes the application of new medical knowledge to improve healthcare. AMCs have also become the almost exclusive source of highly educated and qualified physicians, nurses, and allied health professionals in the United States.

Along the way, particularly in the half century since the introduction of Medicare, AMCs have also become enormously large business enterprises. In some urban areas, these centers have become the largest nonfederal employer in the region. As a result of this evolution, AMCs have become something quite a bit more complicated and embedded in the "real world" of highly competitive medical care delivery than they were intended to be when first conceived in the late nineteenth century. Long ago, AMCs ceased to be the small, fraternal enclave of medical scholars providing virtually free care to the local "charity" hospitals where they trained the next generation of physicians and scientists. Most AMCs are now sprawling enterprises employing thousands of faculty and tens of thousands of workers of all types.

As inherently hybrid, multimission organizations, AMCs make unique contributions to society that should ensure their existence and even prosperity far into the future. However, the "hybrid" nature of the organizations also threatens their very existence. As healthcare providers, AMCs compete in an increasingly Darwinian marketplace with equally large and capable healthcare service organizations that can devote all of their energies and resources to the provision of services. Even at the high "quaternary care" end, these services are increasingly commoditized and priced in a reimbursement environment that forces everyone to operate on razor-thin margins.

As scholarly enclaves, AMCs must compete with universities and research institutions for the very best academic talent. AMCs must live in and harmonize with two very distinct cultures whose end games often seem to be impossibly incompatible. Managing and leading AMCs have thus become an exercise in survival and the exquisite art of balancing competing missions, constituencies, business realities, and cultures. All of these must be aligned to achieve the fundamental aspiration of adding unique value to society and improving the nation's health.

Given the massive investment this nation has made in AMCs and their profound societal and economic impact, it is surprising that relatively little has been written about them as societal and economic entities. Articulating who we are, what we should be, and how we can fulfill that destiny is a vitally needed work of scholarship. In this regard, this work, *Pursuing Excellence: Preserving America's Academic Medical Centers,* by Arthur M. Feldman, MD, PhD, is a seminal contribution. To my knowledge, Dr. Feldman has made the first comprehensive effort to assess in one work the mission, values, opportunities, and challenges of modern AMCs as they face a world in the twenty-first century that is very different from the world they were created to address in the twentieth century.

Feldman has looked at AMCs dispassionately from the point of view of how well they have or have not met their aspirations; however, he maintains his passion for what they could and should be. He adjusts his lens at different times so that the reader can understand the centers from multiple perspectives—from their academic and translational role, their role as economic forces and employment engines, and their role as generators of biotechnology. He has provided a highly readable history of the external forces that have shaped and altered AMCs. He reviews concisely how those forces challenge the fidelity with which these centers can adhere to the unique purpose that they can serve in society. Given the potential for a book covering the subject to be overly dry, overly polemical, or overly "whiny," the author has also done a remarkable job of taking an objective observer's view and mixing it appropriately with his own "insider" view as a distinguished professor and scholar, as well as successful academic leader.

Our enterprise needs a cohesive written work that states in explicit terms who we should be, how well we are doing in achieving that aspiration, and how we might best address the challenges that face us in the future. *Pursuing Excellence* comes as close to achieving that goal as any work that I have encountered in the recent past. This book is a good and important read for anyone aspiring to excel as a leader within an academic medical center. We are indebted to Dr. Feldman for taking on this daunting challenge and discharging it so effectively.

Edward J. Benz, Jr., MD

Contents

Acknowledgments

This book was made possible by the patience and support of countless friends and colleagues in academic medicine who took the time over lunches and dinners and on the phone to share with me their experiences in leading divisions, departments, and schools. Some conversations were brief and others were far more in depth, but all of them contributed to my understanding of the complex workings of America's many academic medical centers. Many of these conversations were facilitated by three organizations that provide a format for physician leaders to interact both academically and socially: the Association of University Cardiologists, the Association of Professors of Cardiology, and the Association of Professors of Medicine. In the case of the Association of Professors of Medicine, Web linkages provide a unique opportunity for department of medicine chairs to communicate with their colleagues in order to address questions of importance across the broad spectrum of academic medicine.

Particular thanks go to Charles Porter, Gervasio Lamas, James Young, Marvin Konstam, Douglas Mann, Barry Lembersky, Edward Benz, and Michael Bristow, who have allowed me to pick their brains about structure or restructuring at their institutions. Special thanks also go to Andrew Epstein and his colleagues at the Bard Group, (Navigant Consulting) who nursed me through a "change project" at my institution and taught me a great deal about restructuring academic medical centers and the daunting challenge of trying to change academic culture.

I also acknowledge the help of numerous colleagues in industry who provided me with background information that allowed me to compare and contrast the "business of industry" with the "business of medicine." Special thanks go to Guido Neels, Ginger Graham, and Jan Leshly, who provided important insights into the structure and organization of the medical device and pharmaceutical industries and how they allocate funds, identify and evaluate new opportunities, and manage their various enterprises. Special thanks also to Susan S. Lefkowitz, who provided an outlook on the financial structure of various health delivery systems and academic medical centers.

I would also like to thank Kristine Mednansky, who believed in the value of this book, and the group at Taylor & Francis that brought it to life. Their support has been indispensable. The staff of the library of the Thomas Jefferson University provided continuing help in tracking down sometimes arcane references. This book would not have been possible without the superlative support of two individuals: my editor, Kathleen O'Hara, who took what several initial readers described as an encyclopedia and molded it into a coherent plan for change, and Marianne LaRussa, who worked tirelessly to translate my hieroglyphics into the English language. Finally, I am eternally grateful for the love and support of my wife, Susan, and my daughters, Emily Kate and Elizabeth Willa, who put up with my many nights and vacations on the computer and who make whatever I do worth doing.

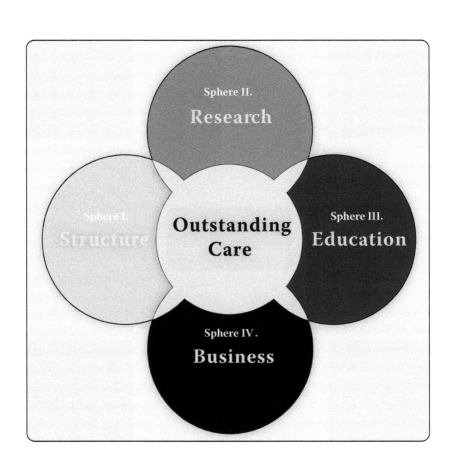

Sphere II.
Research

Sphere I.
Structure

**Outstanding
Care**

Sphere III.
Education

Sphere IV.
Business

Introduction

'Tis no idle challenge which we physicians throw out to the world when we claim that our mission is of the highest and of the noblest kind, not alone in curing disease but in educating the people in the laws of health, and in preventing the spread of plagues and pestilence.

Sir William Osler
McGill Medical School, January 8, 1895 [1]

In the summer of 1964, my father was hospitalized on the Marburg Medical Service at The Johns Hopkins Hospital in Baltimore for 6 weeks because of an infection on one of the valves of his heart. I became friendly with the interns and residents and watched each morning and evening as they marched in their starched white jackets and slacks or skirts from room to room reviewing the progress of each of their patients. The doctors and interns were attentive, responding to any needs of my father; they appeared committed, confident, compassionate, and highly competent.

A week after his admission to the hospital, my father was wheeled out of his room and taken to the historic amphitheatre called Hurd Hall, where his "case" was presented by a resident and discussed by Dr. Philip Tumulty, one of the finest diagnosticians of his era. Like a half century of Hopkins students before them, many of these young physicians would go on to make substantive contributions to the field of medicine through their research or clinical discoveries. Little did I know that some years later I would be sitting in a seat in Hurd Hall and caring for Dr. Tumulty's patients on the wards.

Witnessing the level of care at Hopkins profoundly affected my early image of what being a doctor was all about. I later realized that this experience informed my ongoing passion and commitment to the delivery of outstanding patient care and to academic medicine; this book came about as a result of that commitment. I wrote it because I and many of my academic colleagues know that the academic medical center's mission of providing outstanding patient care and the means to do that is in a critical state that has not been seen since the founding of America's great teaching institutions a century ago.

Funded by a gift from a Baltimore philanthropist, The Johns Hopkins Hospital opened its doors in 1889 and its accompanying medical school admitted its first class in 1893. The Hopkins Hospital and its university and its affiliated medical school formed the model for the creation of academic medical centers (AMCs), or academic health centers, in the United States. These centers provided care to patients regardless of race, gender, or socioeconomic background; they served as the primary training sites for the next generation of clinicians and the home of clinical and basic research that led to transformational changes in patient care. After World War II, AMCs grew as the National Institutes of Health (NIH) supported the costs of research and the accompanying infrastructure.

In addition, the health insurance industry evolved, providing physicians with fees for their services; reimbursements were especially robust for high-cost, high-technology services provided in large part at America's AMCs. As a result, the size of the clinical and research faculties at many AMCs increased substantially [2]. Even moderately sized academic medical centers had dramatic impacts on the economic, medical, and social health of populations in their regions [3]. All was well in the AMC; it flourished, became the standard bearer of care, and was able to fulfill its original societal mission in its community.

By the late 1990s, the fortunes of the AMC began to change, resulting in startling implications for the healthcare industry and, in particular, threatening the core mission of providing outstanding patient care. This alarming trend started with limitations on reimbursements for patient care due to changes in federal regulations, increased competition from community hospitals, external economic pressures, enhanced governmental and public scrutiny, and disadvantageous changes in the traditional financial support systems of AMCs. These combined factors began to take their toll.

Academic leaders began to recognize that the future of AMCs was threatened by changes in the healthcare marketplace and by decreases in public and private support for their educational and research missions [4–6]. The literature became filled with pessimistic views on the health of America's AMCs: "Academic Health Centers: The Making of a Crisis and Potential Remedies" [7], "The Perilous State of Academic Medicine" [8], "Academic Medicine: Boom to Bust" [9], and "Changing Economics of Health Care Are Devastating Academic Medical Centers" [10]. These pessimistic predictions were consistent with the news in the lay press reporting shortfalls and cuts at numerous academic medical centers in geographic locales as diverse as Texas, Boston, and New York [11–15].

Financial problems resulted in the University of Minnesota, George Washington, Indiana, Saint Louis, and Tulane Universities selling their hospitals to for-profit entities. At Georgetown, the financial problems in the medical center became so serious that the university was forced to sell $100 million in bonds to replace reserve funds that it had spent to subsidize hospital losses [16]. Universities jettisoned their academic hospitals for fear that losses in the health system would put the university endowments at risk [16]. Moody's and Standard & Poor's lowered the credit rating of many academic hospitals and healthcare systems making it more difficult for them to borrow money [16]. However, no event raised as much concern as the bankruptcy of the Allegheny Health, Education and Research Foundation (AHERF) and MCP Hahnemann University medical school in 1998—the first bankruptcy of an American AMC [17].

The economic problems of AMCs continued into the twenty-first century. The University of Tennessee Health Science Center in Memphis was recently described as "sick, suffering from aging infrastructure, an inability to pull in top job candidates and dwindling state funds" [18]. The University of Connecticut Health Center reported a $22 million deficit due at least in part to the need for a modern teaching hospital to replace its outdated 224-bed John Dempsey Hospital [19] and the University of Medicine and Dentistry of New Jersey announced that it would not renew the contracts of 18 pediatricians due to a "fiscal crisis" arising from a "large budget deficit" [20].

In addition, the hospital of the University of Medicine and Dentistry of New Jersey reported three straight years of $40 million losses. At the West Virginia University Health Science Center, an outside report noted that the AMC was plagued by "serious leadership and productivity issues" in the Anesthesia Department; an "alarming deficiency of cardio-thoracic surgeons"; an "alarming lack of surgeons in key areas," including trauma, urology, and transplantation; an erosion of operating margins; an atmosphere of "uncertainty and leadership confusion"; and a "lack of cohesive and unified leadership structure" [21].

The financial challenges of today's healthcare economy have severely challenged many AMCs and, as pointed out in an article in the *Chronicle of Higher Education,* they have been asked to "cut back on expensive research, teaching activities, and clinical innovations, or face growing deficits and in some cases, extinction" [22]. The high cost of a medical education has made it increasingly difficult to recruit talented students to academic careers, talented clinicians and scientists have increasingly left academia for positions in the private sector, the public's trust in AMCs has decreased, and continuing turnover in academic leaders has obviated the ability of AMCs to pursue their academic mission. Even AMCs with large endowments are now feeling significant economic pressure because of the global crisis in financial markets.

The global meltdown in the financial markets in 2008 also had a disastrous effect on America's AMCs because many elite AMCs had covered operating expenses using the income from robust endowments. In addition, all AMCs are now faced with caring for a larger number of uninsured patients due to the marked increase in unemployment rates, annual fundraising has lagged behind historic levels, state support for higher education has diminished, and students are finding it increasingly difficult to pay tuitions for graduate school, medical school, and the allied health sciences. As a result, AMCs across the country have frozen salaries, cut budgets, increased tuitions, and delayed needed capital improvements [23–26].

Over the past several decades, the overwhelming challenges of the healthcare environment have led to a change in the underlying culture of the AMC. The unflagging attention to providing outstanding patient care has been replaced by missions more consistent with expediency of care than of quality of care. Although multiple experiences and conversations led to the work that culminated in this book, one event stands out as illustrating the need for readdressing the role of the AMC. It occurred when a senior physician–administrator pointed out to a room full of academic physicians that the keys to the future success of their AMCs were a strict adherence to what he referred to as the four *A*s: affability, availability, affordability, and accessibility. I immediately wondered what had happened to the four *C*s that I had been taught: compassion, confidence, commitment, and competence—hallmarks that were the foundation of my training as a physician.

The grave challenges facing America's AMCs led me to ask an audacious question: How can AMCs compete, survive, and continue to fulfill their societal missions in a highly competitive and hostile marketplace? To answer this question, it was important to understand how successful AMCs differed from less successful AMCs in their core mission of the delivery of outstanding patient care, their organizational and economic structure, their ability to support innovative research and effective education of the next generation of clinicians, and the approaches they took to finance their teaching and scientific enterprises. In addition, it became critical to understand how lessons learned by academic scholars in business and management could be applicable to AMCs and how local and federal governments can be leveraged to support the missions of AMCs.

The efforts to answer this question led to the development of a radically different model for achieving success in academic medical centers: restoring the delivery of outstanding care as the core mission and focus of AMCs. This core mission is supported by focusing efforts on four intersecting spheres of action:

1. developing an integrated structure;
2. pursuing and supporting disease-related research;
3. educating the healthcare workforce; and

4. focusing attention on the "business" of medicine, recognizing that "no margin equals no mission."

Each of these spheres is necessary but not sufficient to support the core mission. All four must work together synergistically in order for the AMC to prosper. Ironically, we will see that many of the fundamental concepts on which each of the four intersecting spheres is built are not new; rather, they were first described by the plans for The Johns Hopkins Hospital in 1875 and by Abraham Flexner in 1910.

Evaluating the Health of America's Academic Medical Centers

In order to evaluate the issues facing the AMC today properly and write this book, a comprehensive understanding of their function, evolution, and historical context was required—as well as a thorough understanding of the "health" of the organization itself. Evaluating the financial health of an AMC is a challenge because, unlike those of public companies, their economic data are not readily available. It is difficult to assess the flow of funds among the medical school, the hospital, and the faculty practice plan (the organization responsible for billing and collecting revenues), and some AMCs have a diverse array of "nonmedical" businesses that provide capital for the AMC but are often not included in its financial statements. It is even more difficult to understand the finances of an AMC when the hospital and the medical school are not integrated as well as when parts of the academic hospital are "owned" or "leased" by outside groups, including physician practices, because each entity then reports its finances separately.

The Association of American Medical Colleges provided important data on the average finances at AMCs but did not provide information regarding individual hospitals or individual medical schools, and the information is self-reported [27]. Some of the most relevant data were obtained from reports in the lay press because the press often has the finances and the clout to obtain data that are impossible for an individual to obtain.

Other important sources of information regarding the overall health of AMCs were trends in NIH funding to medical schools and hospitals that until recently was available for individual AMCs [28], public disclosure of "profit" margins of various academic medical center hospitals, and published support for AMCs from state and local governments. Unfortunately, even state allocations to AMCs are often difficult to follow due to marked differences in how states and academic medical centers show faculty salaries and benefits, Medicaid payments and federal grants, and disproportionate share hospital payments on their individual balance sheets. Information regarding endowment support was available from the capital campaign status reports published each year by the *Chronicle of Higher Education.*

Further information on the overall health of the AMC was obtained from extensive reviews of the literature, investigative reports in the lay press, and visits to many AMCs over the past 4 years. Demographic data from the Association of American Medical Colleges, the Association of Academic Health Centers, and the American Medical Association were also very helpful. Critical information came from conversations with hundreds of academic leaders as well as past and current leaders of major U.S. pharmaceutical and device companies and AMC-related businesses. Healthcare consultants and, in particular, Dr. Andrew Epstein of the Bard Group (Boston) provided additional important background information for this text.

Wherever possible, we have included references to articles in the lay press, studies in the peer-reviewed and non-peer-reviewed scientific and business literature, monographs published by authoritative national organizations, testimony before state legislatures, and numerous textbooks on the history of medicine and from the fields of business management, organization, and leadership. However, to ensure confidentiality and at their requests, we have not annotated the many comments provided by AMC faculty. This has allowed us to provide anecdotes that provide a unique insight into the workings of the AMC.

Why Delivery of Outstanding Patient Care Is the Core Mission of the Model

A distinguishing feature of each of America's great AMCs is an uncompromising focus on providing outstanding patient care. This leads us to the primary message of this work: Success in the AMC's clinical mission is necessary and obligatory for success in the academic mission, including education and research.

In some respects, this concept of the primacy of outstanding patient care is not new. In his letter to the trustees of his new hospital, the Baltimore philanthropist Johns Hopkins wrote: "It will be your special duty to secure for the service of the Hospital, surgeons and physicians of the highest character and greatest skill." In other respects, a model that establishes providing outstanding patient care as the core mission for building the success of an AMC is a radical concept because many academicians view the AMC as having a tripartite mission of research, education, and patient care and they struggle to allocate resources.

In today's competitive healthcare market, some institutions are able to support all three missions, but most are not so fortunate; as a result, limited resources are spread across the three missions. Because AMC revenues are a zero sum game, shifting resources from one mission to support another mission inhibits the ability to pursue excellence in any one of the tripartite missions. By contrast, we will see throughout this text how focusing on the core mission of providing outstanding patient care can allow AMCs to compete effectively in the healthcare marketplace while at the same time enhancing an AMC's ability to excel in research and education also.

The principle of a single core mission effectively enhancing the ability of a complex and multidisciplinary organization to excel across a diverse array of missions or products is not new in the world of business. In 1993, Isaiah Berlin published a landmark book, *The Hedgehog and the Fox* [29]. The unifying concept of the book was that hedgehogs succeed because they simplify a complex agenda into a single idea, principle, or concept that guides everything that they do. In his best selling comparison of good and great companies, Jim Collins found that successful companies succeeded because they were able to focus their efforts on a single core mission determined by identifying what they could be best at, what drove their economic engine, and what they could be deeply passionate about [30].

Therefore, the model presented in this book uses the core mission of providing outstanding patient care as the central defining principle, supported by the four circles or spheres of action intersecting and providing support for the nucleus or core mission.

The Four Spheres of Action

Although outstanding patient care serves as the core focus of many if not most of America's great AMCs, it is difficult to achieve without the synergistic interaction of four fundamental spheres of action: structure, research, education, and business. Although AMCs approach each of these fundamental spheres differently, strong arguments will be presented that an AMC cannot fulfill its societal mission and provide outstanding patient care without successfully addressing each of the four spheres of action and linking them to the core mission. Indeed, we will see that when an AMC loses sight of that core mission, it may abrogate its societal responsibility.

This book is laid out in four main sections that represent each sphere of action. Each section has three chapters that address the complex issues present within each sphere. These complex issues must be addressed in order to achieve the best possible results in each sphere, thereby ensuring the future health of the AMC.

Section 1—Sphere of Action: Structure

In his seminal study of America's AMCs published in 1910, Abraham Flexner noted the importance of the structure of the AMC and in particular its relationship with its accompanying hospital. The report noted that "a hospital under complete educational control is as necessary to a medical school as is a laboratory of chemistry or pathology....Centralized administration of wards, dispensary, and laboratories, as organically one, requires that the school relationship be continuous and unhampered" [31]. Ironically, during the past two decades, many AMCs that were once integrated have separated into their individual components as universities have jettisoned their affiliated hospitals in the fear that financial downturns could adversely influence university endowments. Few of the plans for new medical schools include an association between the medical school and an academic hospital. Indeed, fewer than half of today's academic hospitals have a direct relationship with their affiliated medical school.

The relationships of the various parts of the care delivery system within a given AMC are also often ambiguous. Academic physicians work in departmental silos rather than in cohesive, collaborative, and integrated multidisciplinary teams. However, it is now becoming clear that the current structures of many AMCs are not effective; the following facts can be noted with regard to structure:

- Contemporary AMCs require higher levels of integration among and between the component entities to succeed as a distinctive clinical enterprise in a competitive market.
- Departmental silos are anachronistic at a time when patient care must be multidisciplinary and collaborative.
- AMCs with the highest levels of performance and the best reputations were founded as or are evolving toward highly integrated systems.
- Integrated systems are more able to meet the current challenges facing AMCs and better achieve the goal of providing outstanding patient care.
- A separation of the hospital and the medical school makes it more difficult to take advantage of market opportunities, align vision and strategy across all parts of the AMC, invest in the academic missions of the AMC, and rationally invest in capital improvements.
- Restructuring is not simple and requires a shared vision across the entire AMC regarding the core goals and missions.

There is no perfect structure for any single AMC. However, recognizing that success in the core mission is necessary for success in the academic mission, it is imperative that AMCs undertake self-analysis and restructuring. In Chapters 1, 2, and 3, I will present three fundamental concepts upon which the ideal structure for each AMC can be built while supporting the core mission of excellence of patient care:

Chapter 1 describes the need to integrate the economic and administrative structure of the teaching hospital, the medical school, the practice plan, and the university.

Chapter 2 addresses the need to create a care delivery system that seamlessly links the various components of the healthcare delivery system that have an impact on the care of patients with a specific disease.

Chapter 3 discusses developing a new generation of physician leaders with the authority, the knowledge, and the courage to lead change.

Section 2—Sphere of Action: Research

Over the past century, fundamental discoveries from academic medical centers have resulted in transformational changes in the way that clinicians care for patients with a vast array of diseases. These discoveries have been as diverse as the development of the polio vaccine or the development of novel treatments for some forms of breast cancer. More recently, new scientific discoveries and breakthroughs in technology, including the sequencing of the human genome and advances in stem cell biology, have provided potential opportunities to enhance dramatically our ability to treat human disease in the future. Positioned at the center of both basic and clinical research, AMCs should be poised to translate these scientific breakthroughs into outstanding new methods of patient care that can provide a competitive edge in the healthcare marketplace.

However, it must be remembered that the "best healthcare" cannot be confused with "high-technology healthcare": The highest level of technology might not necessarily be the best healthcare for a given patient. Unfortunately, external and internal impediments now challenge the ability of even America's foremost AMCs to fulfill their research goals.

In a monograph titled, "A Broken Pipeline? Flat Funding of the NIH Puts a Generation of Science at Risk," representatives from six of America's most prestigious AMCs noted that "even as substantial advances appear within our grasp—including breakthroughs in Alzheimer's disease, lung cancer, and depression—they are at risk of slipping away because the NIH is experiencing a dangerous slowdown in funding—one that is unprecedented in the history of the nation's biomedical research enterprise" [32]. These concerns are supported by the following findings:

■ There has been an unprecedented decrease in NIH funding for each of the past 5 years.

- Only 8 out of every 100 scientists submitting an NIH grant will be funded.
- Both young and established investigators are leaving AMCs to pursue careers in industry.
- Well-endowed AMCs have lured teams of funded scientists from smaller AMCs rather than seeking young and less established investigators.
- The difficulty in obtaining NIH funding has caused junior investigators to become conservative in their scientific approaches.
- Physician–scientists have been forced to do more clinical work to support themselves.
- Clinical research has shifted from U.S. academic medical centers to foreign centers.
- High-profile articles in the lay press about conflicts of interest on the parts of scientists and clinicians have led to a loss of public trust.
- The departmental structure of AMCs obviates the development of collaborative and cross-disciplinary research.

In order to regain their international leadership in both basic and clinical science and achieve the core mission of providing outstanding patient care by translating new scientific and technical discoveries into new and novel means of patient care delivery, America's AMCs must address three fundamental concepts:

Chapter 4 discusses fixing the "broken pipeline" of academic scientists and discovery.

Chapter 5 presents the need to resolve the conflict of interest issues that pervade academic medicine.

Chapter 6 describes novel ways to commercialize research discoveries so that AMCs can be less dependent on external funding.

Section 3—Sphere of Action: Education

As part of his landmark study, Abraham Flexner visited each of the 160 U.S. medical schools in existence in 1910. He found that The Johns Hopkins Hospital provided "practically ideal opportunities" for medical education and held the Medical Department of the Johns Hopkins University as a standard. Unfortunately, Hopkins was not typical: The report noted across the United States "an enormous over-production of un-educated and ill trained medical practitioners…in absolute disregard of the public welfare and without any serious thought of the interests of the public" [31].

Flexner blamed the overproduction of ill-trained doctors on "the existence of a very large number of commercial schools…also known as proprietary or for-profit schools." He also noted that although the ideal doctor had to be well educated, "the question is, then, not merely to define the ideal training of the physician; it is just as much, at this particular juncture, to strike the solution that, economic and social factors being what they are, will distribute as widely as possible the best type of physician so distributable" [31].

In response to the Flexner report, state legislatures across the country passed regulations that resulted in the closure of the many proprietary medical schools, and medical educators and hospital officials recognized that education and research improved patient care. By 1925, modern teaching hospitals had been created across the country. After World War II, academic departments increased in size as grants from the National Institutes of Health supported the research efforts of the faculty, many of the patients treated at AMCs paid for their care through health insurance plans, and fee-for-service, third-party reimbursements increased for the high-cost, high-technology services found at many AMCs [33]. Medical school leaders could cross-subsidize the teaching programs of the AMC with the high reimbursements for patient care.

However, over the past two decades, a variety of economic and demographic factors has combined to threaten the educational mission of the AMC. This in turn has threatened the ability of the physician workforce to fulfill its core mission of delivery of outstanding care for patients. Some of the factors include:

- The United States faces a critical shortage in the physician workforce.
- It is increasingly difficult for AMCs to recruit and retain the high-quality physicians needed to teach the next generation of physicians.
- Graduating physicians—over half of whom are women—have sought specialties that are more "family friendly" and offer a more controllable lifestyle, thereby drawing them away from research or primary care specialties.
- The Balanced Budget Act of 1997 capped the number of postgraduate training positions in the United States. This resulted in limited postgraduate training opportunities.
- The high cost of a medical education coupled with high indebtedness and comparatively low salaries for many specialties has had an undue influence on students' career choices.
- New medical schools have evolved without affiliations with research universities, existing medical schools, or sophisticated quaternary hospitals.
- The regulatory agencies that oversee medical education are diffuse and poorly integrated.
- The ability of some AMCs to support the full cost of a medical education for all or a substantial number of their students threatens to result in the development of a two-tiered system of medical education.
- AMCs must face the challenge of incorporating rapidly evolving science and technology into the clinical education of students and graduates.

America's AMCs must focus their efforts on ensuring that the next generation of physicians receives a level of education that allows them to provide outstanding patient care. To do this, they must create a new generation of clinician–educators and clinician–scientists to serve as teachers and role models by excelling in both the art and science of medicine. This will not be an easy task, but it can be facilitated by pursuing three fundamental concepts in Chapters 7, 8, and 9, which provide the framework for the education sphere for future AMCs:

> Chapter 7 looks at how to resolve the physician workforce crisis by expanding current medical schools or building the right kinds of new medical schools.
>
> Chapter 8 addresses the changing demographics of America's trainees.
>
> Chapter 9 describes how to improve the clinical training of America's future workforce by focusing on professionalism.

Section 4—Sphere of Action: Business

In his report to the Carnegie Foundation in 1910, Abraham Flexner pointed out the relationship between finances and the quality of American medical schools. He criticized schools that had poor financial underpinning as well as those that used positive margins to pay "well-to-do" clinicians or "professors in regular practice" or to "pay out fees salaries to some of the most successful practitioners in New York City while the laboratory branches still lack anything like uniform development" [31]. In the years after World War II, NIH funding, lucrative reimbursements from health insurance companies, and robust returns for high-technology services provided at many academic medical centers allowed AMC leaders to fund the many missions of the AMC without focusing on the "business" of the academic enterprise. However, in the mid-1990s, the financial health of AMCs changed dramatically as impediments to financial success multiplied:

- Third-party payers became unwilling to support the academic and research missions of the AMC despite harboring billion-dollar margins.
- Community hospitals became active competitors for high-technology care.
- The Balanced Budget Act of 1997 lowered the financial margin for many AMCs by 35–50%.
- NIH funding decreased substantially between 2003 and 2008.
- At a time when U.S. industry pays nearly $30 billion to support clinical research, the majority of the research is performed outside the United States.
- Many public hospitals closed due to inadequate state or community support.

- AMCs were forced to care for over 60% of the 47 million uninsured patients in the United States.
- Only 30% of U.S. academic medical centers reported positive margins.
- Federal funding fell far short of the dollars necessary to support the education activities of AMCs.
- Rising costs in malpractice insurance fees and large verdicts in states without caps changed the geographic distribution of many physicians and adversely affected AMCs.
- The catastrophic collapse of U.S. and global financial markets has increased the number of patients without health insurance, depleted revenues from endowment portfolios, and decreased yearly fundraising efforts. This has resulted in AMCs having to trim budgets by as much as $100 million.

Although each of the intersecting spheres of action plays a critical role in allowing AMCs to overcome the unique set of internal and external challenges they face in achieving their core mission of providing outstanding patient care, the importance of the business sphere cannot be overemphasized. If Flexner had written his landmark text in 2008, he might have expressed the importance of the AMCs' business mission as "no margin—no mission." In Chapters 10, 11, and 12, I present three specific concepts fundamental to incorporating business practices into the culture of the AMC:

Chapter 10 describes the need to develop new and innovative methods to finance the missions of the AMC.
Chapter 11 presents novel ways in which AMCs can develop strategic regional and global collaborations.
Chapter 12 points out the need to obtain consistent governmental and community support.

A Heritage of Excellence: Continuing the Core Mission

Each Friday morning, a hundred medical residents at Hopkins, a large number of Hopkins faculty and graduates of the Hopkins medical residency across the country, and I take from our drawers a dark blue tie or a scarf emblazoned with a group of small silver shields. Upon each shield is the word *Aequanimitas,* meaning calm in the face of adversity. This was the title of a speech that William Osler presented at the time of his departure for his new position at Hopkins in 1889 to the graduating class of the University of Pennsylvania School of Medicine, the leading center of medical education at the time.

At first, I viewed the tie as a badge of honor worn by those who had survived one of the most demanding medical residencies in the country. However, over time I realized that we did not wear the tie each Friday to mark our membership in the Hopkins fraternity. Rather, we did so as a reminder and a reaffirmation of the heritage of excellence passed on as an unbroken chain from Osler to his numerous successors and the primacy of outstanding patient care in all that we do as physicians, educators, and investigators. Osler's message becomes ever more important today as physicians face increasing adversity.

Subsequent chapters of this book will point out the many changes that have occurred in the field of medicine. In truth, the field has never been without change. Similar to every field of endeavor built on technology, medicine has moved forward and each of these advances has required transformational changes in the way we care for patients.

To some, the changes that have occurred over the last decade have outstripped any that came before them. However, physicians who trained in the 1930s might argue that the introduction of penicillin and other antibiotics in the 1940s might have done more to change the practice of medicine than any group of innovations that have occurred since, and their arguments might well have merit. We will see that although some AMCs have struggled over the past decade to maintain their core missions, others have continuously topped the list of the most outstanding medical centers year after year. It is the goal of this book to present a model that will allow AMCs to continue to deliver the highest quality of care to their patients despite the adversity that surrounds academic medicine.

Thus, the model that is presented is not one that can apply only to some AMCs, but rather is a model that should be applicable, at least in part, to all AMCs. In addition, the reader will see that outstanding patient care is not just about the acute care delivered to a hospitalized patient by doctors and nurses; it is also about public and community health, disease prevention, the effects of poverty and racism on health and disease, issues of nutrition, facilities for care of the elderly, and palliative care and attention to end of life issues.

From a pragmatic standpoint, I have provided the reader with a model that an AMC can utilize to attain success fulfilling its core mission of providing outstanding patient care by addressing the four spheres of action and utilizing the recommendations of each chapter. Many of the issues discussed and even the model we present will raise controversy and discussion; in fact, this is a secondary goal of this work because many of these concerns have gone on for over a decade without adequate attention or debate. Thus, I invite the reader to question my conclusions as well as the model.

However, I hope that this book will bring forth additional emotions: frustration at the inability of some AMCs to take the courageous steps necessary to ensure the delivery of outstanding patient care and anger at the absence of governmental and community support and oversight for a group of institutions that should sit at the very core of our national agenda. I hope that this book will engender debate among healthcare providers, governmental agencies, and the general public while at the same time serving as a call to action for those empowered to effect change in our individual AMCs as well as in our nation's healthcare delivery system.

Arthur Feldman

References

1. Hinohara, S., and Hisae, N., eds. 2001. *Osler's "A Way of Life" and other addresses with commentary and annotations.* Durham, NC: Duke University Press.
2. Stevens, R. 1986. Issues for American internal medicine through the last century. *Annals of Internal Medicine* 105 (4): 592–602.
3. Health News. 2007. Academic health centers measure $3.05 billion impact on three-county region (http://healthnews.uc.edu/news/?/316).
4. Kassirer, J. P. 1994. Academic medical centers under siege. *New England Journal of Medicine* 331 (20): 1370–1371.
5. Carey, R. M., and Engelhard, C. L. 1996. Academic medicine meets managed care: A high-impact collision. *Academic Medicine* 71 (8): 839–845.
6. Berns, K. I. 1996. Preventing academic medical centers from becoming an oxymoron. *Academic Medicine* 71 (2): 117–120.
7. Beller, G. A. 2000. President's page: Academic health centers: The making of a crisis and potential remedies. *Journal of the American College of Cardiologists* 36 (4): 1428–1431.
8. Pardes, H. 2000. The perilous state of academic medicine. *Journal of the American Medical Association* 283 (18): 2427–2429.
9. Friedenberg, R. M. 2001. Academic medicine: Boom to bust. *Radiology* 220 (2): 296–298.
10. VanDerWerf, M. 1999. Changing economics of health care are devastating academic medical centers. *The Chronicle of Higher Education* (http://chronicle.com/weekly.v45/i37/37a03801.htm).
11. Greene, J. 2000. Faculty cuts weighed at Texas med school (www.ama-assn.org/amednews/2000/04/24/prsb0424.htm). *American Medical News,* Apr. 24, 9, 11.
12. Goldberg, C. 1999. Teaching hospitals battle Medicare money cuts. *New York Times,* May 6.
13. Pham, A. 1995. In unusual move, Beth Israel to cut 80 management jobs. *Boston Globe,* Dec. 8.

14. Kowalczyk, L. 2000. Beth Israel begins layoffs to counter 1999 losses. *Boston Globe*, D7.
15. Kennedy, R. 1999. New York hospitals braced for cuts. *New York Times*, May 6.
16. http://chronicle.com/weekly/v45/i37/37a03801.htm
17. Wickware, P. 1999. Stanford donation funds for transdisciplinary center. *Nature Medicine* 5 (12): 1338.
18. Sledge, C. 2008. Money woes beset medical school at UT-Memphis. *Tennessean*, Mar. 21.
19. Waldman, H. 2008. Health center deal urged. *The Hartford Courant*, Mar. 19.
20. Stewart, A. 2008. Pediatrics staff takes major cut at UMDNJ. *The Newark Star-Ledger*, Mar. 17.
21. www.health.wvu.edu/rvrr/rvreport.pdf
22. Thier, S., and Keohane, N. 1998. Point of view: How can we assure the survival of academic health centers? *Chronicle of Higher Education*, Mar. 13, A64.
23. Brody, A. 2009. Message from President Brody to the Johns Hopkins community (www.jhu.edu/news_info/news/univ09/feb09/economy.html).
24. Twedt, S. 2009. UPMC shows losses, gains. *Pittsburgh Post-Gazette* (www.post-gazette.com/pg/09044/948799_28.stm).
25. Cordle, I. 2009. Budget cuts, pay freeze on horizon at University of Miami. *Miami Herald*, Feb. 16.
26. Lichter, J. 2009. Med tightens purse strings in recession. *The Duke Chronicle* (www.dukechronicle.com/home/index.cfm).
27. www.aamc.org
28. http://grants.nih.gov/grants/award/research
29. Berlin, I. 1993. *The hedgehog and the fox*. Chicago: Elephant Paperbacks.
30. Collins, J. 2001. *Good to great*, 300. New York: Harper Collins Publishers Inc.
31. Flexner, A. 1973. Medical education in the United States and Canada: A report to the Carnegie Foundation for the Advancement of Teaching, 239. Bulletin no. 4, New York (reprinted by The Heritage Press, Buffalo, NY).
32. www.BrokenPipeline.org. The broken pipeline.
33. Ludmerer, K. 1999. *Time to heal: American medical education from the turn of the century to the era of managed care*, 514. New York: Oxford University Press.

SPHERE OF ACTION: STRUCTURE

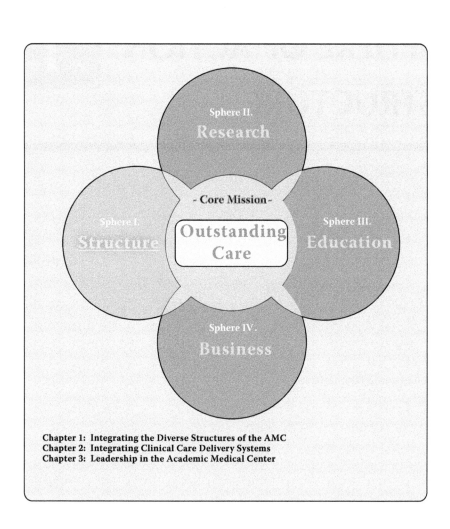

Sphere II.
Research

- Core Mission -
Outstanding
Care

Sphere I.
Structure

Sphere III.
Education

Sphere IV.
Business

Chapter 1

Integrating the Diverse Structures of Academic Medical Centers

The true interests of the Hospital and of the Medical School seem to me to be not only perfectly compatible but inseparable.

Dr. John Shaw Billings
Planner of The Johns Hopkins Hospital, 1875 [1]

Introduction

Although the preceding quote was written in 1875, it is even more relevant today as academic medical centers (AMCs) have become increasingly complex. AMCs can be composed of as many as four separate components: the hospital, the medical school, the university, and the physician practice plan. The physician practice plan is the vehicle through which AMC faculty bill and collect for their professional services. Some medical schools are free standing while others are part of or affiliated with an undergraduate university. The way in which these different entities interact and relate administratively and financially differs at various AMCs. Indeed, it is often said that "if you've seen one AMC—you've seen one AMC."

However, in the current healthcare environment, a cohesive and integrated structure is of particular importance because the relationship among these various entities is integral to the ability of an AMC to achieve excellence in the delivery of patient care. Without integration, there are no checks and balances of power, it is often difficult to align missions, and collaborative comprehensive planning can become problematic if not impossible. This chapter discusses the evolution of the structure of AMCs, examples of AMC structures, how structure can influence the success of an AMC, examples of how some AMCs have restructured, and recommendations for integration.

Evolution of AMC Structure

AMCs first evolved in the early 1900s with the emergence of nonprofit medical schools. Funded by the John D. Rockefeller Foundation, the General Education Board, the Carnegie Corporation, private fund raising, state allocations and affiliated universities, these new medical schools needed patients for their students. The Johns Hopkins School of Medicine owned a hospital that was large enough to provide the appropriate amount of teaching material; however, medical schools without hospitals of their own had to develop relationships with existing nonprofit or municipal hospitals, merge with existing hospitals, or construct modern teaching hospitals with funding from state appropriations [2].

Because private patients were not deemed amenable to receiving their care from medical students, many medical schools affiliated with a public hospital; by 1940, most of the 67 U.S. medical schools had an association with a public hospital [3]. For example, schools in Boston affiliated with Boston City Hospital and New York University affiliated with Bellevue Hospital. In the four decades leading up to World War II, these medical schools and their affiliated hospitals had very small, full-time faculties and grew slowly due to the limited availability of research support and the modest fees received by practicing physicians [4].

After World War II, America's AMCs began to grow. Funding from the National Institutes of Health (NIH) supported the growth of research and a medical school's size and reputation became directly linked with the magnitude of its research portfolio. The establishment of the first national social insurance programs by Congress in 1965 (Medicare and Medicaid) and increased fee-for-service, third-party reimbursement from private or public insurance companies for high-cost, high-technology services provided largely at AMCs substantially increased the finances of most health centers [5]. Nowhere was the growth in technology greater and reimbursement more lucrative than in academic programs in cardiovascular disease, pulmonary medicine, and gastroenterology.

Although subspecialists were highly remunerated for their work, the academic hospitals received even greater benefits because the compensation for the technical component of these high-technology interventions was far more robust than were the professional fees. Between 1960 and 2000, the number of full-time basic science faculty members in U.S. medical schools increased more than threefold and the number of full-time clinical faculty members grew more than 10-fold as both university presidents and medical school deans recognized that physician practice plans and hospital revenues could generate enormous surpluses [6].

Although the post-Medicare/Medicaid period was a great boon to the financial structure of the academic medical center, there were also unintended consequences. First, the same robust reimbursements that fueled the economic fortunes of academic medical centers also resulted in incredibly attractive opportunities in the private practice communities, resulting in talented faculty leaving the AMC. Not wanting to be left out of the largesse from the federal government and private insurance companies, community hospitals rapidly increased their own technologic expertise by recruiting talented physicians from AMCs [7]. In addition, the full-time academic faculty began to compete directly with the community-based physicians for patients to provide much needed teaching material as well as to keep the clinical practice engine of the AMC well greased.

Unfortunately, in the 1980s and 1990s the financial bubble burst on the academic medical center as the "perfect storm" hit academia. The first part of the storm arrived when the government passed legislation establishing the prospective payment of hospital bills for Medicare patients. Instead of the traditional fee-for-service reimbursement in which hospitals and physicians were paid for each day that the patient remained in the hospital, the new prospective payment system reimbursed hospitals based on the patient's diagnosis (diagnosis-related group—DRG) rather than the actual cost of care. If the actual cost to the hospital for the care of a patient was less than the DRG payment, the hospital accrued a profit; however, if the actual cost of care for an individual patient was higher than the DRG payment, the hospital suffered a loss.

The second part of the perfect storm was managed care. For the first time, third-party payers controlled costs by limiting the utilization of medical services. As managed care spread, admissions to teaching hospitals decreased because health maintenance organizations (HMOs) were unwilling to support the social, educational, and research missions of AMCs. Thus, managed care organizations directed their patients to lower cost community hospitals that did not have teaching programs and away from higher cost AMCs. This negatively affected the academic missions of the AMCs.

The final part of the storm was the Balanced Budget Act of 1997, which capped payments to AMCs, including those for postgraduate education. As a result, if an AMC wanted to start a new program or increase the size of its post-graduate training program, it had to support the cost of expansion itself.

In response to the financial stresses placed by the appearance of the perfect storm, many AMCs took a careful look at the relationship of the hospital, the medical school, and the university and attempted to "re-restructure." Some academic hospitals merged: the Brigham and Women's Hospital and the Massachusetts General Hospital, Presbyterian Hospital and the New York Hospital, the Mount Sinai and New York University Medical Centers, Barnes and Jewish Hospitals, Hahnemann University Hospital and the Hospital of the Medical College of Pennsylvania, and the hospitals of Stanford University and the University of California. However, some mergers did not work. For example, the merged UCSF–Stanford Health Care operated at a loss of $176 million during the 29 months that the merger lasted [8].

Other hospitals took very different approaches. The University of Minnesota and Indiana University merged their hospitals with local community hospitals, while Tulane, St. Louis University, George Washington, Thomas Jefferson University, and Georgetown sold or leased their university-owned hospitals to for profit or not-for-profit entities [9]. The University of Kansas Hospital was a part of the University of Kansas system and was led by the dean of the School of Medicine until 1998 when, in the face of significant financial and clinical crisis, the hospital was separated from the university in order to form a new hospital governing authority, bring in professional managers, and enable the hospital to make capital investments without the limitations of the state university system [10,11].

No event so galvanized the academic medical community around a need for change as the announcement in the summer of 1998 that the Allegheny Health System had become the first academic health system in the country to be part of a bankruptcy filing [12]. The university was bailed out only after Tenet Healthcare Corp. purchased eight of the system's Philadelphia-area hospitals; Allegheny's creditors offered a $50 million unrestricted gift to Drexel University's endowment, thus allowing Drexel to take over the medical school; tenured faculty were laid off; and the state contributed substantive support [13]. There was no doubt that AMCs in this country were in crisis and that solutions needed to be found. However, it was unclear what structure would work best for an AMC.

Types of AMC Structures

Although the AMC is composed of the four major components of hospital, medical school, university, and physician practice plan, it is helpful to view the medical school and the university as a common element in the organizational equation. Although the mathematical number of possible combinations among these entities is large, in reality, only a finite number of combinations can exist among American medical centers. These various organizational possibilities have been separated into five distinct groups [14]:

- The medical school, the physician practice plan, and the affiliated hospital or hospitals are "owned" by the same entity (the University of Pennsylvania and the University of Michigan).
- The teaching hospital owns the practice plan, but is separate and distinct from the university and the school of medicine (the Massachusetts General Hospital and Harvard University, the New England Medical Center and Tufts University, and the Dartmouth Hitchcock Medical Center and Dartmouth University).
- The university and the practice plan are a single entity, but have no integration with their affiliated teaching hospitals (the University of Chicago, Columbia University, and Thomas Jefferson University).
- The teaching hospital is owned by the university; however, the physician practice plan is a separate and distinct entity (New Jersey Medical School and the University of Kentucky).
- The hospital, the school of medicine, and the physician practice plan are separate and distinct entities (Northwestern University and the University of Arizona).

Additional factors must be considered when trying to evaluate the various structures that exist in American AMCs. In the case of AMCs where the hospital and the medical school are separate entities, some of the academic hospitals are stand-alone, nonprofit entities that are overseen by an independent board of directors. By contrast, some hospitals, including Hahnemann University Hospital (Drexel) in Philadelphia and USC University Hospital in Los Angeles, are run by for-profit corporations. Alternatively, as in the case of UPMC–Presbyterian Hospital and Georgetown University Hospital, the academic hospital may be part of a nonprofit health system composed of a group of quaternary, tertiary, and/or community hospitals. These health systems may control the expenditures of the individual member hospitals, including the AMC, or each hospital may stand on its own bottom line. In some cases, the multiple hospitals that encompass the health system compete for patients; in other systems, high-technology cases are cared for exclusively at the AMC.

Despite the vast variety of structures, Steven Wartman recently argued that AMCs exist as one of two prototypical models: the fully integrated model, in which the academic, clinical, and research functions all report to one person and to one board of directors, and the split/splintered model, in which the academic and clinical/health system operations are managed by two or more individuals reporting to different governing boards [15]. AMCs have flip-flopped back and forth between these two models as the economics and politics of individual institutions changed. These two prototypes are sufficient for evaluating the effects of structure on the ability of the AMC to meet its primary mission of providing outstanding patient care.

Controversy Regarding the Best Structures for AMCs

For over a quarter of a century, academic leaders have argued about what structure was most effective in supporting the missions of the AMC. In 1982, Dr. Robert Heyssel, president of The Johns Hopkins Hospital, noted [16]:

> The search for the perfect governance and management structure between the teaching hospital and the university and its health colleges is very much like Plato's description of the progression of government from aristocracy through tyranny. Over time, with different people in positions of authority and power and changing circumstances, the perfect can fall to imperfect and then become disastrous. The best way to prevent that from happening is to keep constantly aware of what the businesses are and to maintain the balance of power among those responsible for each. Ultimately, the responsibility for that task resides in the governing bodies.

At the time, the president of Hopkins Hospital and the dean of the Hopkins Medical School reported to different boards—a redundancy in reporting relationships that is often associated with ambiguity in decision making and a decision-making process that appears chaotic and political [17]. However, within two decades, Hopkins would integrate the hospital and the medical school under a single leader.

Other experts clearly disagreed with the view that the hospital and the medical school should be fully integrated. For example, some scholars suggested that changing and uncertain existential situations require that an organization not follow a set pattern, but rather be adaptable to change when the situation requires a different approach [18]. Indeed, some scholars suggested that organizations should "do whatever the situation and environment require, even to the point of encouraging entirely different structures and processes to exist within the same organization" [19].

Some suggested that the administration of the hospital and the medical school should be separate: "We would be better served, I believe, if we left the management of the hospital and budgetary oversight to the vice president and his/her staff, while recognizing the dean as being primarily the academic leader of the faculty" [20]. This separation required a change in the roles of the various AMC leaders: The hospital director would change from the role of academician to that of a businessman in a highly competitive environment, while the role of a department chair would migrate from "that of a business entrepreneur and manager to that of a senior clinician and academician" [20]. Thus, not only the relationship between the hospital and the medical school needed to change but also the roles of the academic leaders.

In 1994, a group of models was conceived by the Working Group on Adapting to Resource Constraints of the Association of American Medical Colleges Advisory Panel on the Mission and Organization of Medical Schools. The group defined models that were very similar to the five models presented earlier [21]. The panel felt that no single model was inherently superior to another. However, simple common sense would lead one to believe that academic medical centers in which the hospital and the medical school are seamlessly integrated would provide enormous opportunities for the development of cutting-edge clinical care based on facilitated translation of research discoveries from the laboratory bench to the patient's bedside, alignment of incentives, and facilitated flow of funds from the hospital to the medical school.

Alternatively, the existence of administrative and financial chasms between the hospital and the medical school would be predicted to inhibit the development of true excellence. From a business standpoint, one can point to companies in which a lack of integration among marketing, sales, and research and development has led to economic misfortune. Until recently, it has been difficult to prove that one or another structure impedes success in the "business" of the academic medical center. However, a review of the available data as well as a recent clinical study support the view that AMCs benefit markedly from tight integration of their different parts.

Although only 44% of America's AMCs have an integrated structure, information can be gleaned from comparing structure and "success" in the academic and clinical arenas that strongly demonstrates the value of integration. For example, with the exception of Washington University (4), Yale (8), and the University of Pittsburgh (9), the top 10 medical schools, based on National Institutes of Health research funding, are integrated with their university hospitals and faculty practice plans (www.nih.gov). Although not integrated, Harvard has a long-standing "brand," a culture of excellence, and an endowment in the billions of dollars that supports its ability to build and achieve excellence in all missions. Though not fully integrated, the University of Pittsburgh School of Medicine is unique in that the many businesses of the UPMC Health System, a $7 billion business, have provided substantial revenues to support the academic mission. At Washington University, positive hospital operating margins are shared between the hospital and the medical school—much as would occur if the two institutions were integrated.

Further support that a unified medical center has benefits comes from the finding that integration is the most dominant model among the 30 most research-intensive medical schools (70% of those ranked 11–20 are integrated, whereas 50% of those ranked 20–30 are integrated). These schools are able financially to support a robust research program using hospital-derived revenues at a time when NIH funding alone cannot support the infrastructure and overhead of a research program. Furthermore, according to *U.S. News and World Report,* 11 of the top 17 hospitals are integrated in some form. Thus, no matter how an AMC is judged, those with integrated structures appear to rise consistently to the top.

Objective data supporting integration come from a recent study undertaken by Mark Keroack, the vice president and director of the Clinical Practice Advancement Center at University Health System Consortium (UHC) in Oak Brook, Illinois [22]. Keroack and his colleagues used a unique scoring system to measure quality of care and safety at 97 university teaching hospitals that are part of the UHC. After ranking all 97 for their quality of patient care, they selected a representative group of top-ranked and average programs. A team with expertise in leadership, nursing, quality improvement, patient safety, and risk management—but blinded as to the ranking of each school—then performed site visits at each of the programs. They interviewed key members of the healthcare leadership team, including board members, hospital leaders, academic leaders, faculty members, residents, and nursing staff. The team then performed sophisticated scientific analysis of interview notes, documents, and interviews in order to identify specific themes that separated the better performing centers. In many ways, this research was similar to the work done by Jim Collins and his research team, which led to the results published in his book, *Good to Great* [23].

Keroack and his team identified a group of themes that were important markers of high-quality AMCs [22]:

The top performers had leaders who articulated the view that patient care was first among the missions of patient care, teaching, and research.
The leaders of the top-performing AMCs focused on pointing out the disparity between where they were and where they wanted to be rather than comparing themselves with competing institutions, and they linked quality to more than simply clinical outcomes.

The top performers viewed excellence as a "source of strategic advantage within a highly competitive marketplace, rather than simply 'the right thing to do'" [22].

The lower ranked institutions seemed unable to resolve their internal conflicts between the missions of patient care, teaching, and research and seemed largely satisfied with the level of quality and safety at their institutions.

The CEO of each of the top-performing institutions was passionate about improvement in quality, safety, and service and took a very hands-on approach to improving these areas.

The top-performing centers were integrated across the multiple components of the AMC.

In two of the top performers, the lead executive in the hospital and the leadership of the clinical departments reported to a single CEO. Although the third leading AMC had a more traditional structure—separation of the hospital, the school of medicine, and the faculty practice plan—the AMC was managed collaboratively with weekly operational meetings of the leaders of each of the three entities. In addition, all three top institutions were "led as an alliance among the department chairs and executive leadership, with joint participation in strategy, program development and performance improvement" [22]. Interestingly, the top institutions did not use financial incentives to reward high levels of performance but rather exerted subtle pressure on clinicians to conform to the institution's core values and core missions—even when there was a mix of private physicians and employed faculty in the AMC. By contrast, the lower performing hospitals displayed tension across the leadership team and a culture of "all persons for themselves" [22].

Examples of Successful Restructuring

Over the past decade, internal turmoil, financial constraints, and the challenging healthcare environment have led a group of AMCs to reevaluate and redefine their structures. At a time when there was enormous confusion as to what structure would best support the missions of the AMC, two of America's premier AMCs—The Johns Hopkins University and the University of Pennsylvania Medical Center—were faced with having to decide which direction to take due to turmoil at both centers. The lessons learned at these two centers provide objective information about the benefits and risks of restructuring [24,25]. More recently, Wake Forest University has taken even bolder steps, although the outcome of its initiatives awaits further evaluations.

Johns Hopkins

At Hopkins, the hospital and the university had been separate since the founding of two corporations by the Baltimore merchant and philanthropist Johns Hopkins in 1867. The chief executive of the hospital reported to the hospital board of trustees while the dean of the school of medicine reported to the president of the university, who in turn reported to the board of trustees of the Johns Hopkins University. The school and the hospital coexisted until the early 1990s when Dr. Michael M. E. Johns, the chair of the Department of Otolaryngology at Hopkins, was appointed dean of the School of Medicine and Dr. James A. Block was appointed president of the Hopkins Hospital.

Dr. Block, a newcomer to Hopkins, was viewed by some as not understanding or supporting the Hopkins culture. Business and culture came to a head when the new chief operating officer of the hospital proposed hiring physicians who did not meet what the faculty viewed as the profile of a Hopkins physician and the hospital and the medical school had large disagreements about how to allocate the costs and overhead associated with new construction [24].

When Dr. Johns resigned in 1995 to become the chief executive at Emory, the board of trustees of both the university and the hospital established a joint committee to evaluate the structure of the two institutions. The story of that effort is described by Morris W. Offit, a long-time member of the university board of trustees [26]:

> The hospital trustees felt that they were the businessmen and that the School of Medicine faculty were academics who didn't understand anything about business. I went head to head with these trustees and said "Hogwash." Johns Hopkins medicine has nothing to do with the bricks and mortar of the hospital[;] it has to do with the quality of the faculty. That faculty is research, teaching and clinical. The chairmen of those departments were the chiefs over on the hospital side. The trustees started to understand. They knew that the marketplace no longer allowed for the luxury of divided governance. Finally, we came up with a configuration where the dean of the School of Medicine became the CEO of Johns Hopkins Medicine. Now the head of the hospital reports to that CEO. So for the first time in Hopkins' history, we clarified the role of the School of Medicine and the hospital. It's working like a charm, and that's why Hopkins medicine is absolutely thriving. The right people are making decisions[;] the CEO of Johns Hopkins Medicine reports to the president of the university. We're the first health system in the country to really pull this all together. This is one of our crowning achievements.

It should be noted that although the hospital and the university could not be "merged," the boards elected to form a new governance structure called "Johns Hopkins Medicine." In 1997, Dr. Edward D. Miller was appointed as the first dean/chief executive officer at Hopkins. Although it is impossible to predict how Hopkins would have fared had it not undertaken reorganization, it has certainly continued to produce and provide during a time of great challenges for academic medicine. Since 1997, Hopkins has constructed new and innovative clinical and research facilities, remained as America's top hospital, and continued to lead the nation's AMCs in funding from the National Institutes of Health. Furthermore, Hopkins has continued as the primary care provider for a large segment of Baltimore's uninsured.

University of Pennsylvania

At the same time that Hopkins was shifting from a separate administrative structure for its hospital and medical school to an integrated administrative structure, the University of Pennsylvania was trying to decide whether to uncouple an administrative structure that had been integrated since 1874 when the University of Pennsylvania had become the first American university to build its own teaching hospital. In 1989, the university recruited Dr. William N. Kelly from the University of Michigan to serve as executive vice president and dean [24]. Kelly formed a health system that included three hospitals and 270 primary care physicians, built two new research buildings and one new hospital building, created a group of suburban outpatient facilities, recruited a large number of new basic science and clinical chairs, created 12 institutes and centers, and markedly increased the level of NIH funding. The purchases of both practices and hospitals were funded in large part by hospital margins and took place at a time of an "arms race" in Pennsylvania: The Allegheny Health System was purchasing a large number of hospitals and physician practices in both western and eastern Pennsylvania as well as two medical schools in Philadelphia.

However, decreasing compensation for physician services and the Balanced Budget Act substantially eroded the positive margin of the hospital and the health system, leading to the bankruptcy of the Allegheny Health System. At the University of Pennsylvania, the purchase of a large number of community practices and hospitals and decreased reimbursements from private and federal employers resulted in a loss of $300 million between 1996 and 1999. In addition, the medical center's debt increased from $170 million in 1992 to more than $800 million in 2000 [24].

In 2000, the University of Pennsylvania decided to replace Dr. Kelly as the leader of the University of Pennsylvania Health System. In order to protect the endowment of the university from ongoing losses at the health center, many of the university leaders felt that the health system and the university should sepa-rate. From an administrative standpoint, it was felt that an independent health system would be more nimble and thus better able to respond to the day-to-day challenges it faced in the competitive Philadelphia marketplace. However, when the leading candidate to succeed Dr. Kelly, Dr. Arthur Rubenstein, insisted on having control of the health system and the school of medicine, the university created "Penn Medicine." Penn Medicine included the school of medicine, the health system, and the medical faculty practice plan under the leadership of the dean/executive vice president. [24]

Rubenstein inherited a health system with a large amount of debt, with little money for growth and development, a location in a city with one of the lowest reimbursement rates in the country, four allopathic medical schools, and a harsh malpractice environment. Nonetheless, Penn has managed to remain a national leader in both clinical care and research. In 2008, the Hospital of the University of Pennsylvania ranked 12th in the *U.S. News and World Report* rankings and number 2 on the list of NIH-funded medical schools in 2005. Furthermore, development efforts have helped fund a group of major construction projects that will provide new and innovative facilities to help provide more seamless patient care, and investment in technology has allowed the hospital to compete effectively in the competitive environment of Philadelphia.

Wake Forest University

Recent evidence suggests that trustees of academic health centers are awakening to the necessity of higher levels of integration. A leading example is Wake Forest University Baptist Medical Center. An ad hoc working group of trustees of Wake Forest University Health Sciences and the North Carolina Baptist Hospital, the closed staff university hospital for the medical school and its faculty approved the reorganization of the components to a medical center model [27]. Both the medical school and the hospital were doing well individually; however, they had missed market opportunities, had difficulty deciding on capital investments, and wanted to invest more in the academic mission. The trustees committed to the reorganization to enable the enterprise to establish and execute an integrated clinical vision and strategy while maintaining the university's autonomy and control over the academic mission.

The Wake Forest model established an empowered medical center board populated by members of the health sciences board and the hospital board and added faculty members. They established the position of medical center CEO, selected by and reporting to the medical center board and overseeing the work of presidents of university health sciences, the hospital, and a newly organized faculty practice. Each executive has a dual reporting relationship to his or her respective boards for fiduciary responsibilities and to the CEO for executive leadership. Although it is too soon to comment on its success, it stands as a recent example of the kind of courageous and committed leadership necessary to achieve success in the contemporary AMC.

Effect of the Staff Model on Structural Integration

Another important structural component of an AMC is the form of its staff model. In the "closed" staff model, most of the physicians at the AMC—regardless of ownership—are full-time members of the academic faculty practice plan, and the hospital is empowered to restrict the number of physicians who can gain privileges at the hospital. By contrast, in the "open" staff model, some portion of the physician staff of the hospital are members of the full-time faculty while other members of the medical staff are not employed by the medical school and are referred to as "voluntary" or "private" staff. The hospital is unable to control the influx of new physicians in the "open" staff model. Voluntary faculty may have faculty appointments and patients are often unable to distinguish whether their physician is a member of the full-time faculty or of the voluntary faculty. Examples of "open" staff models are the Thomas Jefferson University Hospital and Hahnemann Hospital, whereas The Johns Hopkins Hospital and the Hospital of the University of Pennsylvania both use the closed staff model.

In some cases, the relationship between the full-time faculty and the voluntary or private faculty is symbiotic. Physicians who are not members of the full-time faculty may admit their patients to the academic hospital, teach residents and students, provide consultations within the hospital, and care for patients in their outpatient offices. In addition, they may refer their patients to the full-time faculty for highly specialized procedures such as cardiac catheterizations, transplantation, complex surgical procedures, or electrophysiology procedures.

By contrast, voluntary faculty may compete with the full-time faculty for patients, may or may not teach the medical students or the residents, and provide no monetary support for the academic missions of the medical school. In a less integrated center, they may live by their own set of rules and not be accountable for providing the same level of care as the full-time faculty—thereby providing a natural substrate for "town–gown" conflicts, especially when resources are limited. As we will see in later chapters, at some AMCs, voluntary faculty may not be accountable to department chairmen or their political clout may supersede a chair's authority, thereby obviating the ability of the chair to regulate their performance and to ensure quality of care. However, voluntary faculty may have strong political clout when the hospital is not integrated with the university and may see integration as a threat to their autonomy—a possibility that must be factored into attempts at integration.

Recommendations for Integrating AMC Structure

As you can see from the preceding pages, our research has shown that the most effective means of attaining the core mission of providing outstanding patient care can be achieved by integrating the components of the AMC: the hospital, the medical school, the physician practice plan, and the university. Only with integration can contemporary AMCs fund and accomplish their tripartite missions and, in competitive markets, succeed as a distinctive clinical enterprise. The academic health centers with the highest levels of performance and the best reputations were founded as, or are evolving toward, highly integrated enterprises. Even some university-based academic health centers that separated their hospitals in the 1990s to protect the university's endowment are now moving back toward an integrated governance and leadership model. However, this new model requires more than just integration for success: It requires that all elements have an integrated core focus of providing outstanding patient care because success in the clinical mission is an absolute requirement for success in the academic mission.

Restructuring is fraught with challenges in today's AMC. For example, there is no perfect structure for any single AMC and structure alone cannot solve all problems. Great thought must be given to the creation of a new governance structure to ensure that the reorganization is successful. Organization models must be carefully analyzed in terms of benefits and limitations. Inherent internal politics at all AMCS often impede reorganization; therefore, external support services with experience in restructuring AMCs may be required. In terms of leadership, it is a rare executive who is willing to engage in a process that may lead to the change or diminution of his or her role. Thus, restructuring may and often does require leadership change. As a result, the initial impetus for change has most often come from the board of trustees rather than from individual executives.

Nonetheless, there must be both courage and commitment at the level of the board in approaching this sphere of action. Restructuring is not easy and positive effects might not be immediately obvious. In addition, because of complex political factors, it is often useful to have the process driven by external healthcare consultants who have the experience and expertise and a diverse array of methods for effectively bringing about change in complex structures. The following recommendations can serve as a template for achieving integration.

Drive Integration from the Top

Restructuring efforts must come from the top; that is, senior leadership must initiate changes and base them on the clear and well-defined goal of improving patient care. This type of initiative must involve the board of trustees of both the hospital and the university. The boards must commit to and be actively involved in the integration of their AMCs. Indeed, in many cases it may be the board of trustees that actually initiates and drives the process of integration. In these cases, the board should utilize external experts in healthcare management to assist in developing a strategic plan for integration in order to avoid internal politics.

Include All Stakeholders in the Process of Integration

All stakeholders must be involved in the process, including faculty, hospital administrators, university administrators, and department chairs. Where appropriate, community representatives and state legislatures should be involved in the process. In programs that have significant numbers of voluntary faculty, they too should be included in the process of integration. Depending on the process and the situation, faculty, students, and staff may be involved in the strategic planning process. However, even when the reintegration is driven from the level of the board, there must be a sharing of the vision and an assurance that all stakeholders understand the goals and objectives of integration and have a shared vision. To achieve the goals of integration, flexibility will be required at all participant levels.

Develop a Framework for Integration That Can Withstand Changes over Time

It may be helpful for the AMC to utilize some of the "change" models that have been developed within the context of industry. These include methodologies that allow institutions to create a shared need, shape a vision, mobilize commitment, make change last, and monitor progress in order to make change last. Programs that support change include "Six Sigma" (define, measure, improve, and control), "Lean," and the "Change Acceleration Process" (CAP). AMCs that do not have leaders familiar with mechanisms of change may bring in any one of a number of consulting groups to help the organization develop a strategic plan based on a defined algorithm.

Ensure That the Central Focus of Integration Is Improved Patient Care

The ultimate goal of integration is to support the core mission of achieving excellence in patient care. In many respects, it is axiomatic that an integrated AMC can provide the highest level of patient care by aligning the incentives and management across the hospital, the physician group, and the medical school. However, as is true with each of these spheres, integration is necessary but not sufficient to reach the core goal. Interestingly, integration influences each of the four different spheres because alignment of the hospital and university also leads to greater opportunities in and resources for research and education.

References

1. Billings, J. 1875. *Hospital construction and organization. Hospital plans.* New York: William Wood & Co.
2. Ludmerer, K. 1999. *Time to heal: American medical education from the turn of the century to the era of managed care,* 514. New York: Oxford University Press.
3. Dowling, H. 1982. *City hospitals: The undercare of the underprivileged.* Cambridge, MA: Harvard University Press.
4. Petersdorf, R. G. 1980. The evolution of departments of medicine. *New England Journal of Medicine* 303 (9): 489–496.
5. Stevens, R. 1986. Issues for American internal medicine through the last century. *Annals of Internal Medicine* 105 (4): 592–602.
6. Kirch, D. 2006. Financial and organizational turmoil in the academic health center: Is it a crisis or an opportunity for medical education? *Academic Psychiatry* 30 (1): 5–8.
7. Gee, D. A., and Rosenfeld, L. A. 1984. The effect on academic health centers of tertiary care in community hospitals. *Journal of Medical Education* 59:547–552.
8. Stanford Hospital and Clinic Medical Staff UPDATE. 2000. 24 (11).
9. Kane, N. 2001. The financial health of academic medical centers: An elusive subject. In *The future of academic medical centers,* ed. H. Aaron, 101. Washington, D.C.: Brookings Institute Press.
10. Karash, J. A. 1996. KU job cutback denied. *The Kansas City Star,* Feb. 6 (www.firecehelathcare.com/node/8296/print).
11. King, S. 2008. KU Hospital's independent path has led to success. *The Kansas City Star,* Oct. 7 (www.kansascity.com/105/story/312331.html).
12. Maguire, P. 1998. Allegheny's failure sends shocks through academia. *ACP-ASIM Observer,* Dec. (www.acponline.org/journals/news/dec98/failure.htm)
13. Aaron, H. 2000. Brookings Policy Brief 69. The plight of academic medical centers.
14. Levine, J. K. 2002. Considering alternative organizational models for academic medical centers. *Academic Clinical Practice* 14 (2): 2–5.

15. Wartman, S. 2007. *The academic health center: Evolving organizational models.* Washington, D.C.: Association of Academic Health Centers.
16. Heyssel, R. 1984. The challenge of governance: The relationship of the teaching hospital to the university. *Journal of Medical Education* 59:162–168.
17. Allison, R. F., and Dalston, J. W. 1982. Governance of university-owned teaching hospitals. *Inquiry* 19 (1): 3–17.
18. Weisbord, M. 1975. A mixed model for medical centers: Changing structure and behavior. In *New technologies in organization development,* ed. J. Adams, 211–254. La Jolla, CA: University Associates.
19. Hastings, D. A., and Crispell, K. R. 1980. Policy-making and governance in academic health centers. *Journal of Medical Education* 55 (4): 325–332.
20. Petersdorf, R. 1987. Some thoughts on medical center governance. *Pharos* Fall:13–18.
21. Culbertson, R. A., Goode, L. D., and Dickler, R. M. 1996. Organizational models of medical school relationships to the clinical enterprise. *Academic Medicine* 71 (11): 1258–1274.
22. Keroack, M. A., Youngberg, B. J., Cerese, J. L., Krsek, C., Prellwitz, L. W., and Trevelyan, E. W. 2007. Organizational factors associated with high performance in quality and safety in academic medical centers. *Academic Medicine* 82 (12): 1178–1186.
23. Collins, J. 2001. *Good to great.* New York: Harper Collins.
24. Kastor, J. 2003. Governance of teaching hospitals: Turmoil at the University of Pennsylvania and the Johns Hopkins University. *American Journal of Medicine* 114 (9): 774–776.
25. Kastor, J. 2001. Mergers of teaching hospitals: Three case studies. *American Journal of Medicine* 110 (1): 76–79.
26. Warren, M. 2000. *Johns Hopkins, knowledge for the world.* Baltimore, MD: the Johns Hopkins University.
27. http://www.wfubmc.edu/ceo

Chapter 2

Integrating Clinical Care Delivery Systems

A teaching hospital will not be controlled by the faculty in term-time only; it will not be a hospital in which any physician may attend his own case. Centralized administration of wards, dispensary, and laboratories, as organically one, requires that the school relationship be continuous and unhampered. The patient's welfare is ever the first consideration: we shall see that it is promoted, not prejudiced, by the right kind of teaching.

Abraham Flexner, 1910 [1]

Introduction

It would be easy to blame the problems of today's AMCs on the unwieldy structural relationships that exist among the hospital, the medical school, and the university that were described in Chapter 1; however, the structure of the medical school itself often precludes the ability of AMC physicians to provide outstanding patient care. The modern American medical school consists of numerous clinical departments that often operate in their own individual silos. This nonintegrated structure presents a number of different challenges to achieving the core mission of providing outstanding patient care. For example, at some AMCs, the same procedure may be provided in multiple departments without the development of common protocols and without an assessment of which group of physicians does it best.

Another example of how a lack of integration across different departments adversely influences patient care is the geographic separation of closely related specialists. As a result, patients must travel from one outpatient location to another and go through a registration process at each location; their care is often interrupted as the patient has to wait for the different physicians to communicate with each other regarding his or her care. In this chapter, we will look at the historic structure of the medical school, the evolution of the physician practice plan, types and examples of integration, and recommendations for integrating care across departmental boundaries.

Medical School Structure—A Historical Perspective

When Osler, Halsted, Welch, and Kelly established the departmental structure of The Johns Hopkins School of Medicine in 1893, the medical school consisted of only four clinical departments: medicine, surgery, pathology, and obstetrics and gynecology. Abraham Flexner described the model at Hopkins when he recommended [1]:

> There will be one head to each department—a chief, with such aides as the size of the service, the degrees of differentiation feasible, the number of students, suggest. The professor of medicine in the school is physician-in-chief to the hospital; the professor of surgery is surgeon-in-chief; the professor of pathology is hospital pathologist. School and hospital are thus interlocked.

In the hospital, all clinical care was overseen by the chairman of the department of medicine or the chairman of the department of surgery. The number of physicians in each department was very small and the department chiefs often saw each of the patients on their particular service. Indeed, Osler warned of the potential consequences of the early rise of specialists and their separation from their parent departments when he noted [2]:

> The student-specialist may have a wide vision—no student—wider—if he gets away from the mechanical side of the art and keeps in touch with the physiology and pathology upon where his art depends. More than any other of us, he needs the lessons of the laboratory, and wide contact with men in other departments may serve

> to correct the inevitable tendency to a narrow and perverted vision,
> in which the life of the ant-hill is mistaken for the world at large.

Thus, even at the turn of the century, Osler cautioned against thinking in silos rather than integrating care.

Throughout the twentieth century, the departmental structure of the medical school changed as an increasing number of individual departments were formed. In the early part of the century, new departments formed, including pediatrics and psychology. These were followed later in the century by departments of neurology, rehabilitation medicine, radiology, and anesthesiology.

After World War II, individual fields of specialization arose in the disciplines of medicine and surgery. In departments of medicine, subspecialty divisions formed in cardiology, gastroenterology, infectious diseases, pulmonary medicine, critical care medicine, rheumatology, endocrinology, medical genetics, clinical pharmacology, hematology, oncology, and emergency medicine. Most of these subspecialties remained embedded in the departments of medicine, although departments of emergency medicine and oncology became separate departments in many institutions. In departments of surgery, subspecialty divisions arose in critical care medicine; cardiothoracic surgery; plastic surgery; transplant surgery; urology; ear, nose, and throat surgery (otorhinolaryngology); and neurosurgery.

By contrast with departments of medicine, most of the surgical subspecialties became separate departments. As a result, many medical schools have over 20 different clinical departments. By the 1960s and 1970s, some departments, including medicine and surgery, became larger than entire medical schools had been a decade earlier; however, the administrative structure of medical schools did not change to accommodate these marked differences. As a result, departments often became independent fiefdoms that further entrenched the silo model—often battling each other for the limited resources that exist in today's AMCs.

Historic Departmental Structure Can Impede Delivery of Outstanding Patient Care

This traditional departmental structure impedes the delivery of outstanding and seamless patient care. In addition, it limits the ability of individual departments to develop shared accountability for quality of care and to collaborate in the care of a patient, as well as impedes the ability to ensure that quality rather than politics is the deciding factor as to who provides specific services.

The inefficiency of the current departmental structure is highlighted by the ongoing controversies between cardiologists and radiologists at many AMCs about who will image the heart and the peripheral vasculature. Radiologists and cardiologists perform a variety of invasive and noninvasive procedures to image the heart. Radiologists argue that these lie in their domain because they believe that they hold the exclusive franchise on "imaging" within an AMC. However, cardiologists also provide the same services in the private practice community and in some AMCs and believe that they have rights to the franchise by virtue of the fact that they are the ones who care for the patients and who must interpret the tests in order to make clinical decisions. Because they perform the same procedures, the "turf" battles between radiologists and cardiologists become an important case study for understanding how the silos of academic medical centers influence decision making and the "business" of medicine and can impede the core mission of providing outstanding patient care.

If an AMC uses the core mission of providing outstanding patient care to adjudicate internal conflicts, the choice that an administrator must make regarding who should perform cardiovascular imaging becomes quite simple. The development of an integrated program makes the most sense. Radiologists can bring their expertise in imaging while cardiologists can provide their expertise in the anatomy of the heart and the various disease processes, resulting in a "product" that is far superior to what either group could offer alone.

Unfortunately, at a time when it is well recognized that collaborative and multidisciplinary approaches provide the best care for patients, the American College of Radiology has not concurred that collaboration in cardiac imaging is appropriate [3]. Furthermore, the leaders of many AMCs have allowed politics—rather than the core mission of providing outstanding patient care—to guide their decision-making processes, resulting in one of the two silos capturing the franchise for cardiovascular imaging without a mandate for collaboration and compromise.

Evolution of the Practice Plan

Historically, individual clinical departments of medical schools were responsible for doing their own billing and collections from patients or insurance companies. Sometimes these billing operations existed within the medical school and at other times they were carried out by outside organizations. When the financial operations were outside the university or medical school, they were led by the department chairman and overseen by an independent board. Although the department was expected to provide a "tax" to the dean and to the university to support the academic missions of the schools, at many medical schools the individual department chairs had authority over the use of the remaining resources; this gave them a large amount of authority and power.

Today, almost all medical schools have unified the billing operations of their individual departments under a single practice plan, largely to facilitate compliance with federal regulations and billing guidelines. The majority of these practice plans are subsidiaries of the parent university, although some are owned by the hospital and a smaller number remain independent. For example, at Georgetown, the practice plan was sold, along with the university hospital, to a health system that included the Washington Hospital Center; at the New Jersey Medical School, the practice plan is separate from both the university and the hospital.

Regardless of "ownership," there are important variations in the structures of the different practice plans. Some practice plans maintain each department in individual financial silos; each department keeps its own profits but also is responsible for any losses. These practice plans do not cost-shift to support underperforming departments or specialties that receive poor remunerations for providing their services. Thus, although a neurosurgeon may have a yearly salary of $1,000,000, a general internist in the same institution may have a salary of $100,000 per year despite the fact that the neurosurgeon receives many referrals from colleagues in internal medicine or that the internist provides the postoperative care for the neurosurgical patient.

This nonintegrated approach to practice plan management is very effective at maintaining the high revenues accrued by some specialists, including neurosurgery, orthopedic surgery, ophthalmology, and ear, nose, and throat. However, it disadvantages physicians who do not perform procedures and work at the lower end of the economic ladder, including general internists and family physicians. It is not surprising that under this model it is becoming increasingly difficult to recruit and retain general internists.

At the other end of the spectrum are practice plans that operate as multispecialty group practices. Under this model, decision making occurs at the group level, resources are shared across the various practice specialties, and there is transparency among the multiple elements of the practice plan—much like the operations in a successful business. However, the totally integrated multispecialty group practice model exists at only a relatively few AMCs, including the Mayo Clinic, an institution where this type of culture has existed for decades.

The multispecialty group practice model provides an opportunity for rational cost sharing and supports the recruitment and retention of outstanding clinicians in all fields. As one might imagine, moving from one end of the spectrum (independent practice plan units) to the other end (multispecialty group practice) is a herculean task. Any restructuring efforts are immediately impeded by the entrenched economic culture of most organizations and the fear of many specialties that restructuring will cut into their economic status. Nonetheless, common sense would suggest that, like a business, an AMC could operate most efficiently if the many departments were integrated in a logical fashion. As we will see later in this chapter, clinical care service lines may provide an answer to these challenges.

Types of Integration

Scholars in the fields of business management and economics have defined two forms of integration across business entities: vertical and horizontal integration. Vertical integration has been defined as the degree to which a company owns its upstream suppliers and its downstream buyers [4]. In the AMC, vertical integration brings together all of the different specialties that participate in the global care of a patient with a given disease and therefore includes specialists who receive large remunerations for providing their services, as well as those who receive limited remuneration. For example, a vertically integrated vascular center would include vascular surgeons, interventional radiologists, and interventional cardiologists, as well as general internists trained in vascular medicine who might opt to treat the patient medically before pursuing surgical or interventional options.

It makes intuitive sense that from the standpoint of patient care, having all of the appropriate physicians in the same place at the same time, with a common support staff and apparatus, provides the best opportunity to deliver seamless and safe care to patients with any given disease. However, because the various groups that participate in a vertically integrated system have very different levels of remuneration and provide different skills, the challenges to implementing vertical integration are great, resulting in few AMCs pursuing this level of integration.

By contrast, horizontal integration occurs when a business takes over a group of competing companies that provided the same services. In an AMC, horizontal integration among different clinical departments would consist of the integration of physicians whose levels of reimbursement are approximately the same, who perform similar diagnostic or therapeutic techniques, who have similar cultures or personalities, and who utilize the same—usually expensive—institutional resources. Steven Levin, a healthcare consultant, has recently referred to this type of academic integration as "lateral" integration [5]. Examples of lateral integration include the development of sleep disorder centers by neurologists, pulmonologists, and psychiatrists; development of spine centers by orthopedic surgeons and neurosurgeons; and the creation of vascular centers by neurosurgeons, interventional radiologists, cardiologists, vascular surgeons, and neurologists.

Lateral integration facilitates the rationalization of care, allows practice management to be streamlined by pooling facilities and personnel, permits standardization of care and credentialing criteria among the different specialties, and mitigates internal competition. Lateral integration is relatively easy to accomplish because it "almost always simply replicate[s] or extend[s] traditional academic or clinical structures rather than integrate[s] them administratively and financially into new more efficient and patient-centered models of care" [5]. Lateral integration does not lead directly to an increase in market share. When the centers include only specialists who undertake invasive procedures and not noninvasive physicians, the formation of laterally integrated centers may actually limit a patient's options and provide a lower standard of care.

Examples of Integration across Clinical Departments

The Cancer Center

One of the first clinical groups to provide an integrated approach to finances and delivery of care were cancer centers. These centers integrated the work of medical oncologists, radiation oncologists, and oncologic surgeons and were often both horizontally and vertically integrated. When patients look for the best centers for the treatment of cancer, many seek care from or are referred to one of the integrated "cancer centers of excellence" that are federally designated and funded by the National Cancer Institute of the National Institutes of Health.

By contrast with the traditional academic departments, these centers are often multidisciplinary, cross many departmental barriers, and have a broad agenda that includes basic and clinical research, excellence in patient care, training and education, development of new technologies, and cancer control and prevention. Unlike a department chair, the leader of these federally designated cancer centers is a manager who sits in a high position in the AMC, reports to the most senior authority in the medical center, and has complete control over the space, the budget, and the resources of the center. In some cases, the cancer center director runs a free-standing institute and reports to the university president or to an independent board. Examples of these highly integrated cancer centers include Memorial Sloan-Kettering, Roswell Park, Dana Farber, and M. D. Anderson.

It would be nice to think that the integrated structure found in these federally designated cancer centers came about because university or hospital leaders decided to develop a structure that provided the best possible care for patients. However, altruism played no role in the development of the cancer center structure. In reality, the multidisciplinary and collaborative structure found in today's federally accredited NCI cancer centers was mandated by the National Cancer Act passed by Congress in 1971 [6]. The bill was passed due to the strong lobbying of a group of leading citizens, including Mary Lasker, Sidney Farber, Laurence Rockefeller, Benno Schmidt, and Ann Landers, and a panel of consultants as well as the senatorial leadership of Senator Ralph Yarborough [6].

In order to develop the financial and organizational structure for the new cancer centers, this group of concerned citizens studied the leading cancer programs of the time—all of which were free-standing institutions, including Roswell Park, Memorial Sloan-Kettering, and M. D. Anderson. Based on these studies, the federal legislation mandated that the cancer center director control all funds, including those associated with philanthropy, indirect costs, and clinical revenues and that the individual have a level of "institutional authority" appropriate to manage the center [7]. As a result, AMCs had a choice: Develop a cancer center that fully integrated physicians and scientists from multiple disciplines or do not have a federally designated cancer center on campus.

That integration works is seen by the fact that, according to *U.S. News and World Report*, five of the six top cancer programs in the country have physician-led cancer centers (and hospitals) geographically distinct from the parent organization's hospital and, in some cases, financially and administratively separate from their affiliated university (M. D. Anderson Cancer Center, Memorial Sloan-Kettering Cancer Center, The Kimmel Cancer Center of Johns Hopkins Hospital, Dana-Farber Cancer Institute, and the Fred Hutchinson Cancer Center of the University of Washington). Thus, it would appear that, based on the cancer center experience, clinical and financial integration across the multiple disciplines that provide care for patients with the same disease could provide unique benefits for AMCs and result in the delivery of outstanding care for patients.

Recent Examples of Vertical and Lateral Integration at AMCs

Several AMCs have begun to develop vertically integrated programs. For example, the Department of Transplantation at Mayo Clinic, Jacksonville, Florida, includes transplant surgeons as well as transplant nephrologists, hepatologists, pulmonologists, critical care specialists, and heart failure cardiologists [5,8]. At Hershey Medical Center, the Heart and Vascular Institute blends both horizontal and vertical integration. The institute consists of six divisions—each of which includes physicians in different specialties that provide the same service: imaging, interventional procedures, general cardiology, electrophysiology, cardiac surgery, and vascular medicine (Penn State's Milton S. Hershey Medical Center College of Medicine, Heart and Vascular Institute) [9].

Although participating faculty maintain appointments in historic departments (medicine, surgery, and radiology), the institute oversees all practice operations, revenues, compensation, recruitment, and academic initiatives. However, it reports to a large oversight committee composed of the chairs of medicine, surgery, radiology, and neurosurgery as well as key leaders from the medical center—a reporting structure that may not allow the institute director the freedom and latitude to make rapid and timely decisions. Emory University has formed a vertically integrated transplant center that delegates to the center director the authority and responsibility for the activities of all members of the center and dedicated resources, including clinical and research space, and reports to the CEO of Emory Healthcare, the dean of the School of Medicine, and the director of the Emory Clinic. The traditional stakeholders in transplantation medicine, including department chairs, are included as members of an "advisory board" that includes the chairs of medicine and surgery and key members of the hospital administration [5].

A New Model for AMC Integration: The Clinical Service Line

As AMCs have worked to establish vertical integration, there has been a recognition that the most effective means of developing integration is to focus on the clinical experience of the patient by establishing an integrated structure that has the core mission of providing outstanding patient care. Although the complex politics of the AMC can easily impede efforts to integrate programs to improve efficiency, it is hard to argue with efforts designed to improve patient care. In addition, because the goal of integration is patient care, these types of efforts cannot possibly be successful without the active collaboration of academic departments, hospital leadership, nursing, and hospital-based services.

In our modern lexicon, this type of integration, which is both vertical and horizontal in nature, has been called a "clinical service line." Although the concept of a service line is new to academic medicine, it is not new in the context of American businesses. For many years, business leaders have recognized that the various components of a company cannot exist in economically and administratively separate silos, but rather must work collaboratively to fulfill the core goals [10]. These collaborations are facilitated by transparent finances that allow each entity to understand the cash flows of the overall organization, by linking integrated functions through a product or service line approach, and by ensuring horizontal accountability for quality control and product delivery [11–13].

The service line approach in an AMC provides many of the same advantages seen in a business. It aligns incentives across groups that have common interests, provides better alignment between the historical medical school departmental structure and the organizational structure of the hospital, and affords an opportunity to align patients geographically with their physicians in the inpatient and outpatient venues. For example, when cardiologists and cardiothoracic surgeons share outpatient and inpatient space, the care for the preoperative and the postoperative outpatient, as well as for the hospitalized patient, becomes far more efficient because all parts of the team are able to collaborate seamlessly in the care of the patient.

In the larger perspective, a successful cardiovascular service line might also include endocrinologists who specialize in diabetes and obesity (important risk factors for coronary artery disease), vascular surgeons, radiologists specializing in state-of-the-art imaging, rheumatologists who treat patients with vasculitis, and nephrologists who specialize in hypertension. Thus, patients can truly receive "one-stop shopping."

This approach to AMC organization also makes sense from a financial standpoint. Traditionally, medical school administrators balance the finances by "cost shifting" dollars from highly remunerative practices to poorly remunerative groups independently of their intrinsic relationship. For example, losses in the Division of Infectious Diseases might be "balanced" by contributions from Cardiology or from Rehabilitative Medicine—whichever group has positive margins. However, these entities share almost nothing in common. Therefore, if the cash flow in a division of infectious diseases is diminished in a given year, it makes far more sense to "cost share" by borrowing money from transplant surgery, orthopedic surgery, or general surgery—programs that could not survive without excellent support from infectious disease specialists.

The service line approach streamlines the administrative structure of the medical school by providing opportunities for the service line directors to have responsibilities on both the hospital and academic sides of the street. By narrowing the reporting structures of the service line to a single individual or to a small committee, it is possible to focus the efforts of the service line leadership. A service line structure also has enormous benefits for the hospital. Teams of nurses, social workers, case managers, pharmacists, administrators, and other support staff can focus on one area of clinical "excellence," establish consistent care plans and procedures, establish defined therapeutic regimens, and establish evidence-based medical protocols.

Most importantly, service lines providing seamless and well-integrated clinical care in an environment in which all of the needed specialists and support staff are present are the best model for the delivery of excellent patient care. In fact, the National Academy of Sciences and the Roadmap for Medical Research of the National Institutes of Health have both called for medical schools and universities to develop interdisciplinary programs aimed at curing human disease [14]. Patients want to feel that their care is well organized and that they are interacting with physicians who bring the most up-to-date knowledge and treatment approaches to their care [15]. A service line approach could also give AMCs a competitive edge against for-profit clinical carve-outs that organize specialists from different disciplines around a single disease entity and provide payers with packaged coverage [16].

The development of a service line provides a unique opportunity for the AMC because it is difficult if not impossible to establish a fully integrated service line in the context of a community hospital: Physicians work in small groups that are autonomous economic and legal units, hospital organizations have little control over the individual practices, and the practices are not integrated with the hospital, thereby obviating the ability of the hospital and the physicians to share costs. Clinical integration should be something that can be effected in the context of group practice plans in an academic health center. Unfortunately, the cultural, financial, and governance issues that exist in the traditional AMC limit the development of clinical integration, so only a handful of academic centers have made substantive inroads in developing seamless patient care.

Early Efforts in Developing Service Lines

Modeled after product lines in many industries, service lines began to gain popularity in the 1980s as a means of improving patient care, providing cost-effective care across multiple sites of care and multiple specialties, and obviating the silo structure of many hospital administrations [17,18]. However, these efforts were not universally successful because, in some cases, they were associated with increased administrative costs and, in other cases, they led to periods of administrative disruption with little evidence of a beneficial effect [17,19]. More recently, as AMCs have become increasingly challenged by decreased reimbursement for patient care and teaching, some university and hospital administrators have begun to readdress the value of the service line approach in terms of its ability to decrease costs. However, few AMCs have shared their experiences with service line development, thus making it difficult to evaluate their success.

The New York–Presbyterian Hospital

In January 1998, the New York and Presbyterian Hospitals merged and began operations as the New York–Presbyterian Hospital. This merger was carried out in order to increase quality, improve patient access, and enhance fiscal stability at a time when there was a deteriorating financial environment for teaching hospitals [20]. Senior management was challenged by having to work with two separate and independent medical faculties and physician practice organizations, different cultures at the two institutions, and physician concerns that the merger would erode their identities and weaken their clinical programs. To face these challenges, AMC leadership decided to try to bring the two groups together through the development of service lines and their efforts were detailed in an article in *Academic Medicine* [21].

To fit the unique structure of the New York–Presbyterian Hospital merger, the service lines were designed to be flexible, were physician led, and had a governance structure that brought as many people as possible to the table. The components of the service line were designed to work in a transparent environment with responsibility for strategic planning and quality review. Each service line was treated as a small business unit with responsibilities for all parts of the product line, including nursing. Thus, service line chiefs had responsibility and authority more akin to the world of business than to that of the typical departmental chair or division chief. To motivate the faculty and department chairs to participate, hospital leaders gave priority in capital investment to service line projects if the physicians would commit to specific improvements in quality and medical management and work with hospital groups to improve customer service and revenue realization.

That the experiment in service line development worked in the short term was suggested by the finding that the hospitals saw an increase in discharges, a reduction in length of stay, and a decrease in the cost of caring for each patient. However, it must be noted that a decade after the development of the service line concept at New York–Presbyterian, the long-term success of their service lines has not been reported.

The Cleveland Clinic

Believing that integration could best be achieved by significantly restructuring the organization of the AMC into a service line structure, the leadership of the Cleveland Clinic recently took the courageous step to redefine their traditional departmental structure completely. Indeed, not only did the Cleveland Clinic decide to restructure itself, but it also decided to do so by eliminating the entire departmental structure that had been in existence for a century [22]. The initiative to restructure came about after several years of work by a strategic task force as well as numerous meetings of smaller organizational groups and focus groups.

These early initiatives gained buy-in from many key individuals because all of the leaders were asked to participate in the process. However, some of the physicians had reservations about the new structure because many department heads and section heads were fearful of losing their power and influence within the AMC. The initiative was given direction and focus by the CEO of the clinic, Dr. Delos M. Cosgrove.

Several important differences exist between the structure being developed for the Cleveland Clinic and that at the institutions described previously. First, each service line or institute is led by an individual supported by a steering committee having responsibilities for strategic planning, execution, service development, space, and philanthropy; however, the single institute leader has significant authority and responsibility. The service lines at the Cleveland Clinic have matrix relationships with hospital-based functions such as nursing, radiology, and pathology and strong horizontal accountability on the part of all entities. Importantly, this type of integration is facilitated by the fact that the clinic has a salaried staff model with total integration between the hospital and the doctors. Hopefully, the Cleveland Clinic will share its successes and its failures with other academic centers because it will be important for other centers, their leaders, and their boards to understand whether the Cleveland Clinic's efforts are truly the future of academic medicine.

Service Lines Can Achieve the Core Mission of Improved Patient Care

Unfortunately, the service line concept is new and there is not an extensive database to support its value. However, some recent data are available to suggest that service lines will successfully fulfill their mission. In his study of the factors that differentiated the most successful AMCs from those that were only moderately successful, Keroack found that the top-performing programs were characterized by multidisciplinary approaches to problems and the use of multidisciplinary teams [23]. The top-performing institutions also demonstrated what Keroack refers to as a "blend of central control and decentralized responsibility" [23].

By contrast, at the less successful institutions, neither chairs of the clinical departments nor board members felt engaged in the missions of the AMC. Rather than taking on audacious tasks such as the creation of service lines across all elements of the institution (as has been accomplished at the Cleveland Clinic), the lower performing institutions tended to take on a small number of less controversial projects and often used complex methodologies to assess the success or lack of success of their efforts. The underperforming institutions were also found to have staff who did not feel engaged and were sometimes characterized by rivalries across different disciplines—a phenomenon totally lacking in a service line structure because of the complete integration of disciplines that cared for the same group of patients.

Although Keroack did not study service lines per se, the integration of multidisciplinary units found at the highly successful AMCs clearly suggested the potential benefits of a service line approach. Nonetheless, it will be incumbent upon each institution implementing service lines to measure outcomes, including faculty satisfaction, patient satisfaction, clinical outcomes, financial performance, and other metrics in order to demonstrate objectively the success or failure of their efforts.

Recommendations for Integrating Care across Departmental Boundaries

Several lessons can be learned from recent attempts at integrating clinical care within an AMC—including service line development—as well as from integration projects that have taken place in the worlds of business and finance. These are discussed in the following sections.

AMC Leadership Must Be Completely Engaged in the Concept of Fully Integrated Patient Care

Integration of clinical care and the concept of clinical service lines often meet resistance from traditional academic leaders, including chairs of departments and directors of subspecialty divisions; therefore, clinical integration must be driven by senior leadership, including the dean or the chief executive of the hospital. The board of trustees must also be involved in the decision-making process at multiple levels to ensure success. Because of the complexities involved in integration and the need to change culture, senior leadership may find value in bringing in outside consultants to move the process forward, especially when faced with obvious resistance.

Service Lines Must Develop Mechanisms to Protect or Change the Historic Department Structure

The largest challenge to the creation of a service line and/or the development of a seamless integration of clinical services is the necessity to protect or change the historic department structure of the AMC. Indeed, a dean correctly noted [24]:

> The issue involving leadership around service lines is undoubtedly the most critical issue now facing academic centers and medical schools. The cultural transformations that need to take place for

more effective leadership will be extremely difficult to implement, particularly because of the sensitivity of clinical department chairs about shared leadership and governance.

Some AMCs have approached this problem by creating a matrix reporting structure for a single service line director. First developed in industry to allow for lateral responsibilities across a traditional management hierarchy, the matrix structure has been embraced by academic medical centers because of its perceived ability to facilitate the creation of service lines without disrupting the existing departmental organization of academic institutions [25,26]. Many industries have abandoned the matrix structure because of its complexity and inability to deliver positive results. Matrix structures have too many people involved in decisions, a lack of clarity of individual roles, difficulty in aligning objectives, a lack of empowerment, and multiple reporting lines. Indeed, a study of AMC service lines identified a matrix reporting structure as a major impediment to success [24].

Creating a system in which the service line director reports to a dean or provost can cause equal problems when appointments and promotions, finances, and recruitment are maintained in the traditional department. When individual faculty members receive support of any kind from both the service line director and the department chair, the creation of a service line functionally adds another silo to the AMC. Faculty members, staff, and students can play the chair and the service line director against each other or may get different opinions from the two, resulting in confusion and ambiguity. In addition, the creation of a service line may make it more difficult for a department chair to fulfill goals and expectations because the service line may add another silo for him or her as well.

Some authorities have suggested that AMCs should begin their efforts toward integration with one or several centers that have strong leadership and that represent programs in which the AMC plans to invest the most resources [5]. This approach can limit the level of institutional angst and identify "early acceptors" of the new strategy. This is particularly true when the affected department chairs have bought in to the concept. However, developing service lines in a limited context will preclude the ability to bring all of the necessary participants to the table. If individual departments believe that they have the ability to opt out of integration efforts, the ability of senior leadership to move from a single to multiple service lines will be significantly impeded. Furthermore, for many AMCs, the ability to develop even a limited number of service lines is problematic without substantive institutional restructuring.

Another potential solution to the conundrum of how to link the existing department with the service line is to identify clinical chairs as service line directors or to assign the responsibility for a service line to two chairs. For example, the chairs of medicine and surgery might be charged with managing the cardiovascular service line because vascular surgery, cardiothoracic surgery, and cardiology are all located in their domains. Because it is critical that the educational missions of the various clinical disciplines be maintained, a dual-leadership role for two chairs might be more effective than a single service line director in ensuring that education is included. A far different approach has been that taken by the Cleveland Clinic, in which a complete reorganization resulted in no departments of medicine or surgery after realignment into a full service line paradigm.

Unfortunately, few data exist to indicate which pathway works best. Therefore, it will be of critical importance for healthcare scholars to study carefully the ongoing efforts at the Cleveland Clinic and at other AMCs to develop service lines in order to understand which elements work best for the overall mission of the AMC: providing outstanding patient care. In addition, all institutions must display a great deal of flexibility as they evaluate their own efforts so that they can quickly implement change if their initial efforts are not successful.

AMC Leadership Must Identify and Give Responsibility and Authority to a Service Line Director or Directors

Physician leadership has been shown to be critical for the success of the service line [17,27]. Therefore, the same efforts to recruit outstanding department chairs or division directors must be put into identifying a service line director or directors. Because "decision by committee" may not provide effective leadership, a service line director or directors must be clearly identified and provided with the authority to hold ancillary services accountable. For example, a cardiology service line must be able to hold hospital-based services such as radiology, anesthesiology, and laboratory medicine accountable for their actions. However, the service line leader must establish clear governance for the service line. Effective governance requires complete transparency of information—including financial information—among all participants of the service line and an opportunity for all participants to participate in the decision-making processes, recognizing that decisions can be made without consensus.

The reader will notice some ambiguity in my use of "director or directors." In the beginning of the research for this book, I assumed that a single service line director, independent of the department chairs and reporting to senior leadership, would be the most effective form of leadership for a service line. However, conversations with department chairs, service line leaders, and industry consultants have led me to believe that what works well for one institution may not work for another. Although there is no ambiguity in the view that clinical services must be aligned and seamless, how an institution gets there is very unclear, even among the so-called "experts."

There is a general consensus that matrix reporting is inefficient; however, there is far less agreement on whether the service line director should be a chairman, a division chief, a new recruit, or an existing member of the faculty and whether responsibility should be shared by two individuals. In the short term, these decisions must be made within the culture of an individual AMC. Furthermore, it appears that a process that involves all departments is more logical than one that involves just a single department. However, we will only be able to understand what works best once a large number of AMCs have "experimented" with various models of integration and shared the results of those experiments with their colleagues.

Regardless of the specific structure, the service line director must provide leadership opportunities for each of the composite parts of the service line. For example, a cardiology service line should provide leadership positions for the chief of cardiology, the chief of cardiothoracic surgery, the chief of vascular surgery, etc. The service line director must hold division directors accountable but should carefully define their responsibilities while also ceding to them the required level of authority to accomplish their tasks. In addition, the various members of the service lines should have adequate opportunities to meet and discuss issues in an open and transparent manner.

One important component of a successful service line is that the service line leader has responsibilities and authority for both outpatient and inpatient operations. This is often a stumbling block when the hospital and the medical school are not integrated; however, it is important because it provides a seamless experience for the patient. Indeed, it is unlikely that a service line will make economic sense unless the multiple elements of the AMC are integrated. In addition, the service line should integrate all of the individuals involved in patient care, including nurses, social workers, case managers, physical therapists, and pharmacists.

The Optimal Service Line Includes Administrative and Economic Integration

Regardless of leadership, without integrating finances across the members of the service line, the service line does not represent vertical integration. Only through financial integration can the less remunerative specialties be incorporated into the service line concept. Financial integration of the service line provides an opportunity to rationalize cross-subsidization across the various specialties of the medical center.

Creation of Service Lines Must Consider
Education of Students and Residents

AMC leaders have criticized service lines on the basis that they may hinder the educational experience of students and residents; however, the service line might actually improve the educational experience as students see care from a multidisciplinary standpoint rather than just from the perspective of one specialty. During the first 2 years of medical school, the students are taught in integrated blocks based on organ systems. That is, they learn the biochemistry, physiology, and clinical pathology of each organ system in a unified approach.

By contrast, during the clinical years, the educational experience is not integrated across the various specialties. The development of service lines provides a unique opportunity to reevaluate the clinical experience and to develop novel approaches to ensure that the core clerkships are able to support the full spectrum of medical care through an integrated rather than a rigid, single-discipline structure.

Service lines can also facilitate opportunities for both residents and students to participate in clinical research by allowing freer movement of research faculty and trainees across the different disciplines of medicine. The technologic advances in the translational and clinical sciences have pulled down the walls that have traditionally separated the various departments; thus, a service line approach can enhance the clinical and translational research enterprises of all participants. For example, the amalgamation of a cardiology program having a rich basic science program with a cardiothoracic surgery program, a vascular program, and a radiology program having a paucity of basic science research provides a unique opportunity for the programs to link at the translational research level just as they are linked at the clinical level. This provides a competitive opportunity for the AMC because it allows new discoveries to be brought rapidly to a multidisciplinary clinical arena.

References

1. Flexner, A. 1973. Medical education in the United States and Canada: A report to the Carnegie Foundation for the Advancement of Teaching, 346. Bulletin no. 4, New York (reprinted by The Heritage Press, Buffalo, NY).
2. Hinohara, S., and Hisae, N., eds. 2001. *Osler's "A Way of Life" and other addresses with commentary and annotations*, 378. Durham, NC: Duke University Press.
3. Physician community unites around imaging resolution at AMA Annual Meeting. 2005 (www.acc.org/aadvocacy/advoc_issues/imaging_063005.hm).
4. http://en.wikipedia.org/wiki/Vertical_integration

5. Levin, S. A., Saxton, J. W., and Johns, M. M. 2008. Viewpoint: Developing integrated clinical programs: It's what academic health centers should do better than anyone. So why don't they? *Academic Medicine* 83 (1): 59–65.
6. http://cancercenters/cancer/gov/documents/CCSG_Guide12_04.pdf
7. Rettig, R. 1977. *Cancer crusade: The story of the National Cancer Act of 1971.* Princeton, NJ: Princeton University Press, 375 pp.
8. The Mayo Clinic. Transplant programs at Mayo (www.mayoclinic.org/transplant) (Jan. 5, 2008).
9. www.hmc.psu.edu/heartandvascular (Jan. 5, 2008).
10. Slater, R. 1999. *Jack Welch and the GE way.* New York: McGraw–Hill.
11. Case, J. 1998. *The open-book experience: Lessons from over 100 companies who successfully transformed themselves.* New York: Basic Books.
12. Liker, J. 2003. *The Toyota way.* New York: McGraw–Hill.
13. Charan, L. 2002. *Execution—The discipline of getting things done.* New York: Crown Business.
14. The National Academies Council on Interdisciplinary Research. Facilitating interdisciplinary research. Washington, D.C., National Academies Council on Interdisciplinary Research. 2004. National Institutes of Health Office of Portfolio Analysis and Strategic Initiatives, Division of Strategic Coordination. NIH roadmap for medical research. http://nihroadmap.nih.gov (accessed Jan. 4, 2008).
15. ABC News/Kaiser Family Foundation/SUA Today. 2006. Health care in America. 2006 Survey. Available at www.kff.org/kaiserpolls/pomr101606pkg.cfm (accessed Jan. 4, 2008).
16. Gee, D. A., and Rosenfeld, L. A. 1984. The effect on academic health centers of tertiary care in community hospitals. *Journal of Medical Education* 59:547–552.
17. Parker, V. A., Charns, M. P., and Young, G. J. 2001. Clinical service lines in integrated delivery systems: An initial framework and exploration. *Journal of Healthcare Management* 46 (4): 261–275.
18. Shortell, S. M., Anderson, D. A., Gillies, R. R., Mitchell, J. B., and Morgan, K. L. 1993. Building integrated systems—The holographic organization. *Healthcare Forum Journal* 36 (2): 20–26.
19. Byrne, M. M., Charns, M. P., Parker, V. A., Meterko, M. M., and Wray, N. P. 2004. The effects of organization on medical utilization: An analysis of service line organization. *Medical Care* 42 (1): 28–37.
20. Skinner, D. B. 2002. Evolution of an academic medical center to an academic health system. *Journal of the American College of Surgeons* 194 (1): 1–7.
21. Corwin, S. J., Cooper, M. R., Leiman, J. M., Stein, D. E., Pardes, H., and Berman, M. A. 2003. Model for a merger: New York–Presbyterian's use of service lines to bring two academic medical centers together. *Academic Medicine* 78 (11): 1114–1120.
22. Young, J. M. 2007. Personal communication.
23. Keroack, M. A., Youngberg, B. J., Cerese, J. L., Krsek, C., Prellwitz, L. W., and Trevelyan, E. W. 2007. Organizational factors associated with high performance in quality and safety in academic medical centers. *Academic Medicine* 82 (12): 1178–1186.

24. Epstein, A. L., and Bard, M. A. 2008. Selecting physician leaders for clinical service lines: Critical success factors. *Academic Medicine* 83 (3): 226–234.
25. Larson, E., and Gobeli, D. 1987. Matrix management: Contradictions and insights. *California Management Review* 29:126–138.
26. Crist, T. B., LaRusso, N. F., Meyers, F. J., Clayton, C. P., and Ibrahim, T. 2003. Centers, institutes, and the future of clinical departments: Part II. *American Journal of Medicine* 115 (9): 745–747.
27. Longshore, G. F. 1998. Service-line management/bottom-line management. *Journal of Health Care Finance* 24 (4): 72–79.

Chapter 3

Leadership in the Academic Medical Center

> I recommend that the organization of the Hospital shall be on the Military or Railroad plan, i.e., that it shall have one head, and only one, who shall receive his directions from, and be responsible directly to the Board of Trustees, and that all orders and instructions which the Board may make relative to the discipline and internal management of the Hospital shall be issued through him. This Officer should be a competent medical man, and a man of executive ability.
>
> **John Shaw Billings**
> *Planner of The Johns Hopkins Hospital, 1875* [1]

Introduction

Although the AMC at the turn of the century might have been amenable to a leadership structure similar to that of the military or the railroad, as described by Dr. Billings, the complexity found in today's AMC makes it unlikely that leadership strategies can be defined in such a straightforward model. Unfortunately, few objective assessments have been made of the value of different leadership structures in the AMC. This is in marked contrast to the wealth of data available on leadership strategies in the world of business. For example, Amazon.com lists over 53,000 titles related to "business" leadership, but only 33 titles related to leadership in academic medical centers—half of which are not specifically related to the search term.

As AMCs face increasing economic challenges and begin to integrate their various entities, the development of an effective leadership structure becomes increasingly important. Indeed, integration and restructuring cannot effectively be undertaken without a significant change in the leadership structure. In this chapter, we will look at recent data confirming that the current leadership structure needs to be revised, discuss the organizational impediments to effective leadership that are found at many AMCs, describe a model that can improve the role of leaders in today's AMCs, and present recommendations on how to transition from our current structure to a new leadership paradigm. This new leadership structure strengthens the ability of the AMC to focus on the core mission of providing outstanding patient care.

AMC Leaders Face Formidable Challenges

Although business scholars have not carefully studied the leadership structures of the AMC, substantive information supports the notion that current leadership structures are not effective. For example, the average tenure of a dean of a U.S. medical school—the individual generally presumed to be the senior academic official at an AMC—is less than 4 years, which is 1 year less than the median tenure of CEOs of Fortune 500 companies [2]. Arthur Rubenstein, dean of the University of Pennsylvania School of Medicine and executive vice president for the health system, attributed the relatively short tenure of medical school deans to "a combination of dean burnout because of the intensity and time requirements of the job as well as the challenges associated with maintaining the favor of a broad range of constituents—including faculty, students, donors and the university leadership—in a challenging environment and with limited resources" [2]. Claire Pomeroy, vice chancellor for human health services at the University of California, Davis, and dean of the university's School of Medicine similarly noted [2]:

> Being a dean is challenging. First, you have to balance these really diverse missions—academics, research and a complex clinical delivery system—which takes a wide spectrum of skills. We're all more expert in one of those areas than in others, and it's very hard to find the person who is comfortable talking with the HMO providers as meeting one-on-one with first-year medical students. There's a lot of culture clash that goes on and it's really hard to satisfy all those constituencies for a long period of time. Secondly, one of the main

jobs of being dean is getting people the resources they need in those diverse missions, and recently they have been inadequate resources. You're constantly battling to get the resources that your organization needs to be successful and you don't meet everybody's needs.

A recent survey by the Council of Deans of the Association of American Medical Colleges provides additional insights into the challenges facing AMC leaders [3]. A majority of respondents noted that the role of dean was impacted most by the decline in the resources available to medical schools following an era of abundance, the increased competition that AMCs faced in the clinical arena, and a reliance on clinical revenues to support medical education. One dean noted that this change resulted in a shift from "being what I'd call more of an academic deanship to more of what I'd call a marketplace CEO" [3]. The majority of respondents also noted that a major impediment to surviving both as a dean and as a medical school in the new healthcare environment was the failure of the AMC environment to align the dean's responsibilities with the authority to manage. The respondents noted three factors that could be assessed to evaluate the dean's potential for leading the institution in a time of change [3]:

1. Does the dean have adequate support from higher management to serve as a change agent?
2. Does the dean have sufficient authority over the clinical enterprise?
3. Does the dean have enough internal leverage to pursue the school's mission effectively?

Institutional stability was also seen as an important component of a successful tenure as a dean. Two-thirds of the respondents noted that, to be effective, a dean needed support from above as well as stability in senior leadership in both the university and the hospital. Indeed, four of eleven former deans had resigned their positions due to institutional instability. Additional obstacles to success were a "failure of will on the part of the institution to endorse the dean in initiating change" and university leaders who "distance themselves from the dean, who, in turn, becomes expendable" [3]. As one former dean noted [3]:

There's got to be a clear understanding between whoever is doing the hiring and the candidate as to what the university or the institution wants accomplished, and ideally, there is an understanding that the resources and political support that will be necessary to achieve those objectives will be forthcoming, if not forever, for three years, for five years, whatever the time frame may be to accomplish the changes.

A major cause of the early departure of deans has been the intense conflicts that arise between the academic and clinical missions at many AMCs. One dean summed it up best when he said [3]:

> If I am in charge of both the hospital and the medical school, I don't have to arbitrate[;] I just say that's what's going to happen. I may have people below me, one says we don't want the students, the other says I want the students, but there's somebody who has the authority to make the final decision....If you have split administrations, how do a man and wife decide? They argue it out. They fight it out. If you have one person calling the shots, it's easy....It is the central governance problem in academic medicine today.

The chairpersons of the clinical departments face challenges no different from those of the dean. In the early parts of the twentieth century, the chairs of clinical departments had God-like status. They spent their time caring for patients, teaching, and pursuing research and, because of the relatively small size of most departments, their administrative roles were limited. As AMCs grew in both size and complexity, the job of the department chair became increasingly administrative and far more intricate. Because departmental practice plans remained independent, the chairs of the large departments had considerable autonomy and authority.

In the mid- to late 1990s, the independent department practice plans began to merge together into unified practice plans. Although these practice plans often did not work as integrated entities—that is, revenues were not shared across the traditional departmental barriers—they did have leadership teams. In some cases, the boards of the practice plan consisted of the entire group of clinical chairmen; in others, the practice plan was managed by a committee of chairs.

Regardless of structure, major decisions regarding clinical finances began to be made by the group of departments rather than by the individual chairs. At the same time, the economic and administrative separation of academic hospitals from their affiliated medical schools further diminished the role of the department chair. Chairs found themselves with similar levels of responsibility, but substantially less authority and a reporting structure to a large number of administrators—many of whom had different agendas [4]. In some AMCs, a department chair may need to discuss a single business opportunity or recruitment with a dean, a practice plan director, a practice plan CEO, a hospital CEO, a hospital COO, a hospital CMO, and a provost in order to achieve the necessary buy-in and support. This inefficient and cumbersome leadership structure usually results in nothing getting done.

The failure to define their roles clearly and to provide them with the necessary level of administrative authority has led to marked instability among department chairs and deans. This has led to job insecurity, which in turn causes many potential leaders to turn away from leadership opportunities and those who accept the mantle of leadership to do so for a relatively short period of time [5,6]. For example, in the 1970s, the average tenure for chairs of departments of medicine was 5.272 years. However, between 2000 and 2006, the average tenure of a chair of medicine had fallen to 3.997 years—less than the term of most start-up packages and contracts [6]. This average tenure is shorter than that of university presidents (8.5 years), chairs of obstetrics and gynecology (7.5 years), and the chief executive officers of Fortune 500 companies (~5 years) [2].

There might be some consolation in the fact that chairs of medicine do have a slightly longer average tenure than do NFL head coaches; however, the coaches have substantially higher salaries and often longer contracts [7]. However, like NFL head coaches, Department of Medicine chairs sometimes move on to other "teams" as a dean or as a chair [6]. When asked how they might advise current chairs, a group of former chairs responded in the following ways: "Don't think of a chair as a permanent position; evaluate your effectiveness regularly; plan your exit; consider your next career move as soon as you become chair and reevaluate your plan regularly; don't threaten to resign; and negotiate an exit package at the time of appointment or reappointment" [8].

A lack of job satisfaction is also found among the chairs of other medical specialties. A survey in 2002 found that 22% of chairs of obstetrics and gynecology departments were "somewhat/very dissatisfied with their positions" [9]. They also noted "emotional exhaustion" and female chairs reported working more hours per week than their male counterparts [9]. Even chairs of ophthalmology, a group that is usually thought of as having higher job satisfaction, reported scores on a recent survey that reflected low personal achievement, emotional exhaustion, and a high risk for career burnout [10,11]. These results were consistent with a study evaluating burnout in chairs of departments of otolaryngology, who identified stressors that had resulted in decreased job satisfaction, including hospital and department deficits, billing audits, loss of key faculty, staff dismissal, disputes with the dean, and being a defendant in a malpractice case [12].

It has been noted that "the current environment of academic medicine—with increased demands to do more with less—has made [these] chairs particularly susceptible to developing burnout" [10]. During his presidency of the Association of American Medical Colleges, Jordan Cohen said, "As unprecedented reforms pull our complex organizations in new directions, the department chair is arguably the linchpin bearing the most stress" [13]. According to Wilson, "Department chairs, once managing partners who set the research agenda, determined the clinical direction, and designed creative educational programs, find themselves in the role of 'shop stewards,' ensuring the work output, setting the hours, organizing call schedules, settling disputes, negotiating wages, and scuffling for directorships with the administrators" [14].

The 5-Year Rule

At a national meeting of department chairs, I had lunch with a group of colleagues: Three had just become chairs for the second time and two had recently become chairs. The conversation turned to what one colleague referred to as "the 5-year rule." A neophyte, I asked what they meant by this expression. One colleague replied, "That's when the money from your recruitment package runs out and you find that there really aren't any other funds at your disposal so you have to leave or begin to fire everyone that you hired over the past 5 years." Because deans at many schools do not have enough resources to support all of the school's departments, a common strategy is to put together a recruitment package that provides opportunities for only short-term growth and recruitment. At the end of 5 years, the dean must shift the resources to other departments, leaving few resources to support the extended packages of the new division chiefs and investigators who were recruited during the later years of the 5-year package. When the dollars that come from the medical school drop precipitously, the department is left to stand on its own two feet.

This strategy fails for two reasons. First, no research program can stand on its own without institutional support and, second, unexpected budget downturns can occur, resulting in an inability of the medical school to fulfill its 5 years of obligations. Thus, as pointed out by my colleagues, the real meaning of the 5-year rule is that, before reaching the 5-year window, a departmental chair should begin to look for what one of my colleagues described as an "exit strategy." Thus, it is not surprising that the average tenure of a chair is less than 5 years.

Although one can look humorously at the 5-year rule, a closer examination reveals that it can have a significant impact on leadership in the AMC. Like deans and department chairs in academia, corporate CEOs also have a relatively short tenure—only about 1 year longer than that of a medical school dean. However, there are distinct differences between a corporate CEO and a dean. For example, corporate CEOs generally do what they were trained to do; that is, they manage people and companies. Thus, when a CEO leaves a position, he or she has the opportunity to go to another position in the same or a different industry.

By contrast, AMC leaders are trained to be clinicians, investigators, or both rather than business leaders. Those in higher leadership positions, including deans, vice presidents, or even chairs of large departments, are often unable to continue their research or clinical activities at a level that would allow them to be competitive on a full-time basis and thus it is very difficult for them to transition readily back into a general faculty position. Unlike CEOs in corporate America, deans and department chairs do not have "golden parachutes"—exit packages or stock options that allow them to transition from one job to another without personal financial sacrifices and often allow them to land quite comfortably into retirement. The average age of today's AMC dean is 58, so, in most cases, he or she is neither old enough nor financially stable enough to retire after stepping down from deanship.

As a result, many former deans populate the offices of healthcare consulting firms, venture capital funds, the pharmaceutical industry, and large multinational executive search firms. More importantly, the uncertainty of their future also leads deans to be risk averse. They avoid initiating unpopular changes in structure or culture that could shorten their tenure, believing that deferring decisions about implementing major change could appreciably prolong their tenure [15,16].

Cultural Impediments to Effective Leadership

Because faculty, and in particular senior faculty, were taught from medical school to be self-sufficient and independent and because promotion in an AMC is based singularly on individual achievement rather than on a commitment to a collective goal, the faculty by definition becomes an impediment to change— particularly when that change involves moving to a more collaborative environment and a team approach to both clinical care and science. Institutional power and influence are directly related to the money that any individual brings to the institution from grants or from clinical revenues.

At large AMCs with thousands of faculty members, governance is often more rational because any single physician or group of physicians has less influence on the economic integrity of the whole. However, at smaller AMCs—over half of the current 125 medical centers—smaller overall research portfolios, hospital margins, and endowments are associated with a smaller margin between revenues and expenditures. Thus, any single investigator or clinician can have a real or perceived impact on institutional finances if he or she leaves the institution. As one dean noted [3]:

> The problem…is that your survival frequently is dependent upon the faculty at large, their judgment; and, you know, that can make it difficult to take the bold steps you may need to take at a time when there's a lot of change going on around you. [There is] always the fear that you're going to upset too many people, and the more people you upset, the less you could manage.

Another dean noted from a more academic business standpoint: "Well, the problem with academe [is that] academe is a compendium of a thousand small business people,…most of whom place their own interests at least on a par with the interests of the institution at large. And so, consequently, the first question they may ask is, well, how does this affect me?" [3]. Thus, to be successful, a dean must have some type of leverage over the faculty; resources and authority are the two levers that can most successfully be used to effect change.

Another cultural impediment to effective leadership in an AMC—one that is rarely discussed because it is viewed as politically incorrect to do so—is the presence in some AMCs of voluntary faculty over whom the dean or hospital president has no control. Many have likened leadership in the AMC to an effort to "herd cats"; one can describe efforts to lead a voluntary faculty as "herding tigers."

Voluntary faculty do not care about academic awards, promotion, nomination to leading academic societies, research support, or research space. Their salaries are not controlled by the dean and they often include technical services in their practices that compete directly with those housed in the AMC, such as imaging facilities. Although they often enjoy the opportunity to teach and can "draft" off the esteem associated with being a faculty member at a prestigious university, voluntary faculty also have an open opportunity to move their practice to another hospital—especially when multiple AMCs or quaternary teaching hospitals compete in the same geographic region. The portability of their practice often gives them a level of influence in the AMC that is out of proportion with the actual financial impact of their practice.

Although no objective data to assess the true role of voluntary faculty in any single AMC exist, it is interesting to note that of the top hospitals on the *U.S. News and World Report* list, most have so-called "closed staff models" in which only full-time members of the faculty practice plan receive hospital privileges. How leadership in open-staff models deal with voluntary faculty—or how good they are at herding tigers—can often supersede the ability to provide excellence in patient care as a marker of success or failure of an AMC leader.

Structural Impediments to Effective Leadership—The Loosely Coupled System

Although scholars in the fields of business and management have not studied AMCs per se, some of their work is directly applicable to the structure of the AMC. For example, the structure of an AMC is very much like the organizational structure that Orton and Weick first referred to as a "loosely coupled system" [17]. In such a system, "individual elements have high autonomy relative to the larger system in which they are imbedded, often creating a federated character of the institution....actions in one part of the system can have little or no effect on another or can unpredictably trigger responses out of proportion to the stimulus" [17]. The individual elements of a loosely coupled system are poorly integrated because each element focuses on itself rather than upon the whole. Furthermore, the central authority is derived from the members rather than the individual parts of the entity receiving their authority from a centralized structure. Indeed, one might define the loosely coupled system as an anarchy rather than an organization.

Numerous situations can occur in a loosely coupled AMC that obviate the ability of its leaders to make the right decision at the right time. For example, one colleague described a recent episode at an institution in which the chief of the division of cardiology decided that his group was not getting its fair share of discretionary dollars available to the department. Based on a strategic plan, the chair of the department had decided to invest some of the department's discretionary dollars in the recruitment of two very promising young clinician scientists and a new development person to enhance the department's fundraising efforts. However, the chief of cardiology wanted to raise the salary of his clinical group, despite the fact that their productivity had remained relatively flat over the previous 2 years and that they were already at the 75th percentile of salaries for academic divisions.

When the chair of medicine stood his ground, the chief of cardiology took his concerns to the dean of the medical school and to the CEO of the hospital. Fearing that the hospital's cardiology program could be at risk if the chief of cardiology left for a competing hospital, the CEO agreed to provide additional dollars to the division. However, because the hospital and medical school finances were a zero-sum game, the hospital withdrew some of its support to the dean, who in turn decreased support to the department. As a result, the chair was unable to pursue the department's strategic goals.

A second challenge that faces the loosely coupled AMC is what John Isaacson has referred to as the difficulties in building alliances between "church" and "state" [18]. Isaacson uses these terms to define the two halves of the AMC: the professional half (the church) and the managerial half (the state). In church–state organizations, the mission-driven professionals define the directions of the organization and provide the innovation to move the organization forward from a technology and knowledge standpoint, and the "state" handles the business of the institution.

Because AMCs were often relatively simple structures without complex finances, external regulation, or competition, the job of administration was relatively straightforward and the members of the church often failed to recognize the value of the state. Indeed, the state was often populated by individuals who had "retired" from the church. As a result, the faculty generally held a relatively low opinion of the administration. However, as AMCs have become increasingly complex financial organizations, inherent conflicts have arisen between management and faculty, resulting in constant tension and disingenuous behavior on both sides. These conflicts become even more disruptive when management lacks sophistication and a high level of business skills.

Perhaps the most important impediment to managing a loosely coupled AMC is what has variously been termed "jurisdictional proliferation," "semi-autonomous units," or "turf" [19]. In loosely coupled systems, there are not only departments, divisions, and schools but also centers, institutes, and programs. Each of these entities lives in a microenvironment with its own leader and administrator. Each unit has worked to develop its internal structure and relationships, which may or may not mesh well with the structure of the overall federation. Microalliances between these various centers and departments may provide some opportunities for collaboration; however, in many cases, these individual structures polarize rather than unite the whole.

For example, the faculty and managers in the departments of radiology, neurosurgery, and cardiology might fiercely resist the efforts of the medical center to purchase all of its imaging equipment from a single vendor because each individual department has a relationship with a specific vendor that provides them with research support or because they believe that one piece of equipment is better than another. However, by purchasing all of the equipment from a single vendor, the hospital might be able to negotiate a cost structure that can save millions of dollars.

Therefore, in loosely coupled systems the end game becomes the ability of management to convince the individual stakeholders that each will profit by collaborating—an accomplishment that requires a large degree of transparency in terms of how profits are utilized. By contrast, in a tightly coupled AMC, the purchasing would be done by the institution with input from the physicians but without impediments.

Leading around the Edges

Although it is clearly recognized that AMC leadership is challenged, there is little agreement about how AMC leadership can best fulfill their goals. One group has recently recommended an approach first put forward by Albert Hirschman in 1967 [20]: "trait taking and trait making." In this context, AMC leaders are advised to acknowledge the historic semiautonomous status of the various parts of the AMC while looking for opportunities to move the organization gradually toward a more integrated approach to education, clinical service, and research [21]. AMC leaders work to keep the institution within its "safety zone" and manage by building synergies between units [22].

The first element of a management system that recognizes rather than changes the existing structure of a loosely coupled system is referred to as "protecting" the AMC [21]. Protecting the institution requires four actions on the part of an AMC leader:

recognizing the support and authority that derive from sensitivity to the needs of the existing system;
creating space to build leadership;
authorizing leadership colleagues as surrogates; and
building a modern "church–state" organization.

This involves establishing a system of fairness in the decision-making process so that all elements feel equally protected, and making the decision-making process transparent.

The second element of leadership is referred to as "creating space to build leadership." This part emphasizes the need of an AMC leader to be an administrator—a manager as well as a leader. Leaders must recognize that the high level of inertia found in many loosely coupled AMCs will keep ongoing activities moving forward during times of change, while the organizational cultures that make change so difficult can also keep the AMC relatively stable as long as high-priority risks are mitigated. By assembling a group of individuals who have a long-term history with the AMC and mixing in a group of new recruits, AMC leaders can identify surrogates who can help lead the institution.

AMC leaders must also attract strong business and managerial talent who can help develop new strategies for survival. In addition, AMC leaders must identify new sources of money by active fundraising or by merging or phasing out ineffective business units. The most difficult hurdle faced by AMC leaders is the effectiveness of many individuals in the AMC to preserve the status quo. This is especially true in light of the short term of office of most AMC deans and department chairs, which allows many opponents of change simply to wait out their tenure. Gilmore recommends creating windows of opportunity for bringing departments together by establishing collaborative research or clinical projects between different departments or by finding novel opportunities to initiate change through new buildings, the physical move of a department, the installation of a new information system, or the recruitment of new chairs [21].

Can the Traditional Academician Lead?

As the business of medicine has become increasingly complex, it has been argued that a new type of physician leader is needed. Scholars have pointed out that the traditional measures of talent that have been used to identify candidates for leadership positions in academia—demonstrated excellence in patient care, teaching, and/or basic or clinical research—do not adequately measure the ability of an individual to succeed in today's complex and competitive healthcare environment [23,24]. They point out that the successful academician has advanced in the academic environment by focusing on goals that have required significant autonomy whether it is in the physician–patient interaction or the management of an independently funded research program. By contrast, administrators usually advance in their careers by pursuing graduate degrees in business or management, perfecting their managerial and leadership skills through job opportunities, and demonstrating an ability to build collaborative teams that can focus priorities toward attaining a defined vision or goal.

Thus, it has been proposed that there is a misalignment between the clinical and/or research skills that a potential academic health center leader is graded on and the capabilities in business and leadership skills that may be far more important to the future success of the institution. These views have led to the belief that the traditional academician is not prepared to lead today's complex academic health centers and it has led some organizations to choose businessmen rather than physicians as leaders of both the academic medical centers and their governing boards.

However, based on the research for this book, I would take strong exception to these opinions. The suggestion that modern academic medical centers need a new leadership phenotype is inconsistent with the success at many of today's most accomplished AMCs, where the centers are led by individuals who have previously demonstrated excellence in biomedical and/or clinical research as well as in clinical care. Returning to one of the basic tenets of this book—that the future of academic medical centers will be dependent on their ability to provide the highest level of patient care across the entire spectrum of an individual's disease—it would appear axiomatic that the best stewards of excellence in care are individuals who have demonstrated excellence in the clinical and research arena throughout their careers.

Thus, it is not surprising that most of the top U.S. academic medical centers and their hospitals are not led by businessmen but rather by highly accomplished physicians or physician–scientists: Victor Dzau at Duke, Arthur Rubenstein at the University of Pennsylvania, Samuel Their at Harvard, Edward Miller at Hopkins, Toby Cosgrove at the Cleveland Clinic, Dennis Cortese at the Mayo Clinic, Michael Johns at Emory, Herbert Pardes at New York Hospital, Edward Benz at the Dana Farber Cancer Center, and Michael Bishop at the University of California, San Francisco, to name a few.

It is important to look at these individuals as scientists, clinicians, and leaders rather than simply to assess their ability to read a balance sheet. Each of these individuals demonstrated success in leading large research endeavors, national societies, and prestigious departments before moving up the academic ladder. However, it could also be argued that they led their departments at a time when academic chairs had far more responsibility and authority than they have today. Thus, our challenge is not to produce a new type of leader, but rather to ensure that today's up-and-coming leaders are given the opportunity to have responsibility, authority, and mentoring at each level of their careers in order to prepare them for future leadership positions.

Redefining Leadership in the AMC

How can we define, develop, and support the AMC leaders of tomorrow? First, I would argue that we must ensure that our leaders are able to focus on the core mission of the AMC: providing outstanding patient care. In order to carry out the core mission effectively, the AMC leader should be a "competent medical man" (or woman), as Dr. Billings described in 1875. However, AMCs must take additional important steps in order to ensure that their leaders can succeed in fulfilling the core mission by restructuring the leadership paradigm in such a way that AMC leaders can lead the organization rather than "leading around the edges" of a loosely coupled system because such a system is unlikely to work in the increasingly challenging and competitive healthcare marketplace. Toward this end, AMCs should approach realigning their leadership paradigms by following several key principles described in the following sections.

These recommendations are in large part consistent with those that were made by a group of senior leaders in academic administration, health policy, institutional management, and healthcare systems that came together under the auspices of Cap Gemini Ernst & Young US, LLC; the University of Virginia; and Emory University under the banner of the Blue Ridge Academic Health Group to discuss the challenges that face chief executive officers of academic health centers (AHCs) [25].

Empower AMC Leaders Based on Lessons from Industry

At a time when the business of many academic medical centers is clearly challenged, key leaders have a high turnover rate, and many academic centers have negative margins, important lessons can be learned from following leadership development strategies proven to facilitate the development and sustainability of some of the world's great companies. Businesses differ in their leadership structures in that they have a "culture of discipline" that mitigates against the need for hierarchy, bureaucracy, and excessive controls [26]. This is especially important in large corporations with multiple subsidiaries, where individual subsidiaries—analogous to AMC departments—have great levels of autonomy.

While requiring a level of accountability for achieving both individual and core goals, successful businesses create an environment that fosters innovation [27], an ability to move new agendas forward rapidly [28], and expectation that employees will take responsibility for quality and productivity and an entrepreneurial spirit [29]. Managers are encouraged to try new approaches repeatedly and to take risks as well as to change course rapidly if new approaches are not successful [26]. They look for every potential opportunity to lower costs and are expected to process all opportunities fully. Most importantly, they give managers the resources necessary to get the job done as well as the necessary level of authority to manage their group.

Universities must pass on to deans and deans must pass on to chairs and division chiefs a level of authority that matches their responsibilities. When physician management teams are brought together to develop strategic initiatives, address institutional problems, deal with fiscal emergencies, or set the agenda for the institution, the teams must be allowed to have open dialogue and debate, must put self-protection aside for the good of the institution, and must be able to see institutional funds flow in a transparent fashion in order to make informed decisions. Chairs and division chiefs must be empowered as managers and given the authority to make key decisions, the ability to allocate resources, and the opportunity to raise funds through entrepreneurial ventures.

In his study of publicly traded companies that had transitioned from "good to great," Jim Collins found that during the pivotal transition years, these companies had what he described as "level 5 leadership" [26]. Type 5 leaders

> are ambitious for their companies but not for themselves;
> set up their successors for even greater success;
> allow vigorous debate in the search for the right answer;
> display a compelling modesty;

confront the brutal facts of the current reality while maintaining absolute
faith in the ability to succeed;

have an incurable need to produce sustained results;

approach tasks with a workmanlike diligence; and

more often than not, come from within the institution.

The leaders of these "good to great" companies did not "create alignment,"
"manage change," or "motivate the troops." Instead, they led by demonstrating that persistent efforts focused by a core mission can lead to tangible results
that, over time, result in development of momentum and significant change. In
addition, they establish a culture of discipline that gives people both freedom
and responsibility to take actions consistent with the overall priorities and core
mission of the group—a freedom that the current structure of many AMCs
lacks [26]. These characteristics apply to each of the leaders of America's great
academic centers listed previously.

Empower Leaders through the Development of Service Lines

One method that could facilitate the development of stronger linkages across
departmental silos and serve as a catalyst for more global restructuring of leadership responsibilities in the AMC is the development of service lines. Although
the service line construct was discussed in Chapter 2, it is relevant to discuss it
also in the context of academic center leadership because, if successful, the service
line concept can have a dramatic impact on the traditional leadership structure
of AMCs and empower a new leadership paradigm within the organization.

Successful businesses are not hierarchical but rather are horizontally integrated through development of management teams that provide a forum for
active dialogue and debate so that the realities the business faces can come to
the surface; at the same time, they have leaders who hold the individual groups
accountable [28]. Although successful businesses allow for debate, they do not
await consensus and business leaders are always able to make decisions regardless
of their popularity. Decisions are neither arbitrary nor capricious and are made
in a manner consistent with the clearly defined core mission of the institution: in
the case of the AMC, the ability to provide outstanding patient care. The development of a service line concept facilitates the organization and management of
multidisciplinary teams focused on improving the quality of care by focusing
efforts on a single disease entity.

One of the first studies of physician leadership for clinical service lines was
carried out by Epstein and Bard [30]. They found a wide variance in the goals
and expectations set for the service line leaders despite the fact that all of the centers had the same overall goals of increasing market share, volume, and revenue.

Some service lines were "virtual"—little more than a name and a telephone number; some integrated management and some integrated clinical programs through interdisciplinary teams. Only a few service lines had full integration with centralized clinical, financial, strategic, and operational functions. Second, all of the service lines studied used a "matrix structure." As a result [30],

> [Most of the service line leaders] lacked decision making power in one or more of the following areas and had to cede authority to a related academic or hospital leader: influence or authority over academic appointments; span of budgetary authority (up to and including profit and loss accountability); authority over allocation of clinical and research space and equipment; influence or authority over clinical productivity and quality expectations.

One chair noted: "I guess I'm concerned that if you take oncology and cardiology away from me, I'm going to be left with rheumatology and endocrinology and general internal medicine, and where am I going to find my money and resources?" [30]. As a result of the push back from the historic power structures in the institution, few of the service lines included in the study provided their leaders with the requisite authority to meet the overall objectives [31].

The study also found that the academic medical centers used relatively informal processes to "identify, evaluate, and select service line leaders" [30]. Even when the institution established a search committee, the committee did not create a job description or goals, as would occur in most external searches for a department chair or a dean. Cardiovascular service lines tended to select internal candidates and cancer service lines sought leaders through a national search process. This disparity was most likely because heart service lines wanted someone who would help maintain and grow their referral base and cancer service lines preferred someone who had a national reputation and would be attractive to National Cancer Institute review committees.

The selection of a service line leader was also influenced by the fact that the leader's job was "vitally shaped by the AHC's strategic, structural, and political context" [30]. Programs seeking someone with a national reputation sought external candidates, whereas those that focused on building a larger local referral base tended to seek candidates internally. Because of the matrix organizational model, most of the cardiology centers interviewed sought leaders who had "the capacity to influence others and build collaboration across departmental, disciplinary, and organizational lines"; cancer centers had the added need to identify individuals who were comfortable in all aspects of the cancer center, including bench research, clinical research, and patient care [30].

The institutions evaluated by Epstein differed from the Cleveland Clinic, where traditional academic departments have all but disappeared and each service line has a defined leader. Only time will tell which leadership structure is more effective; therefore, it will be imperative that scholars in business and management have full access to study the success or failure of these very different service line models.

Train the Next Generation of AMC Leaders

Another mandate that has come out of the many efforts to understand the complexities of leadership in the AMC is the urgent need for younger individuals who have didactic training in the "business of medicine." The absence of physician involvement in both strategic and tactical planning at the national, local, and institutional healthcare levels is believed to be one of the root causes of the problems in the current healthcare system [32]. In order to participate, scholars have suggested that physicians must gain the necessary "business" skills [32]. In response to this need, a variety of programs have been developed. These include traditional introductory programs that are part of continuing medical education programs, Internet-based programs, certificate programs, and on-site programs at individual AMCs. Each type of program has both strengths and weaknesses.

Continuing medical education programs have been held or more often are offered at national meetings. Alternatively, 1- to 2-week intensive management seminars are held by renowned academic institutions, including the Harvard Business School, the Wharton School, and the Kellogg School. Both of these types of programs have been criticized for being overly superficial and not providing the necessary skill set needed by tomorrow's leaders. For example, continuing medical education programs have been criticized for lacking the personal interactions and team building skills that are often of importance in loosely coupled systems [32]. The 1- to 2-week courses provide an intense educational experience, are well structured, give an approximation of the skills necessary for physician leaders to be successful, and allow the participants to concentrate on their efforts for a dedicated period of time. However, they are often attended by only a single faculty member rather than by a group. Similarly, physicians can access interactive Internet educational sites on their own schedules; however, the encounters are often sporadic and do not allow for team building, while at the same time reinforcing the autonomous behavior already ingrained in the physician culture [32].

Physicians may also choose to undertake a more comprehensive program that leads to a certificate of medical management (CMM), a master of government administration (MGA), a master of health administration, or a master of public health. Certificate programs include local programs such as those housed at the University of Kentucky [32], the University of Texas-Southwestern, and the Johns Hopkins University. Some of these programs can be accessed without travel through a Web-based program. Degree-granting programs can often be pursued during a single long weekend every month or two—with added interactions through Web-based opportunities or teleconferences.

One of the best alternatives for educating the next generation of leaders is internal leadership training programs [33]. Although costly for the host institution, these programs have the advantage that they can be focused on the unique needs of the institution; can teach skills that are needed for the particular tasks at hand; can "train" a large number of leaders at one time, thereby allowing them to begin to work together as a team by breaking down organizational boundaries that may separate them; and can be very effective in changing the organizational culture. These programs are built on the experience of successful industry training programs [34,35]. Successful companies have continuously trained their own leaders and planned the succession of those leaders into progressively more senior positions; this has allowed them to maintain and continually align their institutional visions and goals [26].

Recent initiatives have focused on training at the medical student and resident levels rather than waiting for physicians to complete their training and then matriculate into academic faculty positions [36,37]. These programs tend to recruit students who have work experience in areas such as investment banking and healthcare consulting and who set their career goals on managing hospitals or health plans or on pursuing careers in the business or high-technology sectors. It was hoped that these programs would develop a group of future leaders in academic medicine; however, the majority of students found little interest in working with public health needs, academic medical centers, or underserved populations [37,38]. Rather, the students were far more interested in pursuing careers in the for-profit world—an increasing trend among medical school graduates [39].

Perhaps the most important component of training the next generation of academic leaders is that the present leadership must provide opportunities for young faculty to take on projects, try new ideas, and make mistakes. A common tenet of successful businesses is that they constantly try new approaches to improve the productivity and success of the business. Successful companies (Microsoft is a prime example) are well recognized for allowing their employees—especially those in management positions—to take risks as long as the risks are consistent with the overall strategic goals and core missions of the business.

These initiatives provide a learning experience for future senior managers and provide insight into the mechanisms that can help in understanding the processes that are part of strategic decision making as well as in learning when to discontinue an unsuccessful project or when to place more resources in a project that has not yet proven fruitful but shows great promise. Unfortunately, in the hierarchical and risk-averse world of the academic medical centers, young physicians are often precluded from making decisions or in taking initiatives that involve some degree of financial risk.

Empower the Board of Trustees

In its report on AMCs, the Blue Ridge Academic Health Group found that AMC governance bodies (i.e., boards of trustees) should provide stronger leadership and guidance for AMC leaders. They recommended that AMC leaders [25,40]

continue and strengthen efforts to educate governing boards about immediate and longer term challenges facing AMCs;

initiate conversation with board members on their respective roles in the changing economic climate and boundary conditions that enable leaders to act effectively;

ensure that all members of the governance bodies clearly understand conflict of interest issues;

continue to develop performance measures for AMC leadership; and

encourage board members to play an active role while supporting the management team.

However, the Blue Ridge Group failed to point out some of the marked differences between the boards that oversee publicly traded or private companies and those that often oversee AMCs. For example, the boards of private medical schools are commonly composed of large donors or potential donors, community leaders, alumni, and, occasionally, individuals who provide services to the university such as major suppliers, heads of local law firms, or chairs of leading construction firms. In the case of public institutions, the membership is very similar to that of the private AMC, but also includes an assortment of political appointees and prominent members of the community.

These boards often do not bring the level of expertise that is needed by a hospital or university to understand the complex issues and potential solutions in what has become an increasingly complex industry. In addition, members of the boards of AMCs often do not even bring expertise in the core mission of the AMC: providing outstanding clinical care. Thus, although they are expected to oversee the financial investments made by AMCs, they do not have the requisite knowledge to provide the type of support that is required.

By contrast, businesses are often judged by their ability to include on their boards a group of individuals who can bring a high level of expertise in those areas in which the company competes [26]. For example, a survey of Canadian companies in 2006 demonstrated that individuals with relevant industry experience topped the profile list for new directors [41]. In addition, 98% of Canadian companies surveyed offered continuing education for directors run by the board rather than by management in order to enhance the board's knowledge base regarding the particular industry. Board members of most publicly traded companies are required to retire at a preset age and are graded based on factors including attendance at board meetings.

A key element in the selection of board members in successful companies is that they add value to the core mission by including individuals who, by virtue of their experience, can collectively help to guide the direction of the company [42]. For example, a relatively new start-up pharmabiotechnology company might include on its board the former presidents and CEOs of one of the region's largest public pharmaceutical companies, physicians with experience as founders and CEOs of highly successful biopharmaceutical start-ups, physician–investors with experience as investors and board members of successful biotech companies, and scientists with extensive experience in clinical trials and drug development.

By analogy, AMC boards should include individuals with experience in the healthcare industry, large healthcare organizations, the healthcare insurance industry, venture capital, healthcare law, business, finance, and healthcare management. In addition, AMC boards should include physician leaders with past experience in business and entrepreneurial activities or former deans or CEOs who understand the intricacies of the practice of medicine in a large, complex AMC.

Create Leadership Stability

The development of future leaders will also require that institutions recognize the intrinsic damage done when there is a change in leadership every 3 or 4 years. Both deans and department chairs must be provided with contracts that clearly outline their responsibilities, authority, and deliverables, while at the same time providing them with a level of security that will ensure their commitment to the institution. The future of academic medical centers cannot afford to have senior leaders, including department chairs and deans, who see these positions as simply short stops along the career ladder. Furthermore, budgets must be created that recognize that the growth of any department does not stop after 5 years, that basic science programs require external support no matter how robust they are, and that the quality of the recruits serves as the best yardstick for measuring an institution's value.

In addition, recruitment negotiations for senior leadership should include discussions about what a dean or chair will do within the institution once his or her tenure as a leader has been completed. Former deans and chairs can provide rich sources of information, talent, and experience within an academic medical center. More importantly, the knowledge that they have a future at their own institutions will allow them to take entrepreneurial and organizational risks as well as to feel comfortable in making the difficult and sometimes unpopular decisions necessary in order to ensure short-term change and long-term stability.

References

1. Billings, J. 1875. *Hospital construction and organization. Hospital plans.* New York: William Wood & Co.
2. Stuart, S. Route to the top: A snapshot of deans at U.S. medical schools. www.spencerstuart.com/research/articles/113/ 2007
3. Yedidia, M. 1998. Council of Deans survey. *Academic Medicine* 73:631–639.
4. Petersdorf, R. 1987. Some thoughts on medical center governance. *Pharos* 50:13–18.
5. Daugherty, R. 1998. Leading among leaders: The dean in today's medical school. *Academic Medicine* 73 (6): 649–653.
6. Ringenbach, J. L., and Ibrahim, T. 2008. Tenures for department chairs: How short is too short? *American Journal of Medicine* 121 (2): 163–168.
7. National Football League. www.nfl.com
8. Nettleman, M., and Schuster, B. L. 2007. Internal medicine department chairs: Where they come from, why they leave, where they go. *American Journal of Medicine* 120 (2): 186–190.
9. Gabbe, S. 22. Burnout in chairs of obstetrics and gynecology: Diagnosis, treatment and prevention. *American Journal Obstetrics and Gynecology* 186 (4): 601–612.
10. Cruz, O., Pole, C. J., and Thomas, S. M. 2007. Burnout in chairs of academic departments of ophthalmology. *Ophthalmology* 114:2350–2355.
11. Maslach, C., Jackson, S., and Leiter, M. P. 1996. *Maslach burnout inventory: Manual,* 3rd ed. Palo Alto, CA: Consulting Psychologist Press.
12. Johns, M. M., III, and Ossoff, R. H. 2005. Burnout in academic chairs of otolaryngology: Head and neck surgery. *Laryngoscope* 115 (11): 2056–2061.
13. Cohen, J. 1998. Leadership for medicine's promising future. *Academic Medicine* 73 (2): 132–137.
14. Wilson, S. 2005. The academic department of surgery: Between Scylla and Charybdis. *Archives of Surgery* 140 (8): 719–723.
15. Legnini, M. W., and Waldman, E. K. 1999. Preprint for the W.K. Kellogg Foundation, Economic & Social Research Institute.
16. Inglehart, J. Forum on the future of academic medicine 1998. Session III. Getting from here to there. *Academic Medicine* 3 (2): 146–151.

17. Weick, O. 1990. Loosely coupled systems: A reconceptualization. *Academy of Management Review* 15 (2): 203–223.
18. Gilmore, T. N., Hirschhorn, L., and Kelly, M., Challenges of leading and planning in an academic medical center. 1999 CFAR, Philadelphia, PA.
19. www.nationalacademies.org/onpinews/newsitem.aspx?RecordID-12089
20. Hirschman, A. 1967. Development projects observed. Washington, D.C.: Brookings Institution Press.
21. Gilmore, T. N., Hirschhorn, L., and Kelly, M., Challenges of leading and planning in an academic medical center. 1999 CFAR, Philadelphia, PA.
22. Dror, Y. 1989. Memo for system-reforming rules. *Futures.* August
23. McAlearney, A. S., Fisher, D., Heiser, K., Robbins, D., and Kelleher, K. 2005. Developing effective physician leaders: Changing cultures and transforming organizations. *Hospital Topics* 83 (2): 11–18.
24. Peters, R. 1992. When physicians fail as managers. *American College of Physician Executives.* Tampa, FL.
25. Blue Ridge Academic Health Group. 2000. In pursuit of greater value; stronger leadership in academic health centers Report 4. University of Virginia Health System: Gemini, Ernst & Young, LLC.
26. Collins, J. 2001. *Good to great.* New York: Harper Collins.
27. Hamel, G., and Getz, G. 2004. Funding growth in an age of austerity. *Harvard Business Review* 82 (7–8): 76–84.
28. Charan, L. 2002. *Execution—The discipline of getting things done.* New York: Crown Business.
29. Liker, J. 2003. *The Toyota way.* New York: McGraw–Hill.
30. Epstein, A. L., and Bard, M. A. 2008. Selecting physician leaders for clinical service lines: Critical success factors. *Academic Medicine* 83 (3): 226–234.
31. Crist, T. B., LaRusso, N. F., Meyers, F. J., Clayton, C. P., and Ibrahim, T. 2003. Centers, institutes, and the future of clinical departments: Part II. *American Journal of Medicine* 115 (9): 745–747.
32. Schwartz, R. W., Pogge, C. R., Gillis, S. A., and Hollsinger, J. W. 2000. Programs for the development of physician leaders: A curricular process in its infancy. *Academic Medicine* 75 (2): 133–140.
33. Morahan, P. S., Kasperbauer, D., McDade, S. A., Aschenbrener, C. A., Triolo, P. K., Monteleone, P. L., Counte, M., and Meyer, M. J. 1998. Training future leaders of academic medicine: Internal programs at three academic health centers. *Academic Medicine* 73 (11): 1159–1168.
34. Vicere, A. 1996. Executive education: The leading edge. *Organizational Dynamics* 1996:67–81.
35. Garvin, D. A. 1993. Building a learning organization. *Harvard Business Review* 71 (4): 78–91.
36. Paller, M. S., Becker, T., Cantor, B., and Freeman, S. L. 2000. Introducing residents to a career in management: The physician management pathway. *Academic Medicine* 75 (7): 761–764.
37. Sherrill, W. W. 2000. Dual-degree MD–MBA students: A look at the future of medical leadership. *Academic Medicine* 75 (10 Suppl): S37–S39.

38. Kurtz, M. 1992. The dual role dilemna in new leadership in health care management. *American College of Physician Executives,* Tampa, FL.
39. Letourneau, B. 1998. *In search of physician leadership.* Chicago: Health Administration Press.
40. Detmer, D., and Steen, E., eds. 2005. *The academic health center; leadership and performance.* Cambridge: Cambridge University Press, 315 pp.
41. Spencer Stuart. 2006. *Spencer Stuart board index.*
42. Carver, J. 1997. *Boards that make a difference: A new design for leadership in nonprofit and public organizations,* 2nd ed. San Francisco: Jossey–Bass.

SPHERE OF ACTION: RESEARCH

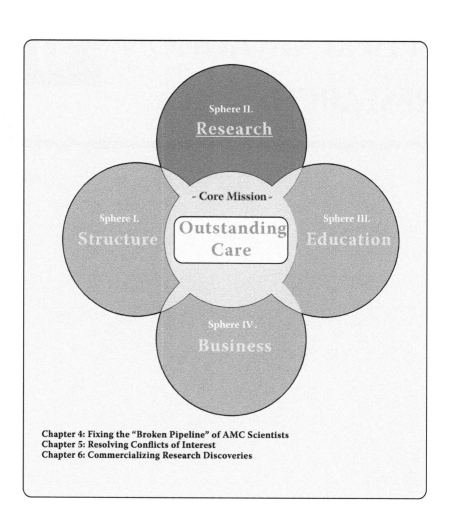

Sphere II.
Research

- Core Mission -
Sphere I.
Structure

Outstanding
Care

Sphere III.
Education

Sphere IV.
Business

Chapter 4

Fixing the "Broken Pipeline" of AMC Scientists

It is their conviction that in no branch of medical instruction is there such urgent need of facilities for practical work, as in the practical laboratory investigation of disease in order to discover improved methods for its relief. They are clearly of the opinion that this clinical laboratory will add materially to the resources of the Hospital for the study and cure of disease and at the same time enable the Medical School to furnish through painstaking, and systematic instruction to those who are to become future practitioners and teachers of medicine [1].

The Board of Trustees
The Johns Hopkins Hospital

Introduction

The preceding excerpt is from a response by the board of trustees of The Johns Hopkins Hospital to a donor of a research laboratory in 1896. Clearly, they recognized the importance of laboratory discovery in improving patient care and discovering cures for human disease. Since that time, transformational discoveries at America's AMCs have been as diverse as the development of the polio vaccine at the University of Pittsburgh, the invention of the cardiac bypass machine at the Jefferson Medical College, the invention and testing of the external and implantable cardiac defibrillators at Johns Hopkins, and the discovery at the University of Pennsylvania that led to the creation of herceptin, a novel new treatment for some breast cancers.

During the past half-century, virtually every new drug and device for the treatment of human disease was tested and evaluated at AMCs. However, as we will see, the research mission of the AMC is now severely threatened, which in turn impacts the core principle on which AMCs were founded. Funding for academic research from the National Institutes of Health has continued to decrease for over 5 years, students and faculty are leaving academia for other opportunities, AMCs have an increasingly difficult time attracting talented investigators, and clinical research has moved from U.S. AMCs to community practices and to sites in other countries. In this chapter, we will look at the causes of this change in America's ability to find new cures for human disease and how some AMCs have taken bold steps to support scientific research, as well as provide recommendations on how AMCs can link research with the core mission of providing excellence in patient care.

Supporting Research in the AMC—A Historical Perspective

Prior to 1900, medicine was taught by proprietary institutions that utilized traditional didactic teaching methods, including lectures and textbooks. These institutions were for-profit entities and the course work was often taught by a handful of physicians who owned the medical school. They had no laboratories, pursued no research, and, in most cases, had no affiliation with a university or hospital.

By the early 1900s, medicine changed with the gradual influx of American students who had trained in medical schools in Europe in which students gained thorough instruction in the scientific underpinnings of medicine as well as learning from experiences in the laboratory and at the patient's bedside. The opening of the Johns Hopkins Medical School in 1893 served as a model for what would become the American system of medical education. Funding for the emerging nonprofit medical schools came from a variety of sources, including John D. Rockefeller's foundation, the General Education Board; the Carnegie Corporation; private fundraising; and the efforts of the presidents of the affiliated universities. Many of the early faculty came from some of the wealthiest families of the times. Both medical educators and hospital officials began to recognize that education and research improved patient care. However, the growth of research in academic departments in America's medical schools was slow due to the meager amount of research support from philanthropy and the modest fees received by practicing physicians [2].

After World War II, contributions from the newly formed National Institutes of Health (NIH) resulted in enormous growth in the size of academic departments and their research activity because the NIH supported the cost of the research as well as the cost of the research infrastructure. Individual academic departments rapidly increased in size with an accompanying growth in power and autonomy in direct proportion to their research budgets. As the NIH began to focus much of its research support on organ-based research, the role of the specialist became increasingly important in the academic community.

At the same time, fee-for-service third-party reimbursement for high-cost, high-technology services increased with the development of new technology, and the revenues accrued from these services could be used to support the research missions of the AMC [3]. By the late 1990s, at least a quarter of the dollars supporting many of America's AMCs came from federal grants and contracts—thus making the academic and financial health of these institutions dependent in large part on grant support from the federal government.

NIH Funding and the Crisis in America's Research Enterprise

Between 1998 and 2003, absolute dollars allocated by the NIH to fund research at American medical schools increased twofold from over $9 billion in 1998 to over $16 billion in 2002—a fact that was trumpeted by the federal government [4]. However, when analyzed based on the change in the value of a dollar, the increase in dollars was only 50%. Of greater concern has been the fact that, since 2003, the NIH budget has remained flat. As a result, when adjusted for inflation and the value of the dollar, NIH funding has actually decreased over the period from 2003 to 2008. For example, in 2004, the NIH budget increased only 3% at a time when the cost of biomedical research and development rose 4.5%, thus resulting in a net loss in research funding [5].

This decrease in NIH funding has substantially affected the ability of individual investigators to obtain support. Between 1998 and 2003 when the NIH budget doubled, the number of grants awarded to new young applicants increased, albeit modestly, from 633 grants awarded in 1998 to 1,787 in 2003

[6]. However, the chance of any single investigator receiving funding on the first try plummeted from 21% in 1998 to 8% in 2006 [5]. Thus, for every 100 scientists who submit a grant, only 8 will be funded. In 1976, the National Heart, Lung and Blood Institute funded 37% of new independent award applications and 59% of renewal awards. By 2006, this number had decreased to 16.5% of new submissions and 29% of continuation grants. Similarly, only 16% of new independent awards submitted to the National Cancer Institute or to the National Institute of Drug Abuse were funded in 2006.

As grants became increasingly hard to obtain, the number of grant applications submitted to the NIH per applicant increased from 1.23 in 1998 to 1.38 in 2006 [5]. Over the same time period, the average age of individuals awarded their first NIH grant increased for investigators with PhD (37–42 years of age), MD–PhD (40–44 years of age), and MD (38–44 years of age) degrees. As noted by David Sweatt, chair of the Neurobiology Department at the University of Alabama, Birmingham: "It's just about inconceivable for a brand-new investigator to get an NIH grant funded on their first submission these days…They're having to spend so much time being anxious over funding to the detriment of having time to think creatively about their research" [5]. This anxiety has also led many talented young scientists to leave academic institutions for positions in industry or teaching.

Another important observation regarding research funding in U.S. medical schools is that the amount of research funding varies enormously among the 125 medical colleges. The average support to the 20 highest awardees in 2005 was $258 million. By contrast, the 20 AMCs receiving the lowest levels of NIH support received an average of $6.2 million—barely enough to cover the overhead of a modestly sized research building. Only those schools ranked 55 and higher in NIH research funding received over $60 million in NIH dollars.

Thus, it is quite clear that well over half of all medical schools in the United States receive a level of funding that is less than 15% of that received by the highest funded AMC: the Johns Hopkins University School of Medicine ($394 million). In departments of radiology, more than half the federal extramural funding goes to just eight departments and almost half of academic radiology departments receive no federal funding whatsoever [7]. This enormous disparity between the financial revenues of the "haves" and the "have-nots" is a ubiquitous problem among America's AMCs that will be addressed in more detail later in the fourth section on finance.

The varying resources among different academic medical centers have led to an ominous trend at a time of decreases in NIH funding: the ability of large and well-funded academic medical centers to aggressively recruit funded scientists from smaller institutions rather than seeking young and less established investigators. For example, in 2007, the University of Michigan in Ann Arbor lured a team of 25 scientists, physicians, and graduate students led by Drs. Jose Jalife and Mario Delmar from the State University of New York Upstate Medical University in Syracuse to the newly established University of Michigan Center for Arrhythmia Research [8].

Although Dr. Delmar had been at Upstate for 25 years, the opportunity to increase the laboratory's space markedly, as well as opportunities to link with private endowments for additional funding and the university's investment in state-of-the art shared equipment, was difficult to overlook. However, for the Upstate Medical Center, the loss of $5 million a year in research funding from federal agencies and foundations was potentially catastrophic for its clinical and research programs. Clearly, this is a dilemma between what is good for an individual scientist and what is important for the success of the institution.

An additional threat to the stability of America's academic research programs is what has been referred to as the "boom and bust" [5]. With the release in 1998 of plans to double the NIH budget, many AMCs assumed that the increase in NIH support for research would continue in perpetuity. Therefore, they began an aggressive effort to build new laboratory space. The rationale was simple: More laboratory space would mean more investigators and thus more indirect revenues to support the university overhead. A survey done by the AAMC in 2002 noted that, from 1990 to 1997, American medical schools invested $2.2 billion in new construction. Between 1998 and 2002, new construction had increased to $3.9 billion and the cost of existing and planned new construction was expected to top $7.4 billion by 2007 [5].

At the same time, academic medical centers recruited new scientists to fill the expanding laboratory space and, not unexpectedly, the number of NIH grant submissions increased proportionately. In a survey in 2002, respondents noted that they expected to have added an average of 89,000 square feet of research space between 2003 and 2008, with a projected doubling in annual debt payments for research buildings by 2008 [9].

Thus, a decrease in NIH funding not only affects the research of individual investigators but also can have a negative impact on the medical center and university as a whole, especially in those institutions without state support. Indeed, in 2007, Elias Zerhouni, director of the NIH, noted: "I'd be a lot more careful [now] than I would have been in 1998" and warned that "the situation may get worse before it gets better" [9]. Clearly, there was real reason for concern at many AMCs in 2008 and a compelling argument for the stabilization of NIH funding. The $10 billion allocation to the NIH from the federal government as part of the stimulus package had a positive effect; however, the stimulus dollars are only available for two years and there is still not clarity regarding long-term support. In addition, this short-term increase in NIH funding must be balanced against the catastrophic fall in endowment revenues due to the financial crisis.

"A Broken Pipeline?"

That the failure of Congress to increase funding for the NIH had a calamitous effect on medical research in the United States was well documented by academic leaders from a group of six prestigious universities who came together in March 2007 to present their concerns at a congressional hearing. In a monograph titled, "A Broken Pipeline? Flat Funding of the NIH Puts a Generation of Science at Risk," the group noted that "even as substantial advances appear within our grasp—including breakthroughs in Alzheimer's disease, lung cancer, and depression—they are at risk of slipping away because the NIH is experiencing a dangerous slow down in funding—one that is unprecedented in the history of the nation's biomedical research enterprise" [10].

The report focused on junior investigators, who are the most vulnerable researchers at a time when grant opportunities are limited and who often represent the most innovative and brightest individuals in the research community. This group is also most likely to choose other career paths in order to support growing families and to pay off medical school and graduate school debts. Isla Garraway (MD, PhD), a young investigator at UCLA studying ways to treat prostate cancer using stem cells found in the prostrate gland, noted [10]:

> We all got federal funding to support our graduate studies. After investing in eight years of training followed by many more years of residency, now there's no parachute. Are they going to let us freefall? It doesn't make any sense. Why not support us to the point of independence when we can make potentially huge impacts?

The "broken pipeline consortium" also pointed out how the current funding crisis has trapped young investigators in the proverbial "catch 22." In order to obtain an independent research award (the NIH RO1), young scientists must establish a laboratory, demonstrate their independence from their mentors, and collect enough preliminary data to suggest that their experiments will be successful. Because they are often pursuing new and innovative ways to address biologic questions, the data are often difficult to obtain. Thus, their RO1 applications are often not funded because of an absence of preliminary data. The university or medical school already strapped for cash to support established investigators and increasing overhead is often unable to provide funds for these new and exciting young investigators to tide them over until they have enough data to support an independent award. As a result, notes Rachelle Gaudet of Harvard University, "The current flat funding of NIH is causing even junior people to be very conservative, and it's just not the right time to be conservative" [10].

However, many young scientists are not "dumbing down" their research endeavors and applications but rather are either leaving academia to pursue careers in industry or in laboratories abroad or are leaving science altogether. Brown University's Tricia Serio said, "When I started at Yale, there were 30 PhDs in my program. As far as I know, I'm the only one who stayed in academic science" [11]. For physician–scientists, the lack of NIH funding means that they will have to do more clinical work—a slippery slope that in most cases leads to a full-time clinical position and a total absence of research time.

The failure of the United States to keep pace with the rest of the world has been clearly recognized and succinctly articulated by those who lead both governmental and industry research enterprises. Elias Zerhouni, former director of the National Institutes of Health, noted that "without effective national policies to recruit young scientists to the field, and support their research over the long term, in 10 to 15 years, we'll have more scientists older than 65 than those younger than 35. This is not a sustainable trend in biomedical research and must be addressed aggressively" [10]. Joshua Boger, president of the biotechnology industry group BIO and head of Vertex Pharmaceuticals, was even more forthright when he stated [10]:

> We could wake up one day and find out that U.S. science is not in the lead anymore. To regain the lead at that point would be very, very difficult. Other countries see the connection between basic science and societal benefit with more vigor and conviction than exists in the U.S.

Thus, there is a compelling need for all academic medical centers, their accompanying universities, and the patients they serve to come together with one voice to convince Congress of the need to reevaluate its support for science and discovery in the United States. At a time when the country is supporting a war in Iraq and there are economic problems at home, it is necessary to look to sources other than the federal government—including the vast billions of dollars accumulated by health insurance companies—to support research activities.

When NIH funding first flattened 5 years ago, the elite research institutions were better able to cope with a downturn: Many of the applications submitted by their scientists had historically received priority scores that placed them in the top 10th percentile; they had large endowments that could be used to recruit funded investigators or to support young investigators; or they had lucrative for-profit entities, substantial health system margins, or income streams from patent royalties. However, as the NIH downturn continued for nearly 6 years, even universities with large NIH portfolios have begun to suffer because young investigators tend to score lower on their initial grant applications, all investigators are submitting more grants even within a single funding period, and the general economic environment has also suffered an unprecedented downturn.

At Duke, an institution ranked second in NIH funding, the medical school has responded to funding shortfalls by creating a bridge funding program that provides up to $100,000 to support researchers whose grant proposals are not approved [12]. However, even at Duke, individual faculty members have been adversely affected by the downturn [12]. Furthermore, the marked instability in the financial markets, the collapse of a major financial institution (Bear Stearns) for the first time since the Great Depression, and the crises in the real estate market and mortgage industry threaten the financial underpinning of many academic medical centers. These AMCs depend on endowment income or development dollars to support the overhead on research space as well as the debt service on new construction. Thus, the flat funding at the NIH is beginning to affect all academic health centers adversely and clearly puts the future research productivity of the United States at risk.

The Demise of Clinical Research in the AMC

In 1925, Abraham Flexner noted that clinical research should be an important component of a medical school [13]. Throughout much of the twentieth century, AMCs served as the primary sites for the clinical evaluation of new drugs and devices for the treatment of human diseases. Academicians were viewed as impartial and independent and their participation was highly valued by industry sponsors. It was also thought to be important that the academic thought leaders who participated and led the clinical trials of a new device present the results of their studies to the Food and Drug Administration in order to gain approval for a new drug. In addition, the participation of prestigious academic medical centers in early clinical trials was thought to be important in the eventual sales and marketing of a new drug.

However, over the past decade, a series of reports noted that both internal and external impediments have increasingly limited the ability of academic investigators to compete successfully for participation in clinical investigations [14–16]. A survey from the Thompson Center Watch, a Boston company that covers the pharmaceutical industry, reported in 2000 that substantially fewer clinical trials were being carried out at academic medical centers [14]. Similarly, a large group of articles within the subspecialties of cardiology, oncology, and gastrointestinal medicine published in 15 major journals between 1991 and

1993 and between 2001 and 2003 were analyzed; the probability that an AMC would participate in an industry-sponsored clinical trial significantly decreased between the two time periods [17].

The decrease in the role of academic medical centers in clinical research has come at least in part from an industry shift from using academia to perform clinical research to the use of clinical research organizations (CROs) [18]. This shift was seen by the fact that annual CRO industry revenues increased from approximately $7 billion in 2001 to an estimated $17.8 billion in 2007. In addition, while there are over 1,000 CROs today, the four largest—Quintiles, Covance, Pharmaceutical Product Development, and Charles Rivers Laboratories—are billion dollar companies; two smaller CROs—Paraxel and MDS Pharma Services—are not far behind.

Although CROs played a role in only 28% of clinical trials in 1993, they participated in 64% of all clinical trials in 2003 [18]. CROs often provide an emphasis on speed that comes at the expense of quality [18]. In an era when time-to-market takes precedence over quality, the CROs, at the request of their clients, have continually shifted not only from academic centers to community practices but also from U.S. sites to investigative teams in Eastern Europe—Russia, India, and Asia, where costs are lower, research subjects are more plentiful, and both governmental and institutional oversight is less. This reduction in the participation of AMCs in industry-sponsored clinical trials has enormous financial implications as national spending on clinical trial in the United States was $25.6 billion in 2006 and is expected to increase to $32.1 billion in 2011 [19].

There are internal constraints to the timely performance of clinical trials at AMCs. These include an increased pressure on clinical faculty to generate revenue from patient visits, inefficiency in the operations of internal review boards, failure of promotion committees to recognize the value of clinical research, absence of trained clinical investigators, and inefficient pricing and contracting mechanisms. Pharmaceutical companies focusing on "time to market" have little patience for these delays, which often occur at AMCs.

As a result, contract research organizations and site management organizations find it more expedient and cost efficient to utilize individual physician groups, community hospitals, and/or community-based physician research networks that are not impeded by the slow AMC bureaucracy. Community hospitals often use contract internal review boards such as the "Western IRB," which can provide approval in a fraction of the time that it takes an AMC internal review board to review the same proposal.

Furthermore, neither foreign study sites nor community hospitals spend time negotiating the ownership of intellectual property that comes out of the research and do not focus on the sometimes controversial issues of when and how data from individual sites can be published. Their sole goal is to be able to provide new and innovative investigational therapeutics for their patients and to have the opportunity to gain additional revenues from the clinical trials. Thus, the AMC has lost its leadership role in clinical research and the opportunity to provide its patients with the latest discoveries in therapeutic care and the competitive edge that comes with it.

Another issue that threatens academic clinical research programs is new regulatory processes and increased governmental oversight of research activities. In order to ensure that Medicare is not billed for services that were more appropriately billed to the sponsors of clinical trials, Medicare published standards for carrying out clinical trials that involved Medicare beneficiaries. Although they were intuitively appropriate, these new regulations provided both hurdles and risks for those academic centers supporting large clinical research portfolios. For example, the Centers for Medicare and Medicaid Services (CMS) proposed that "the research study design had to be appropriate to answer the research question being asked in the study and that the study does not unjustifiably duplicate existing studies."

However, as pointed out in a letter from the American College of Cardiology, it is unclear how these criteria might be judged if CMS audited an investigator's study because the requirements were "self-certified" by the investigator and the sponsor [20]. CMS also included stipulations regarding publication of the study results within 3 years, an explicit description of how the data from the study will be generalized to the Medicare beneficiary, and how the entry and exclusion requirements of the study influence the ability to discern the effects of the drugs on underrepresented populations. However, most onerous of the new rules is the need to provide auditable data ensuring that patients are not billed inappropriately. Although such a mandate is both reasonable and fair, the systems needed to ensure such compliance are available at very few academic medical centers, thereby increasing the infrastructure cost of pursuing industry-sponsored clinical research and resulting in another layer of complex bureaucracy.

In the summer of 2003, Rush University Medical Center found errors in the billing process for cancer clinical trials during a routine administrative review of the operations in their cancer program [21]. Within 30 days of identifying the problem, Rush disclosed the errors to the U.S. Attorney's Office in Chicago and undertook an extensive investigation to understand the processes responsible for the error as well as to identify compliance risks for all clinical trials at the institution. Through a settlement agreement with the U.S. Department of Justice and the Office of the Inspector General for the U.S. Department of Health and Human Services, Rush rectified the overpayments it had received but also put in place a compliance program to ensure that ongoing auditing and monitoring programs would mitigate further errors.

Although Rush's settlement with the federal government was the first that focused exclusively on issues of Medicare overpayments in the context of clinical trials, the results of the Rush audit sent a message to all academic medical centers that similar errors would not be tolerated. Therefore, the operational changes put in place at Rush have served, at least in part, as a model for other academic medical centers in the United States and have also raised a flag of caution regarding participation in clinical trials. Thus, these new regulations further discourage institutions and investigators from pursuing clinical research.

Strengthening AMC Research by Linking Research Bench and Clinical Arena through Translational Research

Over the past decade, research focused on human disease has been given a new moniker: translational research or translational medicine. Translational research has three components:

T1: the use of new technologies, including genomics, proteomics, stem cell biology, gene transfer, structural biology and molecular imaging, to understand human pathology and to identify new drug targets;

T2: clinical trials to assess the effectiveness of new therapeutic and diagnostic options; and

T3: the effective and expeditious translation of new discoveries in clinical research to physicians and the communities that they serve.

This new field requires the seamless interaction and collaboration of traditional bench scientists and clinical investigators as well as the participation of experts in clinical practice guidelines, health policy, quality of care, the social sciences, and information technology [22]. Translational research has become a major focus of the NIH's "roadmap" for medical research in the twenty-first century [23]. The most fertile ground for this type of transformational science is the AMCs. Not only can the AMC bring together the many scientific disciplines required to fulfill the goals of translational research successfully, but new discoveries and therapeutic opportunities can also provide a competitive edge for the AMC in competing with community hospitals.

The fulfillment of the promise of translational research for improving the health and longevity of the world's populations depends on the development of broad-based teams of scientists and scholars [24]. However, AMCs often have inherent barriers that interfere with their ability to create effective collaborations [25]. For example, basic science students usually have a single mentor and are not exposed to patient-based and population-based research. Individual departments often receive funding from the medical school based on the number of students enrolled in their programs and do not get credit for students in multidisciplinary programs.

In addition, the training periods for academic investigators are increasingly lengthy at a time when many students have appreciable debt. As noted by Leon Rosenberg, former dean of the Yale School of Medicine and former president of the Bristol-Myers Squibb Pharmaceutical Research Institute, "the path to an M.D./Ph.D. degree is torturous....there has been a progressive increase in the number of years of postdoctoral training required for physicians undertaking careers in research, often stretching to 10 or more [years]" [26].

The standards established by university appointments and promotions committees also impede the careers of translational researchers. Promotion committees characteristically evaluate individuals using a group of criteria: Are they "independent"? What was their "contribution" to the work they published? Are they recognized as being the leaders of the work? Because translational research involves a "team" approach, it is difficult to recognize each individual's contribution using traditional metrics. In addition, it is more challenging to perform experiments in patient populations than it is in model systems or in animal models and there is a higher level of uncertainty that any study in patients will result in a publication in a high-impact journal—a prerequisite for climbing the academic ladder. As pointed out by Catherine Wu, a medical oncologist at the Dana Farber Cancer Institute in Boston, "Translational research deals with patients, and patients aren't a model system. Establishing causality is always a challenge. It's not a slam-dunk that you're going to get into *Science* or *Nature*" [27].

Translational research has additional risks for investigators—particularly those who are early in their careers. Clinical studies take a longer period of time to complete and the number of publications that come from a translational medicine program are often smaller [28]. Translational scientists are also hindered by the historic antipathy between the academic cultures of clinical and basic research. As noted by one medical school dean [29], translational research "requires breaking down of long-standing institutional walls[;] the scholarship of integration has been slower than the other forms of scholarship to gain acceptance as an integral activity of the professorate."

Translational research has also been threatened by arcane regulatory policies. In December 2006, Peter Pronovosst from the Johns Hopkins University published an intriguing study demonstrating that, in a collaborative cohort study that took place predominantly in intensive care units in Michigan, the use of a checklist could markedly improve the rates of bloodstream infection associated with the use of indwelling catheters [30]. The contributing hospitals sent aggregated data on the rate of infections to the statistical core at Hopkins for analysis. After an anonymous complaint, the Office for Human Research Protection (OHRP) at the U.S. Department of Health and Human Services (DHHS) ordered the hospitals to stop sending data because the institutional review board (IRB) at Hopkins had incorrectly classified the study as "exempt from human research protections."

The hospitals continuing to use the checklist needed to complete the IRB process, submit a form called a federal wide assurance indicating that they would comply with the federal requirements for the protection of human research subjects, and receive OHRP approval [31]. OHRP noted that "if institutions are planning research activities examining the effectiveness of interventions to improve the quality of care, then the regulatory protections are important to protect the rights and welfare of human research subjects" [31]. Numerous professional organizations sent letters to OHRP asking that the requirement that quality improvement efforts require informed consent from all participating patients be discontinued. However, the OHRP would not change its decision. As noted by Pronovost, "We have to clarify this issue in a wise way. Focusing on a very bureaucratic, regulatory interpretation rather than evaluating the risks and benefits to patients of a quality initiative seems very unproductive" [32].

Supporting Research by Economically Linking Research and Clinical Care

Many AMCs—especially those in which the hospital and the medical school are not integrated—assiduously ensure that patient revenues are not used to support basic or clinical research. Indeed, many clinical chairs become apoplectic when the dean uses clinical revenues to support investigators or their research. By contrast, two highly successful academic centers—the University of Pittsburgh and the University of Pennsylvania—have followed and publicly supported a very different paradigm. Both Penn and the University of Pittsburgh Medical Center (UPMC) have espoused the philosophy that "in an academic health center, research and clinical success are synergistic and interdependent. A strategic collaboration between the clinical and the academic enterprises will enhance the success of both beyond what would occur with an investment in either alone" [33].

Thus, at UPMC and Penn, the use of contributions from the hospital or the practice plan to support research activities is an integral part of the business plan of the institution. Indeed, it has been noted that "the most important reason for the success of the 2 academic health centers has been the transfer by the University of Pennsylvania Health System and UPMC of significant funds to their respective medical schools" [33].

At the University of Pittsburgh, this novel strategy was first developed in 1972 when Dr. Thomas Detre came to the university from Yale as chair of the Department of Psychiatry. He faced a daunting task because Western Psychiatric Institute, as well as the medical school, had little federal funding or clinical research. They established a core philosophy that high-quality, efficient, and timely care delivered by individuals focused on the clinical aspects of medicine could be seamlessly integrated with the academic missions of the institution. They laid out a strategy in which they would first improve the quality and timeliness of the care provided by the clinical faculty and then utilize the increased incomes from clinical care to attract highly sought-after investigators and their research grants as well as highly skilled clinicians and new technology—all of which would attract more patients and increased revenues in a self-perpetuating cycle [34].

Within a relatively short period of time, Western Psych had dramatically increased its national presence in both clinical care and research as the institute's budget increased from $6.5 million to approximately $60 million and federal research grants increased from $200,000 per year to nearly $13 million [34].

In 1981, following the paradigm that had been successful at Western Psych, Pitt recruited the internationally known physician–scientist and transplant pioneer Thomas Starzl from the University of Colorado. Although Starzl had performed the world's first liver transplant in 1963, liver transplantation was risky business. Insurance companies did not cover the cost of transplants, organ rejection was a major problem, and the surgery was technically challenging. Indeed, the first four liver transplant recipients at Pittsburgh died. However, Starzl had found a wonder drug—cyclosporine A—that substantially decreased organ rejection [35].

After a $230 million investment in 1986 in transplantation and cancer, UPMC was performing more than half of the world's liver transplantations by 1998 and accruing substantial revenues as a result [36]. Today, UPMC is ranked as one of America's top hospitals and the medical school is ranked in the top 10 for NIH funding. At a time when over 50% of AMCs are reporting negative bottom lines, the UPMC health system provided over $170 million of its nearly $650 million margin for the growth of the research program.

An identical approach has been taken at the University of Pennsylvania, where an investment in innovative technology, engineers, and computer scientists led to the development of new, minimally invasive therapies for the treatment of disease of the cardiac valves—resulting in a marked increase in patient volumes, research funding, and industry collaborations. Unlike UPMC, Penn has long sat atop the list of NIH-funded AMCs. However, common strategies have allowed Penn to maintain its place among the elite hospitals and among the highest funded research institutions in the country, despite being located in a highly competitive healthcare environment.

Even during times of fluctuations in NIH funding or clinical reimbursements, these two premier institutions have been able to continue to pursue state-of-the-art research, which in turn has maintained and enhanced the reputation of the medical school and the hospital system, improved patient care, and ensured the stability of the health system.

Funding Research within the AMC

William Mallon was the first to undertake a qualitative study to investigate how, at a time of financial stress, six medical schools allocated institutional funds to their research enterprises [37]. He found that two models of financial management were operative at medical schools and universities: the charity model and the planned-giving model.

Academic medical centers that use the charity model allocate resources to research centers through an informal "hat-in-hand" appeals process. Center directors or chairs appeal directly to the dean and decisions are made "behind closed doors" based on the negotiating skills of the department or institute director, the personal relationship between the dean and the director, and the timeliness of the request. Although the charity model allows flexibility and eschews bureaucracy, it often leads to mistrust, confusion, and poor morale. As Mallon points out, "Department chairs, division chiefs, and other center directors who don't have access to or a voice in allocation decisions to centers may view them as illegitimate, wasteful, or inappropriate rather than as contributing to shared institutional goals that benefit all" [37].

By contrast, the planned-giving model of allocation utilizes a committee structure, a peer-reviewed decision-making process, and an open, transparent funding culture. "The advantage of a planned-giving model is that the university or medical school can make resource decisions based on the relative value of each center compared to all others rather than on a case-by-case basis" [37]. By making the process transparent, the process is accepted as being fair and rational and morale is improved.

Decision making in the planned-giving model is often slow and cumbersome and also weakens the power of the dean who cannot develop a power base from the give and take involved in the hat-in-hand process. Thus, many deans eschew formulaic resource allocation as well as transparency in how funds are used for cross-subsidization. However, at a time when resources for supporting research are limited, AMCs that are able to focus on strategic research initiatives will have a better chance of surviving the current financial environment.

A Model for the Future—Linking AMC Research and the Core Mission of Outstanding Clinical Care

In addition to education and clinical care, research has been historically viewed as one of the three missions of the AMC. In this context, it stands on its own as an identifiable entity without a clear linkage to the other missions of the AMC. In the new model that this book proposes for tomorrow's AMC, research does not stand as a separate and distinct entity but rather as one of the four spheres of action that support the overall core mission of providing outstanding patient care. In this context, hospitals, physician practice plans, universities, and philanthropists do not invest in research for its own sake but rather because there is an understanding that such an investment will have both short- and long-term beneficial effects on the ability of the AMC to deliver outstanding patient care. This model can be achieved through a group of substantive recommendations, which are discussed in the following sections.

AMC Hospitals and Health Systems Must Support Research

AMCs must recognize that research can expand their ability to provide "excellence" in patient care by providing an opportunity for patients to receive cutting-edge care before it is available within the general medical community and that, for patients with diseases for which there is no treatment, participation in a clinical trial provides an opportunity to receive life-saving therapy. In addition, AMCs must recognize that pursuing excellence in research provides a competitive edge over competition from community hospitals; thus, an investment in research by the AMC hospital can enhance hospital revenues as information from the University of Pennsylvania and the University of Pittsburgh has clearly demonstrated.

Hospital leaders must learn from evaluating hospitals and health systems that have recently made substantive contributions to the research mission, including UPMC Health System, which contributed approximately $167 million to the academic mission in 2007; the Duke Health System, which will contribute $30 million per year for 10 years to the medical school to support research; and the Barnes-Jewish in St. Louis, which shares positive margins with the school of medicine.

AMC leaders must also recognize that, even in times of adequate federal funding, AMC research cannot stand on its own because the costs cannot be covered by direct or indirect payments from federal grants and that grants from societies are often not accompanied by robust indirect costs. Therefore, there must be institutional support for the research enterprise.

AMCs Must Enhance Opportunities in Translational Research

Translational research provides important opportunities for AMCs to build new research programs and to link their efforts with those of community physicians. However, this new arena of research often requires AMCs to change some of their policies and procedures. For example, proactive steps must be taken to ensure that promotion committees use a different set of standards to judge the achievements of translational scientists than those used to judge traditional bench researchers. AMCs must also reward collaboration and multidisciplinary research activities. In addition, AMCs must establish metrics to measure the success of collaborative activities, develop multidisciplinary training programs in order to prepare the next generation of clinicians and scientists to enter the field of translational research [38,39], and ensure that resources are provided to develop the ability to disseminate research findings to the community in order to improve day-to-day clinical care [40].

Translational research should be used as a platform for developing closer relationships with primary care practices that serve as potential referral sources of academic centers. The development of so-called primary care practice-based research networks (PBRNs) can provide research arenas in which scientists use traditional and nontraditional methods to identify, disseminate, and integrate knowledge that can improve the ability of a primary care provider to improve the health of his or her patients [41–43]. To be successful in translating research into improvements in community care, AMCs must also work together to change federal regulations in order to obviate the need for informed consent from patients whose de-identified data are used in community-based and hospital-based quality improvement projects while at the same time protecting patient confidentiality and care [44,45].

Recapture Clinical Research

Recent studies have demonstrated that patients receive better care at hospitals that undertake clinical research than at hospitals that do not [46]. Recognizing the importance of clinical research for providing outstanding patient care, AMCs must create an organizational and administrative structure that fosters clinical research by centralizing administrative authority, thus effectively ensuring regulatory compliance, establishing a business-like process for negotiations with research sponsors, and developing seamless integration of inpatient and outpatient research. To achieve these goals, AMCs must invest in information technology that will enhance all aspects of clinical trial efforts.

In the current federal regulatory climate, AMCs must invest in time, people, and resources to develop billing processes that mitigate against irregularities in clinical research billing practices. It has been pointed out that billing for clinical trials is simple in concept [21]:

> Do not bill for services the sponsor is already paying for, do not bill for services promised free, do not bill for services that are for research purposes only, do not bill for services in a research study that is not designed to have therapeutic benefit, and only bill for services that have no external funding source and are medically necessary.

Nonetheless, at a time when federal regulators are assiduously analyzing AMC billing practices, each AMC must carefully develop new systems that ensure compliance with federal regulations, including standard fee schedules that cross all departmental barriers. AMCs must also integrate billing practices between the practice plan and the hospital [19]. An algorithm developed by Rush Medical School may provide a useful model [21].

Although a robust clinical trials program can be used as a platform for building improved relationships with potential referral sources, AMC leaders must recognize that industry sponsors will only bring clinical trials to AMCs if they can provide timely, efficient, and effective enrollment of patients and subjects. Industry's driving focus is "time to market" for new drugs and devices. If patients are not available in U.S. academic medical centers, they are certainly available abroad or at competing community centers.

One impediment to effective clinical trials is delays in approving institutional review board proposals. In the current financial environment, few physicians have the time to participate effectively as members of these boards. As a result, AMCs should outsource these activities to groups, such as the Western IRB, that are far more timely in their decision-making process. Furthermore, when resources are limited, AMCs should rationalize investment toward clinical trials that support the strategic missions of the institution.

Redefine How AMCs Allocate Research Funds

AMCs that do not have large endowments or substantial profit margins from health systems or entrepreneurial activities must rationalize the way in which they support their clinical and basic research activities. They must recognize that, in the current fiscal environment in which many AMCs live, recruiting a group of investigators focused on a specific target can be far more effective in developing centers of excellence than recruiting a group of investigators with different focuses and missions. For example, for a smaller medical school, recruiting a group of five outstanding investigators who focus on cardiovascular research would be far more useful than spreading that same recruitment over five different specialties (e.g., gastroenterology, infectious diseases, endocrinology, rheumatology, and cardiology). By focusing all of the recruitment on cardiovascular disease, a critical mass of investigators could collaborate with one another as well as create programmatic applications.

AMCs must also set aside funds to support young investigators during their transition from training programs to independent investigator awards. In addition, they must focus their investments on areas of scientific research that most closely link with the clinical areas in which they seek to have or already have excellence in patient care. By developing a strategic focus for research that aligns with the clinical mission, an AMC or individual department within an AMC can have a higher likelihood of providing intellectual support for young investigators, develop a rationale for research targets, and ensure that the research program is able to pursue excellence.

References

1. *Minute book of the board of trustees of The Johns Hopkins Hospital.* 1896. 1: 276–278.
2. Petersdorf, R. G. 1980. The evolution of departments of medicine. *New England Journal of Medicine* 303 (9): 489–496.
3. Stevens, R. 1986. Issues for American internal medicine through the last century. *Annals of Internal Medicine* 105 (4): 592–602.
4. http://grants.nih.gov/grants/award/research
5. Couzin, J., and Miller, G. 2007. NIH budget. Boom and bust. *Science* 316 (5823): 356–361.
6. www.nih.gov
7. Hillman, B. J. 2006. Academic radiology, the future of the specialty. *Journal of the American College of Radiology* 2006: 229.
8. June, A. W., and Basken, P. 2008 (January 11). The U of Michigan lures cardiac researchers wholesale from a SUNY camp. *U.S. Chronicle of Higher Education.*
9. Kaiser, J. 2007. U.S. research policy. Med schools add labs despite budget crunch. *Science* 317 (5843): 1309–1310.
10. www.hhs.gov/budget/06budget/nih.html
11. www.BrokenPipeline.org. The broken pipeline, 16.
12. Johnson, M. 2008. Research fund pool runs dry. *Duke Chronicle,* April 11.

13. Flexner, A. 1973. Medical education in the United States and Canada: A report to the Carnegie Foundation for the Advancement of Teaching, 346. Bulletin no. 4, New York (reprinted by The Heritage Press, Buffalo, NY).

14. Campbell, E. G., Weissman, J. S., Moy, E., and Bluemnthal, D. 2001. Status of clinical research in academic health centers: Views from the research leadership. *Journal of the American Medical Association* 286 (7): 800–806.

15. Task Force on the future of Academic Medical Centers. 1999. From bench to bedside: Preserving the research mission of academic health centers. The Commonwealth Fund.

16. Bodenheimer, T. 2000. Uneasy alliance—Clinical investigators and the pharmaceutical industry. *New England Journal of Medicine* 342 (20): 1539–1544.

17. Feldman, A. M., Weitz, H., Merli, G., DeCaro, M., Brechbill, A. L., Adams, S., Bischoff, L., et al. 2006. The physician–hospital team: A successful approach to improving care in a large academic medical center. *Academic Medicine* 81 (1): 35–41.

18. Shuchman, M. 2007. Commercializing clinical trials—Risks and benefits of the CRO boom. *New England Journal of Medicine* 357 (14): 1365–1368.

19. Rubin, E., Lazar, D., Gaich, N., and Haray, D. 2007. *The clinical trials landscape: Limitations, strengths and promise*. Washington, D.C.: Association of Academic Health Centers.

20. Dove, J. 2007. Letter to CMS. 2007. (August 18). Comment on the Center for Medicare and Medicaid Services' (CCMS) draft National Coverage Decision (NCD) memorandum (Draft Memo) or Clinical Trial Policy (CAG-00071R2). American College of Cardiology.

21. Boyd, C. E., and Meade, R. D. 2007. Clinical trial billing compliance at academic medical centers. *Academic Medicine* 82 (7): 646–653.

22. Woolf, S. 2008. The meaning of translational research and why it matters. *Journal of the American Medical Association* 299 (2): 211–213.

23. http://nihroadmap.nih.gov/overview.asp

24. Sung, N. S., Crowley, W. F., Jr., Genel, M., Saliber, P., Sandy, L., Sherwood, L. M., Johnson, S. B., et al. 2003. Central challenges facing the national clinical research enterprise. *Journal of the American Medical Association* 289 (10): 1278–1287.

25. Pober, J. S., Neuhauser, C. S., and Pober, J. M. 2001. Obstacles facing translational research in academic medical centers. *FASEB Journal* 15 (13): 2303–2313.

26. Rosenberg, L. 1999. The physician–scientist: An essential—and fragile—link in the medical research chain. *Journal of Clinical Investigation* 103 (12): 1621–1626.

27. Carpenter, S. 2007. Science careers. Carving a career in translational research. *Science* 317 (5840): 966–977.

28. Garber, K. 2007. Translational Institute unites unlikely partners at Penn. *Science* 317:968–969.

29. Dauphinee, D., and Martin, J. B. 2000. Breaking down the walls: Thoughts on the scholarship of integration. *Academic Medicine* 75 (9): 881–886.

30. Pronovost, P., Needham, D., Berenholz, S., Sinopoli, D., Chu, H., Cosgrove, S., Sexton, B., et al. 2006. An intervention to decrease catheter-related bloodstream infections in the ICU. *New England Journal of Medicine* 355:2725–2732.

31. Kuehn, B. 2008. DHHS halts quality improvement study: Policy may hamper tests of methods to improve care. *Journal of the American Medical Association* 299 (9): 1005–1006.

32. Comarow, A. 2008. Checklists can save lives. *U.S. News and World Report* (http://health.usnews.com/blogs/commarow-on-quality/2008/1/17/checklists-can-save-lives.html).

33. Bowman, M. A., Rubenstein, A. H., and Levine, A. S. 2007. Clinical revenue investment in biomedical research: Lessons from two academic medical centers. *Journal of the American Medical Association* 297 (22): 2521–2524.

34. Levin, S. 2005. Empire building: Starzl's success a model for growth at UPMC. *Pittsburgh Post-Gazette,* Dec. 6 (www.post-gazette.com/pg/pp/05360/628058-85.stm).

35. Starzl, T. 1981. Liver transplantation with use of cyclosporine-a and prednisone. *New England Journal of Medicine* 305 (5): 266–269.

36. Levin, S. 2005. Empire building: Consolidation and controversy at UPMC. *Pittsburgh Post-Gazette,* Dec. 27 (www.post-gazette.com/pg/05361/626262-85.stm).

37. Mallon, W. T. 2006. The financial management of research centers and institutes at U.S. medical schools: Findings from six institutions. *Academic Medicine* 81 (6): 513–519.

38. Lin, M. 2008. Bridging the gap: New grad program teaches students to better interpret research (www.dailycampus.com/home/index).

39. Huskins, C., Weavers, K. M., Gorden, J. F., and Gabriel, S. E. 2008. Training the next generation of translational science teams. *Clinical and Translational Science* 1 (2): 94–95.

40. Westfall, J. M., Mold, J., and Fagnan, L. 2007. Practice-based research—"Blue highways" on the NIH roadmap. *Journal of the American Medical Association* 297 (4): 403–406.

41. Mold, J. W., and Peterson, K. A. 2005. Primary care practice-based research networks: Working at the interface between research and quality improvement. *Annals of Family Medicine* 3 (supp 1): S12–S20.

42. Reinhardt, A. C., and Ray, L. N. 2003. Differentiating quality improvement from research. *Applied Nursing Research* 16 (1): 2–8.

43. Morrison, E., Mobley, D., and Farley, B. 1996. Research and continuous improvement: The merging of two entities? *Hospital Health Services Administration* 41 (3): 359–372.

44. Casarett, D., Karlawish, J. H. T., and Sugarman, J. 2000. Determining when quality improvement initiatives should be considered research: Proposed criteria and potential implications. *Journal of the American Medical Association* 283 (17): 2275–2280.

45. Johnson, N., Vermeulen, L., and Smith, K. M. 2006. A survey of academic medical centers to distinguish between quality improvement and research activities. *Quality Management in Health Care* 15:215–220.

46. Majumdar, S. R., Roe, M. T., Peterson, E. D., Chen, A. Y., Gibler, W. B., and Armstrong, P. W. 2008. Better outcomes for patients treated at hospitals that participate in clinical trials. *Archives of Internal Medicine* 168 (6): 657–662.

Chapter 5

Resolving Conflicts of Interest

Keep the practitioner "out of the clutches of the arch enemy of his professional independence—the pernicious literature of our camp followers, a literature increasing in bulk...." The profession has no more insidious foe than the large borderland pharmaceutical houses.

William Osler [1]

Introduction

As early as the turn of the twentieth century, Osler recognized that the pharmaceutical industry could impact the way that physicians treated their patients. He proposed that an antidote would be "the presence in the community of a body of men devoted to science, living for investigation and caring nothing for the lust of the eyes and the pride of life" [1]. Indeed, scientists have always faced nonfinancial pressures that could bias the interpretation of their results: the need to compete for extramural grants, the desire to climb the academic ladder, and the desire to receive accolades from peers and to win prestigious research awards [2]. There was little oversight because of an incredibly high level of trust in the integrity of scientific discovery and a reliance on the ethical attitudes of individual investigators [3].

In 1980, the playing field changed with the passage of the Bayh–Dole Act [4]. This act not only provided the opportunity for academic investigators who were funded by federal grants and their institutions to commercialize their discoveries but also encouraged them to do so. Scientists now had both an academic and an entrepreneurial interest in their work and relationships between academicians and industry blossomed [5].

AMCs also profited as they developed technology transfer offices to oversee the patenting of new discoveries and the out-licensing of patents to existing pharmaceutical or device companies or to new start-up companies founded by university investigators or the universities themselves. These potential conflicts of interest threatened the historic trust between the AMC and the public and raised concerns that AMCs were providing care driven by financial incentives and not by the goal of achieving excellence. In this chapter, we will look at the different types of conflicts, actions already suggested by the Association of American Medical Colleges, and recommendations to regulate conflicts of interest.

Conflicts of Interest within Physician Groups

Over the past decade, scandals in biomedical research at major AMCs have made the front pages of every major newspaper in the United States, leading the public to question whether physicians and scientists who populate America's academic centers have conflicts of interest that cause them to make decisions regarding patient care or the presentation of research studies that are biased by their personal financial interest. Indeed, a recent article in the *New York Times* suggested that "universities are all but incapable of policing their faculty's conflicts of interest" [6]. These highly publicized events have diminished the public's trust in AMCs and led medical schools across the country to reassess their relationships with industry.

The public's concerns can be best understood by looking at conflicts of interests among four distinct groups of individuals. Each is different and, as we will see, requires separate oversight and regulation:

- clinician investigators who lead or participate in the clinical investigation of new drugs or devices;
- thought leaders who advise governmental regulatory agencies or other physicians about the use of new drugs or devices;
- physicians who may use selected drugs or devices in their practice because of equity relationships with the manufacturer; and
- physicians who may alter their use of drugs or devices due to monetary or nonmonetary gifts from industry.

Clinical Investigators Who Lead or Participate in Clinical Studies

No event had more of an impact on the public's views on academic conflicts of interest than a report in the national press in 1999 regarding the death of an 18-year-old patient. Jesse Gelsinger died after he was treated with gene therapy in a trial led by Dr. James Wilson, a highly respected scientist and director of the University of Pennsylvania's Institute for Human Gene Therapy [7,8]. The study was sponsored by Genovo—a company that Dr. Wilson had founded in 1992 and in which he held equity [9]. Penn's leadership immediately took action, limiting Wilson to nonhuman research and forming an independent panel to review the events of Gelsinger's death. The committee raised serious questions about how human gene therapy studies were being monitored at the institute; it concluded that the institute was not capable of complying with the federal regulations governing clinical trials and recommended that the university review its policies on conflicts of interest [8].

Although public outcries followed the disclosures at Penn, the problem was just one of many to surface in the lay press. In June 2002, the *Washington Post* published an article disclosing that one of the nation's largest and most prestigious cancer centers, M. D. Anderson Cancer Center in Houston, had enrolled 195 patients with cancer in tests of an experimental drug called Erbitux without informing them that the institution's president held a significant financial interest in the company and stood to earn millions of dollars if the drug was found to be effective [10]. Dr. Mendelsohn, the president of M. D. Anderson, had distanced himself from the studies there and certainly, as president of the institution, did not see patients or participate in the clinical trials.

The situation with Dr. Mendelsohn illustrates that conflicts of interests are not black or white but rather a complex set of interactions between physicians and industry that require straightforward and fair policies. For example, without the scientific and entrepreneurial efforts of Dr. Mendelsohn and his colleagues, Erbitux would never have been made available for patients with cancer. However, the issues addressed in the *Post* story added fuel to the national debate and pointed out to AMCs that even the perception of conflict could weaken the public's trust [10].

In May 2000, Donna E. Shalala, then secretary of the U.S. Department of Health and Human Services, released a statement in which she noted [11]:

> Recent reports of problems in gene transfer trials have highlighted the new pressures facing researchers, IRBs, and research institutions themselves...Protecting patient safety, and ensuring informed consent, is a shared responsibility. I want to urge university presidents,

leaders of our academic medical centers, and others involved in biomedical research to take a hard look at oversight of clinical trials,
their partnerships with the private sector, their own ethical guidelines, and the support and guidance they give their IRBs. Public
confidence in clinical trials is essential to the continued advances in
medicine we all hope to see in the next century.

In addition, the Department of Health and Human Services announced
that it would take aggressive steps to mitigate conflicts of interest, including
the support of legislation to enable the FDA to levy civil monetary penalties for
violations of informed consent and other research regulations. However, these
admonitions had little effect; studies demonstrated that conflicts of interest per-
sisted as evidenced by the following:

- Of faculty investigators at the University of California, San Francisco,
  7.6% had some personal financial ties with sponsors who supported their
  research [12].
- A study of papers published by the *New England Journal of Medicine* and
  the *Journal of the American Medical Association* found a strong association between a positive outcome and the presence of a conflict of interest
  among the authors [13].
- A review of studies published between January 1980 and October 2002
  showed that one-fourth of the investigators had industry affiliations
  and two-thirds of the AMCs had equity in start-ups that sponsored the
  research [14].
- Authors who had financial relationships with pharmaceutical companies
  were significantly more likely to reach supportive conclusions than authors
  without industry affiliations [14].
- Only 47% of high-impact journals had policies in 2000 requiring disclosure of conflicts of interest [15].
- Among journals that had conflict of interest policies, few articles actually
  included conflict of interest disclosures [16,17].
- A survey of 250 AMCs in 2000 found no established policies for dealing
  with physicians who failed to disclose conflicts of interest [15].
- In a survey of 10 research-oriented medical schools, only one prohibited investigators from having equity or consulting agreements or holding positions in
  a company that sponsored their clinical or basic research activities [18].
- In a survey of 100 institutions with the most funding from the NIH in
  2000, only 55% required their faculty to disclose conflicts of interest [19].

One would have expected that the overwhelming number of studies suggesting that AMCs were on thin ice regarding their interactions with industry and the efforts by prestigious journals such as the *New England Journal of Medicine* and the *Journal of the American Medical Association* would have led to a greater level of oversight by AMCs and caution on the part of academic investigators. Unfortunately, this does not seem to be the case. In a paper published in February 2006, a research team from Duke University Medical Center, Wake Forest University, and Johns Hopkins University reported that only 48% of U.S. academic medical centers had a formal policy requiring that financial conflicts of interest be disclosed to participants in industry-sponsored clinical trials [20].

Even when conflicts of interest do exist, participants in clinical studies are informed about the conflicts less than half of the time [21]. Also, there is little agreement among institutions about whether disclosures should include the amount of a particular financial interest held by an investigator [22]. Thus, almost a decade after the death of Jesse Gelsinger, AMCs have not solved the problem of conflicts of interest in clinical studies.

Thought Leaders, Regulation of Drugs and Devices, and Clinical Practice Guidelines

Academic physicians have also come to public attention because of their participation in regulatory reviews at the FDA and writing committees for national practice guidelines—despite equity relationships with companies that would directly profit from recommendations made by these committees. In 2001, an article in the *Washington Times* noted that the House Government Reform Committee was "looking into assertions that certain committee members are using the knowledge and influence gained from long FDA tenure and the implied promise of favorable consideration to gain consulting positions from drug makers or employment as designers or directors of late-stage clinical trials" [23]. Noting that these academic clinicians received consulting fees and retainers as high as $200,000, the article quoted one drug company executive who "referred to the advisory committee members' approaches for obtaining such work as 'shakedowns' because a company that refused to yield to requests could doom products that cost tens of millions of dollars to develop" [23].

In July 2004, the National Cholesterol Education Program (NCEP) published its updated recommendations for the use of a group of drugs called "statins" in lowering cholesterol [24]. In the initial publication, none of the authors noted conflicts of interest. However, within one week of publication of the manuscript, articles began to appear in the press suggesting otherwise. These reports led the National Institutes of Health to note on its Web site that eight of the nine authors of the original document had financial ties to pharmaceutical companies that produced statins [25]. The story of the NIH cholesterol guidelines caused even more concern when David Willman, a Pulitzer Prize winning investigative reporter for the *Los Angeles Times,* reported that one of the authors of the NCEP update had received $114,000 in consulting fees from pharmaceutical companies that produced statins between 2001 and 2003 [26]. These findings led one observer to comment that "although one can make a case that the purpose of an industry is to make a profit and not necessarily to serve the public good, it is difficult to accept this as a justification for the behavior of medical scientists and regulatory agencies" [27].

In Minnesota, requirements for public disclosure of industry payments have brought additional conflicts to light. For example, the *New York Times* reported that Dr. Richard Grim, a physician who served on government-sponsored hypertension panels that created guidelines about how best to use drugs for the treatment of hypertension and served on a National Kidney Foundation panel that wrote guidelines about the therapy of patients with kidney disease, received more than $798,000 from drug manufacturers. This included $231,000 from Pfizer, the maker of Lipitor, the most commonly used cholesterol-lowering drug, and Norvasc, a drug commonly used to treat hypertension [28].

Dr. Donald Hunninghake, a member of a government-sponsored advisory panel that also wrote guidelines regarding the use of cholesterol-lowering drugs, received at least $420,800 from drug makers between 1997 and 2003; $147,000 came from Pfizer in 1998. Dr. Grim was quoted by the *Times* as saying, "On your side, you're making a bit of money, but you're also trying to educate the doctors. And in my view, the doctors need a lot of educating" [28].

In October 2008, an article on the front page of the *New York Times* described conflicts of interest on the part of Dr. Charles R. Nemeroff of Emory University—"the most prominent figure to date in a series of disclosures that is shaking the world of academic medicine and seems likely to force broad changes in the relationships between doctors and drug makers" [6]. According to the *Times* article, Dr. Nemeroff had signed a disclosure form promising Emory administrators that he would earn less than $10,000 a year from GlaxoSmithKline but in fact had received income of $179,000 in a single year—17 times the agreed-upon level.

Although Dr. Nemeroff consulted for a large number of pharmaceutical companies, the major "conflict" is that he served as the principal investigator for a 5-year study funded by the National Institutes of Health that evaluated a drug produced by GlaxoSmithKline. This was not the first brush with conflicts for Dr. Nemeroff: In 2006, he "blamed a clerical mix-up for his failing to disclose that he and his coauthors had financial ties with Cyberonics, the maker of a controversial device that they reviewed favorably in a journal he edited" [6].

Unfortunately, the conflicts of interest portrayed in the lay press are not isolated incidents, as evidenced by studies carried out among panels of academic thought leaders that demonstrated that [29]

87% of guideline authors had some form of interaction with the pharmaceutical industry;

58% of guideline authors had received financial support for research projects;

38% of guideline authors received remuneration as employees or consultants for a pharmaceutical company;

58% of authors had relationships with companies whose drugs were recommended by the guidelines they authored; and

55% of guideline authors reported that the guidelines they participated in had no formal process for declaring an industry relationship.

In addition, two-thirds of AMC department chairs reported some form of personal relationship with industry that included serving as a consultant (27%), serving as a member of a scientific advisory board (27%), being a member of a speakers' bureau (14%), serving as an officer (7%), or being a founder (9%) or member of a board of directors of a private or public company (11%) [30].

Physicians Who Use Drugs or Devices in Their Clinical Practice and Hold Equity in the Company That Manufactures Them

In December 2005, a front-page article in *The Wall Street Journal* raised concerns about potential conflicts of interest at the famed Cleveland Clinic [31]. According to the report, more than 1,200 patients at the Cleveland Clinic had undergone a procedure for treatment of atrial fibrillation using a device made by the company AtriCure Inc. The FDA had approved the use of the AtriCure device for soft-tissue surgery, but not for treatment of atrial fibrillation.

However, as strong advocates for the use of the AtriCure device for the treatment of atrial fibrillation, the Cleveland Clinic doctors had been using it for so-called "off-label" indications. Dr. Delose Cosgrove, CEO of the clinic, had lectured about its value at a meeting of the American Association for Thoracic Surgery. The *Wall Street Journal* revealed that a venture capital partnership founded in part by the Cleveland Clinic had a significant equity investment in AtriCure, Inc. and that Dr. Cosgrove sat on AtriCure's board of directors, had invested personally in the venture capital fund that invested in AtriCure, and served as one of the general partners of the fund.

According to *The Wall Street Journal's* investigations, the clinic's potential conflicts of interest came to public attention when the hospital's institutional review board, headed by Dr. Lichtin and Dr. Eric Topol, a famed cardiologist and provost and chief academic officer of the clinic, reported their discovery of the relationship between AtriCure and the clinic to the clinic's conflict of interest committee, which was headed by Dr. Guy Chisholm. Concerned that the clinic's ties with AtriCure could influence a patient's care or the way in which treatment options were presented, the committee decided that patients must be told about the clinic's and its doctors' financial ties to AtriCure.

In May 2006, the board of the Cleveland Clinic took steps to address the conflict of interest concerns that had been disclosed by *The Wall Street Journal* and others [32]. The board announced that it would take on a greater role in evaluating and monitoring industry relationships that might bias research or patient care. It also announced that doctors who had relationships with particular drug or device companies would not be able to participate in the clinic's purchasing decisions and Dr. Cosgrove severed his ties to outside companies and the clinic's venture fund. However, the board did not call for public disclosure of outside relationships of its staff or its trustees. Furthermore, Dr. Topol lost his top post at the clinic's medical school, which also removed him from the conflict of interest committee and the clinic's board of governors. The clinic ascribed this change to an administrative reorganization, but it was viewed by some as a punitive action for Dr. Topol's disclosing the clinic's conflicts of interest [33].

In June 2008, the *Philadelphia Inquirer* published a front-page expose on conflicts of interest on the part of orthopedic surgeons who implanted expensive artificial joints and the multibillion dollar implant industry with profit margins of nearly 20% [34]. Federal investigators had found that in some cases, large consulting fees had been paid to surgeons who had performed little or no work for the company, suggesting that the payments were aimed at convincing them to use the company's products [34]. The article noted that within the Philadelphia region alone, 29 doctors had received a total of $7.1 million. The lion's share of the payments went to a professor at Thomas Jefferson University and a professor at the University of Pennsylvania—at least one of whom held patents within the joint replacement field.

While hospitals and practices informed patients that their doctors had received payments from industry, Charles Rosen, a California spine surgeon who founded the Association for Ethics in Spine Surgery, noted that "to just see the name of a company doesn't have the same clarity of being told that [a doctor] gets $800,000 a year from the company" [34]. A former prosecutor noted that "the sheer size of some of those deals raises questions about whether doctors' decisions were tainted and, ultimately, whether patients were harmed" [34].

Physicians Who May Alter Their Use of Drugs or Devices due to Monetary or Nonmonetary Gifts from Industry

A very different type of conflict of interest that has gained the public's attention over the past several years is the relationship between industry representatives or "drug reps" and individual physicians. In 1999 alone, the pharmaceutical industry spent nearly $8 billion to send sales representatives to physician offices and to exhibit their products at medical conferences [35]. Unlike the conflicts described in the first part of this chapter, these industry-to-physician conflicts do not involve equity, are often not disclosed, and are overwhelmingly common. In rare instances, these interactions involve six- or seven-figure honoraria or lavish, all-expense-paid vacations, but in the majority of cases they simply encompass free pens, lunches, or writing pads. In many cases, pharmaceutical representatives support the many conferences and teaching activities that occur at both community hospitals and AMCs and provide an opportunity to bring well-known experts from other institutions to lecture on their areas of expertise.

However, they have engendered almost as much public attention, largely because they are so ubiquitous: 94% of physicians reported some type of relationship with industry, including food in the workplace (83%), drug samples (73%), payments for consulting or speaking engagements (27%), and reimbursement for meeting costs (35%) [36]. In addition, between 1997 and 2005, the pharmaceutical industry paid more than 5,500 healthcare professionals in the state of Minnesota at least $57 million [28]. The median payment per consultant in Minnesota was $1,000 although more than 100 people received more than $100,000. Furthermore, 16% of physicians reported serving on a speakers' bureau [37], 91% of residents reported receiving promotional material from industry representatives, 54% reported attending lunches sponsored by industry, and 80% reported receiving free meals. In addition, residents reported receiving samples at least twice a year and 80% reported receiving gifts with an average value of $60.

Regulating Conflicts of Interest in AMCs

One of the more controversial issues facing AMCs is the role of small gifts such as pens, pads of paper, and slices of pizza in changing practice behavior. One report noted a direct correlation between the cost of a physician's treatment choices and his or her level of contact with pharmaceutical company representatives [38]. Only 16% of medical residents believed that promotions did not influence the prescribing activities of their peers [39] and meetings with pharmaceutical representatives were associated with requests by physicians for adding new drugs to the hospital formulary and changes in prescribing practices [40]. Furthermore, statistical analysis demonstrated that interactions with pharmaceutical representatives had an effect on the way that individual physicians practiced and prescribed medication [40–42].

By contrast, well-respected academicians, including Dennis Ausillo and Thomas Stoffard from Harvard Medical School, have noted that little evidence supports the contention that gifts are used to cajole physicians into using company products or that such use is medically inappropriate or unjustifiably increases costs [43]. Indeed, they remarked that drugs are "not even close to the top drivers of health care costs" and that "the best approach to optimize cost effectiveness of product prescribing is to promote more, not less, interaction among all stakeholders involved in healthcare delivery, including company marketing reps" [43].

Despite the controversy, some academic medical centers have gone after the low hanging fruit—gifts to physicians and residents—rather than seeking a broad-based resolution of conflicts. For example, the University of Connecticut Health Center banned gifts over $100 and specified that only modest meals would be allowed at educational presentations [44]. The Henry Ford Health System implemented a series of strict and unique policies, including a policy that requires medical, surgical, and pharmaceutical vendors to be certified through a Henry Ford-sponsored certification [45]. Stanford prohibited its physicians from accepting even small gifts like pens and mugs, recognizing that these policies would cost the medical center millions of dollars in industry support, including free meals and support of continuing medical education activities [46].

Despite changes at some AMCs, public frustration has led to mandates by regulatory authorities. In 1993, Minnesota mandated that all pharmaceutical and device companies needed to report relationships with physicians—a mandate later passed in Vermont, Maine, West Virginia, California, and the District of Columbia [36]. More recently, Senators Charles Grassley and Herb Kohl introduced the Physician Payments Sunshine Act, which would require manufacturers of pharmaceutical and medical devices to disclose the amount of money they give to individual physicians. In many respects, this bill would be beneficial for patients, physicians, and the pharmaceutical and device companies.

However, in some states, governmental actions have simply gone too far. Recent proposals by the Massachusetts Senate would ban all gifts and freebies to doctors from pharmaceutical companies, a move that would make Massachusetts the first state in the country to ban such gifts outright [47]. Failure to adhere to the ruling could result in a fine of up to $5,000 and a jail sentence of up to 2 years for practicing physicians who accept a pen, a pad of paper, or a slice of pizza from a company representative.

The proposed Massachusetts ban has been criticized for negatively impacting information flow to practitioners [47]. Academic leaders have also noted that "the language of the legislature's proposed anti-gifting bill is both severe and vague, inviting inquisitors and individuals with personal grievances to harass physicians involved in a large variety of potentially constructive research and educational activities. Such harassment will inevitably inhibit appropriate industry support of these legitimate activities" [48]. Thus, it becomes imperative that AMCs—rather than governmental agencies—regulate these conflict of interest issues to ensure that a physician who accepts a ballpoint pen from an employee of a pharmaceutical company does not wind up practicing the art of medicine in the prison dispensary.

Regulating Industry Support for Educational Activities—Actions by the AAMC

From a pragmatic standpoint, the pharmaceutical industry sponsors many of the educational activities held at academic medical centers and community hospitals. The large number of educational conferences required by the regulatory bodies that oversee graduate medical education cost millions of dollars each year. They provide the best opportunity for trainees to be exposed to nationally respected experts in their fields and have been shown to be increasingly useful [49,50]. Even the free meals that accompany many educational activities are useful because they improve attendance by busy trainees [51].

In April 2008, the Association of American Medical Colleges (AAMC) published the report of its Task Force on Industry Funding of Medical Education [28]. The task force did an outstanding job of presenting recommendations that were both fair and rational. Although the AAMC provided a good start, its recommendations focused only on conflicts of interest that surround educational programs. In brief, the task force recommended that

- distribution of pharmaceutical samples should be centrally administered;
- access by pharmaceutical representatives to individual physicians should be restricted to nonpublic areas;
- interactions with trainees and students should occur only under the supervision of a faculty member;
- industry representatives should provide educational materials only under the supervision of a faculty member;
- representatives should not be allowed to be present during patient care activities without consent;

- AMCs providing CME programs should develop audit systems to ensure compliance with standards of the Accreditation Council for Continuing Medical Education (ACCME);
- all funds should flow through a central continuing medical education office;
- centers should define appropriate standards for participation by their faculty members in industry-sponsored FDA-regulated educational programs;
- all scholarship dollars from industry should flow through a central administrative office;
- industry-supplied food and meals should be provided only as part of ACCME-accredited programming;
- academic medical centers should prohibit their employees from allowing their professional presentations to be "ghostwritten" by industry personnel;
- academic personnel with financial interests should be excluded from purchasing committee decisions when they have a conflict; and
- medical schools should design courses to educate students and trainees about the process of drug development, clinical testing, sales, marketing, and regulatory affairs.

Two recommendations of the AAMC task force have come under criticism from both academicians and industry representatives. The first is the recommendation that "with the exception of settings in which academic investigators are presenting results of their industry-sponsored studies to peers and there is opportunity for critical exchange, academic medical centers should strongly discourage participation by their faculty in industry-sponsored speaker's bureaus." Only a handful of medical schools presently bar faculty members from serving on speakers' bureaus; therefore, if this recommendation is widely adopted, it could transform the relationship between medical school faculty and industry and could "change substantially the way medical education is routinely delivered" [52]. Continuing medical education courses serve as an important means of educating the community physician about how to care for patients with a variety of complex diseases. It is preferable for academic clinicians to present data with which they are familiar than for a community physician to use an industry slide set to present data with which he or she is less familiar.

From a purely pragmatic standpoint, it is becoming increasingly difficult to attract clinicians to academic medicine because of low salaries, poor reimbursement, and uncertain research funding; therefore, obviating the ability of an academic thought leader to earn additional revenue, albeit modest, from speaking engagements will make an academic career even less appealing. Dr. Robert J. Alpern, dean of the Yale School of Medicine noted: "I don't have a problem with doctors making $3,000 or $5,000 a year on the side, but it's a totally different thing when its $80,000" [52]. Therefore, constraints rather than prohibitions would form a far more reasonable policy. One obvious approach suggested by Dr. Alpern would be to set financial or time limits on faculty participation in outside lecturing—something that many institutions have already accomplished.

The second area of controversy is the task force's recommendation that academic medical centers "establish and implement policies that prohibit the acceptance of any gifts from industry by physicians and other faculty, staff, students, and trainees of academic medical centers, whether on-site or off-site." As noted before, prohibiting small gifts to physicians and residents is highly controversial. Also, it seems disingenuous that the task force would recommend prohibiting academic physicians (but not community physicians) from accepting a pen at a national meeting, a slice of pizza for lunch, or a note pad for a desk at a time when every prestigious medical journal, including the *New England Journal of Medicine* and the *Journal of the American Medical Association,* is filled with colorful advertisements that are situated on the back cover or at the very front of the journal to attract maximal attention. Thus, there is a need for careful evaluation of any proposed regulatory actions.

The Great Conundrum: Regulating Relationships between Investigators and Industry

The most difficult challenge facing AMCs is to regulate the ongoing relationships between their research faculty and industry. As David Korn, former dean of the School of Medicine at Stanford, noted at a conference sponsored by the NIH [2]:

> I do not suggest that the commercial exploitation of faculty discovery is limited to biomedicine, far from it. But when faculty or institutional conflicts of interest or commitment occur in computer science or microelectronics, or in schools of business or law—as they do, they do not generate vivid front-page stories in the national media or headlines on the 6 o'clock news.

However, when conflict of interest policies do exist, they span the spectrum from highly permissive to draconian; most AMCs have no policy at all [53]. In many cases, the policies are neither straightforward nor understandable without a law degree. At Harvard, the policies "widely acknowledged to be among the most stringent fill eight closely worded and nearly impenetrable pages" [43,54]. Furthermore, the policies are often not equally applied to all members of the hospital or university staff—especially when the individual in conflict threatens to move his or her practice to a hospital with more lenient conflict of interest policies.

To some, the fix is easy: Simply ban all associations between academic physicians and industry. However, eliminating all relationships between AMCs and industry could have disastrous effects on industry's ability to develop the next generation of drugs and devices. Dennis Ausiello has noted [55]:

> The notion that academic researchers who partner with industry are intrinsically tainted reflects a misunderstanding of the importance and quality of industry research, and the role industry plays in bringing new drugs to the patients who need them. While most of the original insights leading to new drugs and devices likely derive, at least in part, from the work of academic scientists, turning these preliminary advances into FDA-approved treatments required an exceptional investment by industry, and vital partnerships between academic investigators and company scientists.

Using the Core Mission of Outstanding Patient Care to Develop Rational Conflict of Interest Policies

As we have seen in other chapters of this book, the core mission of providing outstanding care to patients can facilitate the ability of AMCs to make critically important decisions—particularly those that are confounded by politics and conflicting agendas among the various communities of the AMC. Resolving the conundrum of conflicts of interest—especially those in clinical research and clinical practice—can be approached by simply keeping in mind the core goal of the institution. Thus, recognizing the need to provide incentives for clinician–investigators and physician–scientists to develop new methods of treatment [56], recommendations are presented that are based on the core mission of excellence in patient care.

From a patient's point of view, the issues are simple. Patients expect that their routine care will be unaffected by real or perceived conflicts of interest; that new therapies will be safe; that adverse effects will be fully reported; that, if they participate in clinical trials, they will have full knowledge of the risks and hazards associated with their participation; and that the investigators who enroll patients in clinical trials and analyze data are not biased by the opportunity for personal profit if the results are favorable [5]. Furthermore, 85% of potential patients said that they thought it was not acceptable for doctors to be paid by drug companies to comment on prescription drugs [28].

With delivery of outstanding patient care as the core focus, the following recommendations can be implemented to regulate conflicts of interest:

No investigator or institution should participate as an investigator or as an investigative site, respectively, in a clinical trial in which the investigator, the institution, or a senior official in the institution holds equity in the study's sponsor.

Academic clinicians who receive more than a threshold amount per year from any company for consulting should not serve as investigators for studies sponsored by that company. That is, they should not participate in the enrollment of patients into the trial or in any way oversee individuals who are responsible for enrolling patients.

Academic clinicians who receive more than a threshold amount per year in consulting fees from any company or have equity of any amount from a company with whom the medical center does business should have no membership on any hospital committee that might purchase or oversee studies that involve any products produced by that company, including an internal review board, a pharmacy and therapeutics committee, or a committee known to order products.

Any clinician who has a consulting relationship or owns equity in a company that provides supplies to the physician's hospital should detail the amount of equity and the amount of consulting fees received each year to every patient undergoing surgery or a procedure that uses a product sold by that company.

AMCs can serve as incubators for biotechnology companies to facilitate the translation of basic science discoveries to the clinical arena; however, for-profit laboratories should be physically and intellectually separate from the non-industry-funded laboratories with separate equipment, data collection facilities, and personnel.

Postdoctoral fellows and junior faculty members should not be allowed to participate in research activities of the for-profit sector.

Academic clinicians and investigators should be allowed to receive honorariums for presenting presentations within their sphere of interest; however, the sponsoring institution and the amount of their honorarium should be declared prior to their presentation. Individual medical schools can develop their own policies to adjudicate conflicts of commitment to ensure that individual faculty members are not absent from campus for an undue period of time.

All publications should disclose the fact that an author of the publication has an equity interest in the company whose product was being tested or has received honoraria or consulting fees from the company. In the case of consulting fees, the author should note whether the accumulated fees were greater than or equal to $10,000.

AMC leadership must be willing and able to take action when the conflict of interest rules are broken and these actions must be prospectively documented.

These simple recommendations ensure that an investigator's entrepreneurial efforts are unequivocally separated from his or her clinical responsibilities. While allowing individual faculty members to pursue entrepreneurial activities, simple policies also ensure that these individuals have no conflicts in terms of enrolling patients into the clinical trials in which they hold equity. However, these policies provide no limitations on an investigator's ability to collaborate with industry or to pursue developmental opportunities for new drugs and devices. If AMCs fail to take action, it is clear that federal regulators will institute policies that may be far more limiting and capricious.

References

1. Hinohara, S., and Hisae, N., eds. 2001. *Osler's "A Way of Life" and other addresses with commentary and annotations,* 378. Durham, NC: Duke University Press.
2. Korn, D. 2000. Conflicts of interest in biomedical research. *Journal of the American Medical Association* 284 (17): 2234–2237.
3. Levinsky, N. G. 2002. Nonfinancial conflicts of interest in research. *New England Journal of Medicine* 347 (10): 759–761.
4. The Bayh–Dole Act of 1980. Patent rights and inventions made with federal assistance. 35 U.S.C. §200–211.
5. Martin, J. B., and Kasper, D. L. 2000. In whose best interest? Breaching the academic–industrial wall. *New England Journal of Medicine* 343 (22): 1646–1649.
6. Harris, G. 2008. Top psychiatrist didn't report drug makers' pay, files show. *New York Times,* Oct. 4, A1.
7. Stolberg, S. G. 1999. U.S. panel moves to force disclosure in gene testing. *New York Times,* Oct. 30, A10.
8. Stolberg, S. G. 2000. Institute restricted after gene therapy death. *New York Times,* May 25, A20.
9. Philipkoski, K. 2000. Penn halts gene therapy tests. *Wired News,* May 24 (www.wired.com/news/technology/0, 1282, 26563,00.html).
10. Gillis, J. 2000. A hospital's conflict of interest: Patients weren't told of stake in cancer drug. *The Washington Post,* June 30.
11. www.hhs.gov/news/press/2000pres/20000523.html; 11.25.2007.
12. Boyd, E. A., and Bero, L. A. 2000. Assessing faculty financial relationships with industry: A case study. *Journal of the American Medical Association* 284 (17): 2209–2214.

13. Friedman, L. S., and Richter, E. D. 2004. Relationship between conflicts of interest and research results. *Journal of General Internal Medicine* 19 (1): 51–56.
14. Bekelman, J. E., Li, Y., and Gross, C. P. 2003. Scope and impact of financial conflicts of interest in biomedical research: A systematic review. *Journal of the American Medical Association* 289 (4): 454–465.
15. McCrary, S. V., Anderson, C. B., Jakovljevic, J., Khan, T., McCullough, L. B., Wray, N. P., and Brody, B. A. 2000. A national survey of policies on disclosure of conflicts of interest in biomedical research. *New England Journal of Medicine* 343 (22): 1621–1626.
16. Krimsky, S., and Rothenberg, L. S. 2001. Conflict of interest policies in science and medical journals: Editorial practices and author disclosures. *Science and Engineering Ethics* 7 (2): 205–218.
17. Hussain, A., and Smith, R. 2001. Declaring financial competing interests: Survey of five general medical journals. *British Medical Journal* 323 (7307): 263–264.
18. Lo, B., Wolf, L. E., and Berkeley, A. 2000. Conflict-of-interest policies for investigators in clinical trials. *New England Journal of Medicine* 343 (22): 1616–1620.
19. Cho, M. K., Shohara, R., Schissel, A., and Rennie, D. 2000. Policies on faculty conflicts of interest at U.S. universities. *Journal of the American Medical Association* 284 (17): 2203–2208.
20. Weinfurt, K. P., Dinan, M. A., Allsbrook, J. S., Friedman, J. Y., Hall, M. A., Schulman, K. A., and Sugarman, J. 2006. Policies of academic medical centers for disclosing financial conflicts of interest to potential research participants. *Academic Medicine* 81 (2): 113–118.
21. Friedman, J. Y., Sugarman, J., Dhillon, J. K., Depuy, V., Pierre, C. K., Dinan, M. A., Allsbrook, J. S., et al. 2007. Perspectives of clinical research coordinators on disclosing financial conflicts of interest to potential research participants. *Clinical Trials* 4 (3): 272–278.
22. Weinfurt, K. P., Friedman, J. Y., Dinan, M. A., Allsbrook, J. S., Hall, M. A., Dhillon, J. K., and Sugarman, J. 2006. Disclosing conflicts of interest in clinical research: Views of institutional review boards, conflict of interest committees, and investigators. *Journal of Law and Medical Ethics* 34 (3): 481, 581–591.
23. Gribbin, A. 2001. House investigates panels involved with drug safety; mismanagement claims spur action. *The Washington Times,* June 18, A1.
24. Grundy, S. M., Cleeman, J. I., Bairey Merz, C. N., Brewer, H. B., Jr., Clark, L. T., Hunninghake, D. B., Pasternak, R. B., et al. 2004. Implications of recent clinical trials for the National Cholesterol Education Program Adult Treatment Panel III guidelines. *Circulation* 110 (2): 227–239.
25. Third report of the expert panel on detection, evaluation and treatment of high block cholesterol in adults. 2004. National Cholesterol Education Program.
26. Willman, D. 2004. The National Institutes of Health: Public servant or private marketer? *LA Times,* Dec. 22.
27. Abramson, J., and Starfield, B. 2005. The effect of conflict of interest on biomedical research and clinical practice guidelines: Can we trust the evidence in evidence-based medicine? *Journal of the American Board of Family Practitioners* 18 (5): 414–418.
28. Harris, G. 2008. Group urges ban on medical giveaways. *New York Times,* Apr. 28.

29. Choudhry, N. K., Stelfox, H. T., and Detsky, A. S. 2002. Relationships between authors of clinical practice guidelines and the pharmaceutical industry. *Journal of the American Medical Association* 287 (5): 612–617.

30. Campbell, E. G., Weissman, J. S., Ehringhaus, S., Rao, S. R., Moy, B., Feibelmann, S., and Goold, S. D. 2007. Institutional academic industry relationships. *Journal of the American Medical Association* 298 (15): 1779–1786.

31. Armstrong, D. 2005. How a famed hospital invests in devices it uses and promotes. *The Wall Street Journal,* Dec. 15, A1.

32. Abelson, R. 2006. Clinic moves to fight conflicts of interest. *New York Times,* May 9.

33. http://hcrenewal.blogspot.com/2005/12/was-topol-fired-for-investigating.html

34. Goldstein, J. 2008. Implant firms pay doctors millions. *Philadelphia Inquirer,* June 30, A1.

35. *Pharmaceutical Representative.* 2000. Sales forces, scripts up in 1999.

36. Campbell, E. G. 2007. Doctors and drug companies—Scrutinizing influential relationships. *New England Journal of Medicine* 357 (18): 1796–1797.

37. Campbell, E. G., Gruen, R. L., Mountford, J., Miller, L. G., Cleary, P. D., and Blumenthal, D. 2007. A national survey of physician–industry relationships. *New England Journal of Medicine* 356 (17): 1742–1750.

38. Caudill, T. S., Johnson, M. S., Rich, E. C., and McKinney, W. P. 1996. Physicians, pharmaceutical sales representatives, and the cost of prescribing. *Archives of Family Medicine* 5 (4): 201–226.

39. Steinman, M. A., Shlipak, M. G., and McPhee, S. J. 2001. Of principles and pens: Attitudes and practices of medicine housestaff toward pharmaceutical industry promotions. *American Journal of Medicine* 110 (7): 551–557.

40. Wazana, A. 2000. Physicians and the pharmaceutical industry: Is a gift ever just a gift? *Journal of the American Medical Association* 283 (3): 373–380.

41. Tenery, R. M., Jr. 2000. Interactions between physicians and the health care technology industry. *Journal of the American Medical Association* 283 (3): 391–393.

42. Noble, R. C. 1993. Physicians and the pharmaceutical industry: An alliance with unhealthy aspects. *Perspectives in Biology and Medicine* 36 (3): 376–394.

43. Policy on conflicts of interest and commitment. 1996. President and fellows of Harvard College, from Faculty Policies on Integrity in Science (www.hms.harvard.edu/integrity/conf.html).

44. UConn considers pharma gift ban, Oct. 25, 2007 (www.fiercehealthcare.com/node/8398/print).

45. Press Release. 2006. Henry Ford Health System to implement strict vendor policies, Dec. 14 (www.fiercehealthcare.com/node/4468/print).

46. Pollack, A. 2006. Stanford to ban drug makers' gifts to doctors, even pens. *New York Times,* Sept. 12.

47. Woolhouse, M. 2006. Ban of gifts to doctors sought. *The Boston Globe,* Mar. 4.

48. Ausiello, D., and Stossel, T. P. 2008. Legislators' cure in need of malady. *Boston Herald,* Apr. 17.

49. Hebert, R. S., and Wright, S. M. 2003. Reexamining the value of medical grand rounds. *Academic Medicine* 78 (12): 1248–1252.

50. Mueller, P. S., Litin, S. C., Sowden, M. L., Habermann, T. M., and LaRusso, N. F. 2003. Strategies for improving attendance at medical grand rounds at an academic medical center. *Mayo Clinic Proceedings* 78 (5): 549–553.

51. Segovis, C. M., Mueller, P. S., Rethlefsen, M. L., LaRusso, N. F., Litin, S. C., Tefferi, A., and Habermann, T. M. 2007. If you feed them, they will come: A prospective study of the effects of complimentary food on attendance and physician attitudes at medical grand rounds at an academic medical center. *BMC Medical Education* 7:22.

52. Harris, G. 2008. Group urges ban on medical giveaways. *New York Times,* Apr. 28.

53. Ehringhaus, S. H., Weissman, J. S., Sears, J. L., Goold, S. D., Feibelmann, S., and Campbell, E. G. 2008. Responses of medical schools to institutional conflicts of interest. *Journal of the American Medical Association* 299 (6): 665–671.

54. Angell, M. 2000. Remarks delivered at HHS Conference on Financial Conflicts of Interest, Aug. 16 (http://aspe.hhs.gov/sp/coi/angell.htm).

55. Shaywitz, D. A., and Ausiello, D. A. 2008. Scientific research with an asterisk. *The Boston Globe,* Apr. 29.

56. Dana, J., and Loewenstein, G. 2003. A social science perspective on gifts to physicians from industry. *Journal of the American Medical Association* 290 (2): 252–255.

Chapter 6

Commercializing Research Discoveries

> It was this determination to become a physiology-based surgeon rather than anatomy-based surgeon that led to the discovery of heparin.
>
> **Dr. Jay McLean** [1]

Introduction

In 1916, Jay McLean, a second-year medical student at Johns Hopkins, discovered heparin while working in the laboratory of Dr. William Henry Howell. Unfortunately, the initial preparations were toxic. However, between 1933 and 1936, Connauglit Medical Research Laboratories, a part of the University of Toronto, perfected a technique that resulted in the production of nontoxic heparin [2]. Although Connauglit was later sold to the Canadian government and then privatized, the discovery of heparin represents one of the earliest discoveries and commercializations of a pharmaceutical within the domain of academia. However, only in the recent past have AMCs recognized the value of commercialization of discoveries for supporting the finances of the AMC and facilitating the delivery of outstanding patient care.

As revenues that support the infrastructure and missions of the AMC have continued to decrease, AMCs have sought new ways of supporting their operations and growth. One mechanism pursued by many AMCs and their affiliated universities is the commercialization of discovery. The value of the commercialization of intellectual property has excited academic leaders in large part as a result of high-profile "hits" that have occurred at some AMCs. For example, the Children's Hospital of Philadelphia, the teaching program for the University of Pennsylvania School of Medicine, raised $182 million from the sale of royalties from a vaccine against rotavirus made by Merck & Co. Inc. [3]. The vaccine had been developed based on research that was performed at the Children's Hospital and licensed to Merck. Northwestern University had an even more lucrative sale of royalties—$700 million—arising from a license to Pfizer for a drug used in the treatment of fibromyalgia.

These financial windfalls could be used to support such things as scholarships for under-represented minorities, funding for recruitment of new investigators, bridge support for talented young investigators who had not yet attained independent extramural funding, and support for innovative pilot studies to test out new basic science or clinical investigations. However, the system might not be as successful as one might imagine; in 2004, universities' revenue from patent licenses was modest, totaling $1.3 billion—just 3% of their total research spending [4].

AMCs have also been challenged in financing entrepreneurial activities at a time when economic markets worldwide are in crisis. Nonetheless, it is important to understand the issues that arise around commercialization of discoveries and how AMCs can best take advantage of the opportunities that exist. This chapter will review the historical aspects of academic–industry collaborations, look at the various ways in which an AMC can commercialize its products, and provide recommendations based on new and innovative models.

History of AMC–Industry Relationships in the United States

Between World War I and World War II, America's pharmaceutical industry developed an independent research capability and began to recognize the opportunities afforded by academic–industrial relationships [5]. "By 1940, a survey by the National Research Council showed that 50 U.S. companies were supporting 270 biomedical research projects in 70 universities" [5]. Nonetheless, many universities espoused the belief that medical discoveries should not be commercialized by academic institutions. In fact, both Harvard and Johns Hopkins had prohibited faculty members from filing patents [6,7]. However, these long-held beliefs began to change in the 1970s. In 1974, Harvard entered into a relationship with the Monsanto Company in which Monsanto agreed to give the school

$23 million in exchange for a license for all discoveries and inventions made in connection with company-funded work [8]. Universities began to lobby for better collaborations between industry and academia.

The seminal event in the history of academic–industry relationships was the enactment of the Bayh–Dole Act by Congress in December 1980 [9]. Prior to the act, the U.S. government owned and managed technology that was developed using federal funds. However, the government rarely pursued commercialization. Indeed, prior to the enactment of Bayh–Dole, the U.S. government had accumulated 30,000 patents but licensed only 5% of them [9].

The act remedied this situation by establishing that inventions made using government funds would be owned by the scientist, who would then assign the rights to his or her academic institution. The individual institutions then were required by law to make reasonable efforts to commercialize the patents; special preference was given to smaller biotechnology companies [10]. Because the act required that inventors receive a share of payments or royalties obtained through academic–industry collaborations and that remaining dollars go to support research or education, there were strong incentives for both the investigators and the AMCs to develop infrastructures to deal with this large influx of patents.

Fortuitously, the Bayh–Dole Act came at a time of an enormous shift in the technology of science that resulted in the emergence of the capability to make synthetic compounds rapidly; sequence DNA quickly, thus leading to the complete sequencing of the human genome; identify new and unique therapeutic targets at the DNA and protein levels effectively and rapidly; and test the relevancy of new findings in genetically modified experimental animals. These innovations led to an enormous increase in the number of clinical trials in the United States (60,000 in 2001 versus 14,000 in 1980) and the development of close relationships between university-based research laboratories and entrepreneurial ventures by university-based faculty [11]. Due in large part to this new technology and to the increased opportunities for entrepreneurship afforded by the Bayh–Dole Act, patent filings by U.S. universities increased from around 180 in 1991 to over 1,000 in 2005, the number of staff members in U.S. offices of technology transfer doubled between 1997 and 2005, and 628 new spin-off companies were created in 2005 alone [12].

Although relationships exist between university-based investigators and industry, academic–industry relationships are particularly prevalent at AMCs. These relationships often come about as a result of the development of personal relationships between industry and university leaders with broad expertise in both basic research and clinical care. For example, a recent study demonstrated that relationships between industry and universities are ubiquitous in academic medicine. Goold and colleagues surveyed department chairs at all 125 U.S. allopathic medical schools as well as at the 15 largest independent teaching hospitals in the United States [13]. Almost two-thirds of the department chairs who responded to the survey (67% of those polled) reported some form of personal relationship with industry that included serving as a consultant (27%), serving as a member of a scientific advisory board (27%), being a member of a speakers' bureau (14%), serving as an officer (7%), or being a founder (9%) or member of a board of directors of a private or public company (11%).

Clinical departments were more likely than nonclinical departments to receive research support or support for training programs and continuing medical education; nonclinical departments were more likely to receive support from intellectual property licensing. More than two-thirds of chairs believed that industry relationships had no effect on their activities, although most believed that a chair should have no more than one substantive industry-related activity to avoid conflicts of commitment. However, these relationships provided a ready opportunity to link industry and academia in order to facilitate the translation of novel findings at the research bench or in the clinic to the actualization of new therapies for patients with disease.

Indeed, William Brody, president of Johns Hopkins University, entrepreneur, and founder of three medical device companies, noted that academic–industry partnerships are an important way to further science. "It's critical for researchers to help companies keep up with innovation," he reported [14].

Converting New Discoveries to New Sources of Revenue

With the ability to own their intellectual property, AMCs began to create new income streams by commercializing discoveries that were made in their laboratories in collaboration with the biotechnology industry. Several different models have evolved for taking early discoveries from the laboratory to the commercial arena. Each has both benefits and shortcomings: licensing, development of spin-offs, creation of biotechnology "parks," and development of AMC-based and -supported biotechnology centers.

Licensing Technology to Industry

The most straightforward means of commercializing a product is to license technology developed in the academic laboratory to a free-standing, for-profit company. In most cases, the university receives a small up-front payment that covers the initial cost of the patent work done by the university (usually outsourced) and a small fee that can be used by the university and the investigators to support new work. In 2005, U.S. universities executed 1,378 exclusive and 2,180 nonexclusive licenses to the biotechnology or device industry. Some universities received substantial license income—for example, $27 million at Harvard, $30 million at the University of Rochester, $49 million at Wake Forest University, $585 million at Emory University, $133 million at NYU, and $12 million at the University of Texas Southwestern Medical Center. Columbia has been a poster child for licensing success. It licensed a patent on a novel way to treat glaucoma to Pharmacia, which in turn developed the blockbuster drug latanoprost—earning the university $20 million in royalties in 2000 alone [15].

However, not all universities receive support from intellectual property licensing and some universities receive very little income, such as $470,000 at Georgetown, $323,000 at the University of Arkansas for Medical Sciences, and $79,000 at the Medical College of Georgia Research Institute. Licensing agreements may also include subsequent royalty fees but rarely include equity in the entity that is licensing the intellectual property.

From a pragmatic standpoint, licensing is the most cost-effective means for an AMC to transfer its technology from the academic home to the clinical healthcare arena. Most university technology transfer operations struggle with limited budgets, high legal fees, and high operating costs [16]. Therefore, because the biotechnology company pays for much of the patent work, the costs to the university are often modest; for example, a provisional patent usually costs between $10,000 and $20,000. However, licensing also has downsides: The inventor has no control over how the patent is utilized or developed, there is no guarantee that the company that licenses the patent will actually use it, and the time between licensing and royalty payments may be extremely long because the process of drug development and discovery is continually weighed down by increasing federal regulations.

Furthermore, the revenues obtained from licensing agreements are not particularly robust. The average income per active license in 2000 was only $64,465, only 43% earned royalties, and only 0.56% of licenses earned more than $1 million [17]. Furthermore, early discoveries are finding it increasingly difficult to pass muster at the patent office. For example, in 2001, the U.S. Patent and Trademark Office, the government agency charged with determining the patentability of inventions, finalized new guidelines that required a patent to demonstrate credible, specific, and substantial usefulness [18]. As a result, patent applications that identify new proteins, methods to regulate cellular processes, single nucleotide polymorphisms, and human genome sequences are no longer receiving favorable reviews at the patent office. Thus, when the information from the basic scientific work reaches the public domain, industry can use the information and control the intellectual property by creating a "final product" such as a device or drug [19]. As Kesselheim and Avorn pointed out [20]:

A major goal of science policy in the coming years will be to create a more versatile body of intellectual property laws for biomedical research that also rewards the seminal work, often conducted in non-profit institutions and funded by taxpayer support, on which newly patented therapeutics, diagnostic tests, and medical devices depend so heavily.

Joint Industry–Academic Development

Another format for moving discovery from the bench to the bedside has been the development of collaborative projects between industry and academia. For example, academia and industry collaborated in

- the development of a bird-flu vaccine from the St. Jude Children's Research Hospital;
- a University of Kansas concept for solving solubility problems of small molecules;
- a new method for fixing broken wrists from the University of North Carolina School of Medicine; and
- a novel chemotherapy derived from a monoclonal antibody for the treatment of colorectal and head and neck tumors from the University of California, San Diego.

Agreements were also developed between Monsanto and Washington University, between Hoechst and Massachusetts General Hospital, and between Novartis and both the Scripps Research Institute and the University of California, Berkley [11].

Novel collaborations that were formed to accelerate the process of finding new small-molecule drugs included an alliance of the Hereditary Disease Foundation, Aurora Biosciences, and academic researchers of the Huntington Study Group to develop small molecules for the treatment of Huntington's disease [21]. The Global Alliance for TB Drug Development includes investigators at the Rockefeller Foundation, the Bill and Melinda Gates Foundation, the World Health Organization, a group of non-U.S. university-based researchers, and several private companies [22].

It was announced recently that AstraZeneca and Columbia University Medical Center would collaborate in a new research project to examine how neurogenesis—the creation of new neuronal cells—in adults might provide new approaches for the treatment of depression and anxiety. One of several new alliances between AstraZeneca and leading academic research centers, the collaboration between Columbia and AstraZeneca in the area of depression and anxiety mirrors an earlier collaboration between the two groups focused on metabolic disease [23]. These types of collaborations bring cutting-edge basic science research together with the ability to perform combinatorial chemistry to develop small molecules that will interact with new target proteins and overcome many of the obstacles that inhibited prior efforts.

However, these types of partnerships fail when the participants do not agree at the outset on the means to handle potentially divisive issues such as structure, control of intellectual property, publication of fundamental research findings, and funding. Success requires flexibility on the part of the involved institutions, periodic scrutiny to assess the effectiveness of the collaboration in fulfilling its goals, and an evaluation of whether the partnership enhances academic inquiry while accelerating the drug development process [24]. In addition, all relations must be open and transparent and investigators must be allowed to publish freely their own and shared findings.

Pfizer and the University of California, San Francisco, also recently announced a novel alliance to advance a broad range of research [25]. The collaboration, which spans several University of California campuses and multiple Pfizer research units, will provide up to $9.5 million in support and will utilize defined templates to facilitate rapid completion of industry–university agreements. The Pfizer–UCSF agreement is unique in its scope and thus should speed the translation of basic research discoveries into drugs and diagnostics for a variety of diseases.

Spinning Off New Companies from Academia

Spinning off new companies from academia can be described as "high risk–high reward." The concept is relatively straightforward. After disclosing an invention to the university technology transfer office, the inventor seeks funding to establish a biotechnology company that will develop the invention for commercial purposes. The development of the new company can be done with or without the help and collaboration of the university technology transfer office; this is gauged in large part by the experience of the inventor (company founder), the sophistication of the personnel in the technology transfer office, and the philosophic views of the university. Regardless of whether or not the AMC participates directly in the founding of the company, the university receives a fee to out-license the technology to the new company as well as equity in the new entity.

A segment of the venture capital community funds these types of early start-up companies; however, the downside is that they invariably take the majority of the seats on the company board, can hold as much as 80% of the total equity in the company, and have equity in the form of preferred rather than common stock. Thus, neither the university nor the inventors receive any remuneration until the holders of preferred stock have been reimbursed for their initial investment as well as interest on the investment. This is usually in the range of 8%—significantly higher than interest rates on a typical loan or mortgage. Nonetheless, the enormous upside to spin-offs accounts for the fact that, between 1980 and 2005, 5,171 new spin-off companies were formed; 628 new spin-off companies were formed in 2005 alone [12].

Examples of successful spin-offs include Stentor, a biotechnology company that the University of Pittsburgh Medical Center (UPMC) helped create using intellectual property developed by a UPMC physician. UPMC sold the company for over $280 million [26]. Pitt started six start-up companies in 2006, eight in 2005, and ten in fiscal year 2004 [27]. The Stentor technology is exciting because it allows radiology images to be viewed on personal computer networks, has now been marketed widely, and has in many ways changed the practice of radiology by providing an opportunity for radiologists to read images at home or in their offices and to transmit the images around the world.

UPMC has also invested heavily in new technology that it perceives will influence the future of medicine and healthcare. For example, in April 2003, it invested in a Virginia-based biotechnology firm whose parent company was involved in producing the cloned sheep, Dolly [28]. In the same year, it also purchased a large bioterrorism research group from the Johns Hopkins University—appropriately believing that bioterrorism research grants would be plentiful in times ahead.

Another highly successful academic spin-off was Myogen, Inc. Founded by a group of University of Colorado faculty in 1996, the university spin-off was funded exclusively with venture capital financing. Although Myogen had starts and stops during its relatively short existence, it was able to call on the deep pockets of some of its venture capital partners and in-license three drugs ready for phase III clinical development. The company went public in 2005 and was sold to Gilead Pharmaceuticals for $2.5 billion in 2006 [29].

Despite the great successes that can be identified in university spin-offs, these entities often face hurdles that they are unable to surmount. In a recent editorial in *Nature Business,* Don Siegel, an economist at Rensselaer Polytechnic Institute in New York, noted that "most technology-transfer offices at universities fail to cover their own expenses, much less generate revenue streams" [4]. Industry is frustrated by disputes over intellectual property rights, the value of intellectual property, and the fact that many technologies are based on multiple patents; thus, with each university wanting a substantial proportion of the profits, the economics become unfeasible.

Academic spin-offs also raise important issues regarding conflicts of interest. Large pharmaceutical companies pay the university for the license and have teams of investigators on hand that can develop the products or buy late-stage products that can go directly into clinical development. However, biotechnology spin-offs usually evolve around far less mature products and need the active participation of the inventors. In order to reward them for their help, young companies provide equity or stock options to the inventors and often to the participating university. This "engenders a powerful but controversial incentive for the investigator and has proved to be one of the most difficult issues for academic centers to manage" [24]. As noted in Chapter 5, these types of conflicts can best be mitigated by always putting the responsibility to an individual patient above the competing interests of financial gain, the demand of entrepreneurs, or economic development [24].

An important limitation of the spin-off approach to commercializing academic intellectual property is that the ongoing worldwide financial crisis has limited the ability of many entrepreneurs to raise money from venture capital groups. Because capital is drying up, many biotechnology companies are starting to cut their work forces and even eliminate drug development projects in an effort to make the cash they currently have last longer [30]. Since the turmoil in the financial markets makes it almost impossible for biotechnology companies funded with venture capital money to go public, the venture capital companies must keep financing their companies longer. As a result, they do not have the money to invest in new companies.

Many venture capital groups that have money are investing in publicly traded companies because their shares have become devalued—again decreasing the amount of money available for new companies. Some large pharmaceutical companies are also watching as venture-backed biotechnology companies begin to run out of money in the expectation that they might be able to buy the company or its drug portfolio at a highly discounted price. For companies seeking to get started, venture capital companies are significantly discounting the pre-money valuation of the start-ups, thereby markedly limiting the amount of equity available for the inventor and the university even if a deal can be brokered. For AMCs that have invested in biotechnology, the downturn in the economic markets is one more constraint on their current finances.

Creating University-Based Biotechnology Companies

Duke University and the University of North Carolina, Chapel Hill, have taken somewhat different approaches to building revenue streams from their intellectual property [31]. Both universities have opened drug discovery centers. These efforts come at a time when the pipeline in many pharmaceutical companies is at an all-time low. As noted by R. Sanders Williams, senior vice chancellor at Duke, "Academia should help them if pharma can't do it all" [31]. At the University of North Carolina, Stephen Frye, GlaxoSmithKlein's former head of drug discovery research, is building the Center for Integrative Chemical Biology and Drug Discovery with the goal of linking the medical school with chemists from the pharmacy school to generate innovative drug research.

Meanwhile, at Duke, Allen Roses, a former Duke professor, left GlaxoSmithKline after 10 years to head up Duke's new drug discovery efforts. Roses' goal is to identify drug research opportunities that the pharmaceutical industry is not pursuing and then to bring them into what is currently a virtual company. Once the new drugs are tested in animal models and humans, he hopes to sell them to pharmaceutical companies that will be able to bring the drugs to market. Duke's ability to develop potential compounds will be helped by the award of one of the first clinical and translational science awards (CTSAs) from the National Institutes of Health—a grant focused on translating basic science findings into therapies that will improve health. UPMC has taken a similar approach by entering into an agreement to join Carnegie Mellon University in developing innovative computer and software research and investment in a Carnegie Mellon spin-off that uses software to help organizations in procurement deals [32].

Using Academic Laboratories as Incubators

Another approach to commercializing discoveries has been to use academic laboratories as incubator facilities to pursue industry-sponsored research. Several universities have developed free-standing research institutes or foundations to separate research activities that are industry related. These include the Draper and Lincoln Laboratories and the Whitehead Institute for Biomedical Research at the Massachusetts Institute of Technology, the Applied Physics Laboratory at the Johns Hopkins University, and the Wisconsin Alumni Research Foundation of the University of Wisconsin-Madison. These have proven successful largely due to a mission that is driven by a donor or sponsor (e.g., the need for the applied physics laboratory to carry out classified military research), a clear focus, and careful oversight and management by the associated university.

However, using an academic laboratory within the confines of the university to support industry-funded research raises significant concerns. Great care must be taken to ensure that there is no cross-talk between the trainees and personnel in the laboratory on the university side and those on the corporate side. This becomes a difficult situation when the proximity of the investigators and the common technology of the laboratory result in sharing of reagents, know-how, or technology. It is difficult to protect conflicts of interest, and it is equally difficult to adjudicate conflicts of commitment because of an inherent incentive for both faculty and staff to spend more time on for-profit activities than on fundamental research at a time when federal grant support is increasingly difficult to obtain.

How AMCs Can Commercialize Technology in Difficult Economic Times

It is important that, at a time when AMCs are financially stressed, they seek new revenue sources; an important one is the commercialization of new technology that comes from the research labs of America's medical schools. The approaches outlined previously have led to successful financial ventures for a number of different AMCs. As noted, however, each of these approaches has limitations and careful oversight is needed to ensure that conflicts of interest do not impede good judgment on the part of institutions and inventors and that decisions are always in the best interest of patients and subjects of clinical trials. However, in the face of a global financial meltdown, when larger pharmaceutical companies are laying off staff and funding from private equity is decreasing, it is becoming increasingly difficult for AMCs to partner early-stage discoveries or spin off successful companies for the development of later stage products [33].

In addition, pre-money valuations by venture capital companies are at an all-time low. Some AMCs will simply wait out the storm. However, it may not be advantageous to wait out the current recession because the clock starts ticking once a patent is issued; therefore, long delays may waste substantial portions of the life of a patent, resulting in limited value once it is time to move toward commercialization. Thus, AMCs must seek ways to commercialize their patents even at times of great financial stress in the U.S. marketplace. The suggestions in the following sections, based on successful programs at a number of different academic institutions, may be helpful in times of crisis in the global financial markets.

Intellectual Property Bundling

Intellectual property bundling is the aggregation of intellectual property from multiple institutions for the purpose of optimizing opportunities for licensing to the pharmaceutical or device industry. Although patents encourage commercialization by giving the ownership rights to new discoveries to their inventors, the patent process often inhibits the exchange of information needed for the collaborative development of new technology. Because so many processes in drug development require pieces of the new technology to come from the work of independent investigators, biotechnology companies must often deal with multiple patent holders in order to develop a single product. As a result, the "downstream" researchers or biotechnology companies must negotiate licensing agreements with each of the different "upstream" patent holders in order to create a viable patent portfolio.

Unfortunately, the costs of these numerous agreements often become prohibitive and sometimes individual institutions are resistant, leading to what is commonly known as "patent thicket." Pooling allows a group of patents from different institutions to be "bundled" together under the control of a single institution, thereby creating a one-step process for potential licensees at a reasonable cost. Technology bundling also allows institutions without the resources to pursue a large number of technology transfer agreements on their own to work collaboratively with other institutions to pursue joint efforts. Collaboration is important; data show that fewer than half of the research universities actively seeking patents break even from technology transfer efforts and two-thirds of the revenue has gone to only 13 institutions [34]. By defining preexisting guidelines for patenting, a consortium of institutions can negotiate more effectively.

The Larta Institute, a private firm specializing in technology transfer and the Ewing Marion Kaufman Foundation of Kansas City initiated the Technology Bundling Project [35]. After reviewing more than 1,500 inventions from six institutions, the project group was able to identify 41 potential bundles made up of 100 different technologies [35]. A similar approach was taken by a group of organizations in New Mexico, including the University of New Mexico, the National Center for Genome Resources, and other nonprofit institutions in the state, to create the Technology Research Collaborative [36]. One of the fundamental objectives of this group was to create institutional agreements that would support the ability of the organization to bundle patents and license them through a single entity [36].

However, it must be noted that these types of collaborative activities are not easy. The various partners must negotiate the relative value of each contribution, negotiate in advance how royalty revenues will be distributed, and identify the added value that comes from collaborating. Furthermore, these agreements often require an outside arbiter to set values and to provide unbiased leadership [37]. Nonetheless, in our current fiscal environment, such collaborative activities present an opportunity to overcome existing challenges.

Development of Cross-Institutional Collaborations in Technology Transfer

Technology transfer has become increasingly sophisticated and complex over the past decade, and AMCs undertaking efforts to commercialize their discoveries face some important challenges. As in many businesses, the ability to obtain venture capital financing or to out-license new discoveries requires the talents of individuals who have at some time in their careers been part of the relatively small world of venture capital and/or the drug-development industry and have demonstrated success in their earlier endeavors. Because many venture capitalists pay as much attention to the "jockey" as they do to the "horse" when they make their decisions about which new biotechnology companies they will finance, the experience level of the inventor or the individual chosen to run the new company is also of great importance. Unfortunately, it is difficult to recruit individuals who have been successful in biotechnology venture capital or in the development and leadership of biotechnology companies before they joined academia.

Another challenge for AMCs developing technology transfer programs is the inherent cost of the patent process and the need to have attorneys familiar with the many different areas of biotechnology—from the synthesis of small molecules to the identification of the relevance of single nucleotide polymorphisms in the human genome. Patent attorneys with this type of expertise are neither inexpensive nor readily available, so technology transfer offices often receive advice from less experienced lawyers that leads them to patent a number of products with little commercial value or to pass on patenting discoveries that might later be found to have enormous value. Indeed, few inventors with whom I have spoken thought that their technology transfer offices provided an optimal level of service.

Technology transfer offices are undermanned and have excessive overhead. This creates an optimal opportunity for a group of AMCs to partner in developing a first-rate technology transfer program staffed with experts in the pharmaceutical and biotechnology business as well as patent attorneys. Partnering would result in decreased overhead costs. The increased number of patent filings would make it cost effective to hire first-rate patent attorneys on a full-time basis or to outsource patent work to a single, high-quality attorney or firm and to explore the process of patent bundling when appropriate.

Indeed, combining patent offices can be just one more part of the collaboration among various institutions that is now encouraged by the NIH and it has recently led to pooling of research efforts across all of Harvard's hospitals and research institutions as well as the efforts of Boston University and Tufts University [38]. At a time when venture capital funding is so difficult to obtain, collaborations among a large group of AMCs may also allow the various schools to contribute to their own venture fund. This would provide small start-up packages to new biotechnology companies and help them until improvements in the markets allow venture capital firms once again to invest actively in early-stage biotechnology at reasonable valuations.

Development of Nonprofit Biotechnology Companies

The Laboratory for Drug Discovery in Neurodegeneration (LDDN) looks like many other biotechnology start-ups. Located in Cambridge, Massachusetts, with a mission of creating new drugs to treat human disease, the laboratory is quite unique because it is not a biotechnology company but rather a not-for-profit entity that sits under the Harvard Medical School umbrella [39]. LDDN began in 2001 with part of a $37.5 million gift from an anonymous donor. By focusing on drugs that are not blockbusters but rather treat specific diseases that affect a smaller number of patients, the center hopes to gain economic rewards. Because LDDN has no shareholders, it does not have the usual pressures for rapid results and because it is a not-for-profit entity, it can seek collaborative help from the many parts of the Harvard Medical School research enterprise.

A unique part of the program is that it funds sabbaticals for Harvard postdoctoral researchers. This allows them to bring their target proteins or genes to the laboratory and work for a period of 12–18 months to develop small molecules that can alter the function of these proteins. Thus, they are able to translate their basic research findings into therapeutic compounds. The research is facilitated by the presence of a large library of compounds, robotic screening systems, and medicinal chemists.

However, like for-profit biotechnology laboratories, LDDN must raise money to continue to support itself through grants and contracts. Future funding will come from licensing deals and royalty streams. In the meantime, its focus on a single disease raises enormous opportunities for fundraising from patients and family members. The application of this type of not-for-profit biotech to other medical centers will require the same type of substantive donation or funding that was used to start LDDN. However, this type of facility might be applicable to funding through a collaborative effort of a group of AMCs and their affiliated hospitals.

References

1. McLean, J. 1959. The discovery of heparin. *Circulation* 19:75–78.
2. Marcum, J. A., McKenney, J. B., Galli, S. J., Jackman, R. W., and Rosenberg, R. D. 1986. Anticoagulantly active heparin-like molecules from mast cell-deficient mice. *American Journal of Physiology* 250 (5 Pt 2): H879–888.
3. Armstrong, M. 2008. Hospitals sells drug royalties. Apr. 25 (www.philly.com/business).
4. Gewin, V. 2005. The technology trap. *Nature* 437 (7061): 948–949.
5. Swann, J. 1988. *Academic scientists and the pharmaceutical industry cooperative research in twentieth century America*. Baltimore, MD: Johns Hopkins University Press.
6. The Johns Hopkins University patent policy. 1951. Meeting minutes, July 10, 1951. Baltimore, MD: The Alan Mason Chesney Medical Archives of the Johns Hopkins Medical Institutions.
7. Meeting of the Harvard University medical faculty. 1923. Meeting minutes, Boston.

8. Ludmerer, K. 1999. *Time to heal: American medical education from the turn of the century to the era of managed care,* 514. New York: Oxford University Press.
9. The Bayh–Dole Act of 1980: Patent rights and inventions made with federal assistance (www.usaid.gov/policy/ads/300/318.pdf).
10. Kirshenbaum, S. R. 2002. Patenting basic research: myths and realities, *Nature* neuroscience supplement. 4 (November): 1025–1027.
11. Martin, J. B., and Kasper, D. L. 2001. In whose best interest? Breaching the academic–industrial wall. *New England Journal of Medicine* 343 (22): 1646–1649.
12. Survey Summary. 2007. AUTM US Licensing Survey FY 2005. The Association of University and Technology Managers (www.autm.net).
13. Campbell, E. G., Weissman, J. S., Ehringhaus, S., Rao, S. R., Moy, B., Feibelmann, S., and Goold, S. D. 2007. Institutional academic industry relationships. *Journal of the American Medical Association* 298 (15): 1779–1786.
14. Brandt, M. L. 2005. Hopkins president: No conflict, no interest. Stanford News Service, Oct. 5 (http://news-service.stanford.edu/news/2005/october5/med-hopkins-100505.html).
15. Mowery, D. C., Nelson, R., Sampat, B. N., and Ziedonis, A. A. 2004. *Ivory tower and industrial innovation.* Stanford, CA: Stanford University Press.
16. Gelijns, A. C., and Thier, S. O. 2002. Medical innovation and institutional interdependence: Rethinking university–industry connections. *Journal of the American Medical Association* 287 (1): 72–77.
17. Thursby, J. 2003. Intellectual property—University licensing and the Bayh–Dole Act. *Science* 301:1052.
18. Utility examination guidelines. 2001. 66 *Federal Register* 1092, Jan. 5.
19. Gluck, M. E. Federal policies affecting the cost and availability of new pharmaceuticals. The Henry J. Kaiser Foundation, July, 2002 (www.kff.org/rxdrugs/3254-index.ofm).
20. Kesselheim, A., and Avorn, J. 2005. University-based science and biotechnology products: Defining the boundaries of intellectual property. *Journal of the American Medical Association* 293:850–854.
21. Moses, H., Braunwald, E., Martin, J. B., and Their, S. O. 2002. Collaborating with industry—Choices for the academic medical center. *New England Journal of Medicine* 347:1371–1375.
22. McCan-Markar, M. Stronger TB drugs expected in a decade. TB Alliance (www.tballiance.org/newscenter/reviewinnews.php?id=452).
23. http://www.astrazeneca-us.com/about-astrazeneca-us/newsroom/all/3095607?itemId-3095607.
24. Moses, H., Braunwald, E., Martin, J. B., and Thier, S. O. 2002. Collaborating with industry—Choices for the academic medical center. *New England Journal of Medicine* 347:1371–1375.
25. Pfizer, UC San Francisco form alliance (www.universityofcalifornia.edu/news/article/17986), June 10 (http://pub.ucsf.edu/newsservices/releases/200806101/).
26. Snowbeck, C. 2005. UPMC, Pitt cash in on sale of high-tech medical firm. *Pittsburgh Post-Gazette,* July 7.
27. Shropshire, C. 2006. Pitt reports number of startup firms drops. *Pittsburgh Post-Gazette,* Oct. 11.

28. Levin, S. 2005. Empire building: Consolidation and controversy at UPMC. *Pittsburgh Post-Gazette,* Dec. 27, A1.

29. Ransom, J. 2006. Deconstructing Myogen's market cap. *Nature Biotechnology* 24:227–228.

30. Pollack, A. 2008. Broader financial turmoil threatens biotech's innovation and cash. *The New York Times,* Oct. 29.

31. Vollmer, S. 2008. Where pharma meets college. *The News Observer,* March 26.

32. Snowbeck, C. 2006. UPMC's expertise for sale around the world. *Pittsburgh Post-Gazette,* Oct. 22.

33. Vollmer, S. 2008. Layoff toll rises at GSK. *News and Observer,* Aug. 5 (http://www.newsobserver.com/business/story/1165312.html).

34. Roe-Dupree, J. 2008. When academia profits ahead of wonder. *New York Times,* Sept. 7.

35. Virtual Bundling Agent, Larta Institute (www.larta.org/ClientsandPrograms/Universities Institutes and Foundations/virtualbundlingagents.aspx).

36. New Mexico Technology Research Corridor Collaborative (www.nmpartnership.com/press-releases/article.php?id=971&title=new+mexico+technology+research+corridor+collaborative).

37. Lyzenga, A. 2007. *Intellectual property building: An opportunity for academic health centers?* Washington, D.C.: Association of Academic Health Centers.

38. Lazar, K. 2008. Harvard medical researchers pool work. *The Boston Globe,* May 30.

39. Alper, J. 2003. Biotech thinking comes to academic medical centers. *Science* 299:1303–1304.

SPHERE OF ACTION: III
EDUCATION

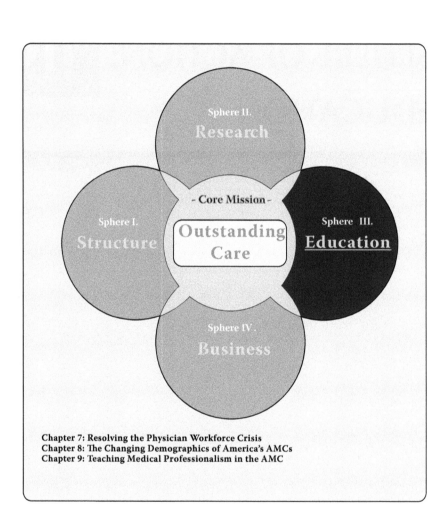

Sphere II.
Research

- Core Mission -

Sphere I.
Structure

Outstanding
Care

Sphere III.
Education

Sphere IV.
Business

Chapter 7

Resolving the Physician Workforce Crisis

> In the first place, the small town needs the best and not the worst doctor procurable. For the country doctor has only himself to rely on: he cannot in every pinch hail specialist, expert, and nurse. On his own skill, knowledge, resourcefulness, the welfare of his patient altogether depends. The rural district is therefore entitled to the best trained physician that can be induced to go there.
>
> **Abraham Flexner 1910** [1]

Introduction

In 1910, Flexner first noted concerns regarding the size of the physician workforce and the need to ensure that qualified physicians practiced in both small towns and large cities. Today, the United States is facing a shortage of physicians that will imperil its ability to care for the ever increasing size of the U.S. population—especially in rural and underserved urban areas [2,3]. These shortages come at a time when 20% of Americans live in regions that have already been designated as health professional shortage areas [4,5]. Only recently has the general public begun to become aware of this brewing crisis. For example, in February 2008 *USA Today* described the plight of Nassawadox, Virginia, where a shortage of surgeons had adversely affected care [4].

This is not just a rural problem; over a dozen states have reported physician shortages or an expectation of physician shortages, a large number of specialties have pointed to shortages in their fields, and many practices in both rural and urban areas have reported an inability to fill vacant positions. The workforce crisis has also had an enormous impact on the AMC, which must increase its ability to train students at the same time that the physician shortage compromises its ability to recruit and retain its own workforce. An unprecedented number of academic positions are unfilled as academic medical centers have an increasingly difficult time recruiting and retaining the high-quality physicians for which they have been renowned [6,7]. This threatens the very foundation on which AMCs were built: providing excellence in patient care.

This chapter will describe the causes of the physician workforce crisis, describe how some AMCs are developing plans to enhance their ability to train physicians, discuss concerns regarding some of the new models being created for some medical schools, and present recommendations to create a national task force to address the physician workforce crisis.

Causes of the Physician Workforce Crisis

The history and causes of the workforce shortage have been detailed by Richard Cooper, a former medical school dean and leading authority on the topic [2,8,9]. In the 1970s, policy makers became concerned that the increased spending on healthcare was driven by physicians—a belief that led to the hypothesis that the economy would benefit if the total physician pool were to be decreased [8]. The Graduate Medical Education National Advisory Committee advised Congress in 1980 of a growing surplus of physicians and predicted a net excess of 70,000 physicians by 1990 and an excess of 140,000 by the year 2000. Governmental support for medical schools ceased and, as a result, so too did the expansion of both allopathic and osteopathic medical schools [10]. Thus, one important component of developing a physician workforce—undergraduate training—was crippled by decreased governmental support.

The decrease in funding for undergraduate training had a profound effect. Between 1980 and 2000 the number of students trained at allopathic medical schools did not change while the population of the United States increased significantly. Thus, the number of physicians per capita graduating from American medical schools markedly decreased [8]. The Council on Graduate Medical Education, a group that just a decade earlier had strongly supported the notion that there would be a physician surplus, reversed its earlier projections and noted that there would be physician shortages in the years ahead [3]. Indeed, the Association of American Medical Colleges recommended that U.S. medical schools increase their enrollments by 30% by the year 2015 [11].

By the fall of 2005, U.S. allopathic medical schools had increased their enrollment levels by approximately 10% [12]. By 2007, 115 of 126 allopathic medical schools had increased their first-year enrollment, which would be expected to increase growth to over 19,000 first-year students in 2012 [13]. Unfortunately, these increases will be insufficient to meet all future needs of the U.S. population, thus threatening the healthcare of the nation [14].

The ability to train more physicians has also been limited by federal restrictions on the number of postgraduate training slots. In the late 1990s the American College of Physicians Health and Public Policy Committee and the Health and Public Policy Committee on Physician Workforce and Financing of Graduate Medical Education made a group of substantive recommendations regarding postgraduate medical education (internships, residencies, and fellowships) in the United States [15]. Unfortunately, the only recommendation that received attention from federal regulators was that the number of postgraduate year 1 (PGY-1) residency positions be decreased. As a result, the Balanced Budget Act of 1997 froze federal funding for graduate medical education at its 1996 level. According to Cooper, "this single action fully accounts for the leveling off of physician supply in 2005 and the projected decline thereafter" [8].

With a cap on the number of postgraduate training positions, even if U.S. allopathic and osteopathic medical schools were able to increase the number of medical students trained each year in the United States, the overall number of practicing physicians would not change substantially. With an increase in the number of U.S. graduates, programs that traditionally filled with international graduates would instead fill their programs with U.S. graduates. Thus, the total number of trainees would remain the same, but would be composed of a higher percentage of U.S. graduates [16]. Because of this, U.S. teaching hospitals must increase their number of postgraduate training slots annually for a period of 10 years to reach a total of 35,000 trainees by 2020 in order even to begin to approach the future U.S. workforce needs [8].

Not all experts agree that there is a shortage. David Goodman has been a leading advocate of the view that current workforce planning has failed to outline explicitly the expected patient or societal effects of training more physicians [17]. Goodman suggests that U.S. healthcare would be better served by investing in coverage for uninsured children and reforming Medicare physician payments to shore up the collapsing infrastructure of primary care medicine. However, other studies have shown that simply increasing the supply of primary care physicians will not result in better outcomes [18–20]. Furthermore, the Institute of Medicine of the National Academies of Medicine, the most prestigious group of health science academicians in the United States, weighed in on the subject in

April 2008 and clearly supported the contention of Cooper and others that the United States was clearly facing a healthcare workforce crisis [21].

Shortfall of Academic Physicians

Just as there is a physician shortage in communities across the United States, there is also a critical demand for physician–scientists, physician–educators, and clinician–investigators (the academic workforce) in virtually all of our AMCs. Furthermore, it is just as important to retain young investigators as it is to retain established investigators. A recent survey by the Association of American Medical Colleges reported that almost two out of every five faculty members leave academic medicine within a decade for more lucrative opportunities in private practice or industry [22]. After 10 years, only half of all academic faculty remained at their medical schools, while 38% had left academic medicine. Of even greater concern was the high attrition rate of young faculty: 43%. Given the high cost of recruiting an individual faculty member and adverse affects of turnover on physician morale and satisfaction, the continuing difficulties in recruiting and retaining young physicians to academic medical centers threaten their integrity and future.

In 2001, CenterWatch, a group that oversees U.S. clinical research enterprises, reported that by 2005 there would be a critical shortage of individuals trained in clinical research [23]. Consistent with this finding, only 8% of principal investigators conducting industry-sponsored clinical research at U.S. academic medical centers are younger than 40 years of age [23] and fewer than 4% of competing research grants awarded by the NIH in 2001 went to investigators who were 35 years of age or younger [24]. This shortage has not gone unrecognized by policy analysts or by the clinical research industry. In 1998, the NIH created a group of awards for new investigators (K23) or those who were at the midpoint of careers in patient-oriented research [25]. In addition, a program (K30) was instituted to provide funds for clinical research training programs at 55 institutions across the country [26].

The most valuable addition to the NIH grants portfolio in terms of improving the number of clinician investigators has been a clinical research loan repayment program that repays educational debts for individuals who spend the majority of their time in clinical research [27]. However, the impact of this program is limited by the fact that it only applies to minority candidates, there are far more applicants than funding, and the repayments only cover a part of the 4-year medical school curriculum. Corporate foundations have also invested in training programs for clinician–investigators [28].

However, even funding for training cannot obviate one of the major impediments to attracting young physicians to careers in clinical research: an absence of financial support for faculty who pursue clinical research. Young faculty members are constantly pressured to see more patients and to take on more clinical responsibilities to support their salary; this provides little time to pursue clinical research [29]. Thus, with continuing cuts in physician reimbursements, it will be increasingly difficult to attract young physicians to academic medicine.

The challenges faced by the clinician–scientist (i.e., an MD undertaking basic science research) are daunting. The concerns for the future of the physician–scientist were aptly laid out by the report of a task force on the future of clinician–scientists at the University of California, San Francisco, in 2001. The report noted that "many [faculty] reported that excessive clinical responsibilities prevented them from working on grants and the projects funded by grants" [30]. Of the respondents, 58% felt that the balance between their clinical and research activities was not consistent with meeting their research goals. One respondent summed it up [30]:

> A successful clinician–scientist, measured as a prominent clinician and scientist, is a difficult task. Clinically, you are competing with full-time clinicians who are protecting their practices to sustain their salaries. Scientifically, you are competing with full-time scientists who are pushing as hard as they can to protect their grant support. In this atmosphere of highly polarized needs, it is a tall order to succeed on both fronts.

More recently, the Association of Professors of Medicine published a report entitled "Recommendations for Revitalizing the Nation's Physician–Scientist Workforce" [31]. The report noted the shrinking and aging of the physician–scientist workforce, as well as pointing out the dramatic generational changes in the priorities of recent graduates and the fact that women find careers as physician–scientists less attractive than do men.

As already described in detail in Chapter 5, the decrease in NIH funding has made it even more difficult to recruit physician–scientists. In a survey performed by the journal *Science* in 2007, Jennifer Couzin and Greg Miller interviewed dozens of investigators at academic institutions across the country as well as six NIH institute directors and agency head Elias Zerhouni. All described "a climate in which young scientists struggle to launch their careers and even the most senior are trimming their research projects" [32]. Edward J. Benz, Jr., the president and CEO of the Dana-Farber Cancer Institute in Boston, noted that what is "chilling" about the continuing decrease in NIH funding is that "we're getting into years 3 and 4 with no end in sight" [32]. As noted by David Seatt, chair of the Neurobiology Department at the University of Alabama, Birmingham, "It's just about inconceivable for a brand-new investigator to get an NIH grant funded on their first submission these days" [32].

However, not only young investigators are adversely affected by the NIH cuts. Couzin and Miller also describe the trials of Alan Schneyer, who at the time of the interview was a 52-year-old reproductive endocrinologist at Massachusetts General Hospital in Boston [32]. While studying the effects of two proteins on reproduction, he serendipitously found that when he eliminated these proteins in mice, they had superior glucose tolerance and a marked increase in cells in the pancreas that make insulin. Although he had a novel finding that had the potential to yield substantial gains in the understanding and treatment of diabetes, his pathway to NIH funding was impeded by the fact that he would have to seek funding from an evaluation group at the NIH that was not familiar with him or his work. After 3 years of trying for NIH grants and failing, he left Massachusetts General to work at a life sciences institute that did not rely as heavily on NIH funding; therefore; he could perform research without worrying about funding.

An innovative approach to training the next generation of academic physicians is being taken by the Scripps Research Institute and Scripps Health in San Diego, California [33]. Recognizing a manpower crisis in the physician community as a whole as well as a critical deficiency in the number of physician–investigators, Scripps is planning to enroll up to 50 students each year in a program that will include traditional medical school courses, rotations at Scripps Health's hospitals and doctor's offices, and training in research laboratories and clinical research programs.

As noted by Eric Topol, who directs the Translational Science Institute and Genomic Medicine Program at Scripps, "Students will have a stipulated interest in becoming physician–scientists, not only for the care of patients but to conduct research to change the future of medicine" [33]. With an annual operating budget of approximately $400 million, the Scripps Research Institute is one of the world's largest independent, nonprofit biomedical institutes with numerous graduate science programs and over 200 students.

The Association of Professors of Medicine initiative took a different approach. It recommended that AMCs direct resources and attention to a focused group of the most promising physician scientists, develop a career-long mentoring program using teams of dedicated mentors, focus on the recruitment and retention of women physician–scientists, and pursue efforts to begin to introduce research during the premedical education and to accommodate a larger number of medical students with research interests [31].

Quality in the U.S. Healthcare Workforce

The need to increase the size of the medical student population has raised concerns about whether an adequate number of qualified students can be found to fill the increased number of training slots. Cooper noted that "unless a pool of young people who do not now seek medical education materializes, there will be too few applicants in 2015 and the years thereafter to sustain quality as it is now measured" [8]. His concerns come from his finding that a ratio of first-time applicants to matriculants of 1.5:1.0 is required to ensure continued quality in the medical student class. Unfortunately, the current ratio is very close to the ideal, suggesting that there is little reserve.

Concern is heightened by the fact that the current ratio of 1.5:1.0 would be significantly higher were it not for the marked increase in applications from women over the past decade because the number of male applicants decreased substantially over this same time period. Thus, when Cooper and colleagues estimate the increase in applications based on trends in the population and postsecondary education, they postulate that a 20% increase in medical school enrollment (far less than the required 40% increase) would result in a decrease in the applicant-to-acceptance ratio to 1.4:1.0—a fall that would make it difficult to sustain the current level of student quality in our medical schools [8]. Interestingly, medical school applications increased substantially in 2007 and 2008 due at least in part to the economic crisis on Wall Street and in corporate America resulting in fewer and less remunerative job opportunities. Nonetheless, AMCs must still focus on programs to attract a broader and more diverse group of students—a process that must begin during secondary school education.

The Challenge of Enhancing the Physician Workforce in Rural Environments

Another important challenge is to ensure that an increased supply of physicians results in improved patient access in both rural and underserved urban environments. Recent studies have shown that U.S. medical students have become increasingly interested in non-primary-care specialties [34,35]. For example, the number of family medicine residents who graduated from U.S. allopathic medical schools fell from 8,232 in 1998 and 1999 to 4,848 in 2004 and 2005 [36]. Although some students consider family medicine early during medical school, the numbers drop significantly during the second-year curriculum as students become more cognizant of the full spectrum of opportunities ahead of them as well as the financial implications and lifestyle opportunities of different career options [37,38].

Even when admissions policies target students with an interest in primary care, studies show that most students opt to pursue a different course once they enter their clinical training [39]. U.S. students also see the care delivered in large quaternary or tertiary hospitals as being more exciting and more rewarding, while the rural environment is seen as being isolated from the exciting innovations and collegial interactions of big-city hospitals. All of these reasons account for the failure to attract young U.S.-trained physicians to practice opportunities in rural areas. In a free market society, it is unlikely that anything short of financial incentives such as tuition remission or enhanced reimbursements for services will entice students to practice in rural or underserved environments.

Increasing Yearly Output of America's Allopathic Medical Schools

Increasing the supply of America's physicians is being approached in a number of ways, including increasing the size of existing medical school classes, creating new medical schools in affiliation with existing U.S. universities, expanding existing medical schools by developing new training opportunities at rural hospitals, and developing new medical schools without an affiliation with a research university or an existing AMC. Although some of these pathways are effective, others raise concerns that some of the new medical schools are very similar to the proprietary medical schools detailed in Flexner's landmark report.

The most straightforward means of increasing the physician workforce is to increase the number of students trained at each of today's existing medical schools. Unfortunately, this approach is limited by the existing infrastructure for both preclinical and clinical education at the majority of U.S. medical schools and the capacity of their physical plants. As a result, a number of different approaches have been taken and many of them raise concerns about the quality of the graduates.

Creating a New Medical School with an Affiliated University without a University Hospital

The first new allopathic medical school to be founded in 20 years was the Florida State University College of Medicine, which opened in 2005 [40]. Florida had a 30-year history of partnering between Florida State University in Tallahassee and the medical school at the University of Florida in Gainesville; 30 students completed their first year of medical school at Florida State University each year and then transferred to the University of Florida College of Medicine campus in

Gainesville for the final 3 years of their education [40]. However, the new medical school was established using a unique blueprint established by the legislative bill. Clinical training would occur at community-based centers, and a new curriculum would focus on the unique needs of Florida's elderly and minority populations. An admission process was designed to focus on identifying applicants from underrepresented populations and a postbaccalaureate program would be developed to give applicants from target populations additional preparation before applying to medical school [40].

The Florida law mandated that clinical instructors be community physicians at existing healthcare facilities. However, in order to participate in the program, community physicians had to participate in faculty development sessions at their regional campuses; course directors were required to participate in planning sessions at the main campus of Florida State. Importantly, the state of Florida allocated $50 million for facilities, $95 million for operating revenues, and a yearly allocation of $38 million. Thus, the state ensured that the funding would be available to support the educational mission of the new school.

Expanding Existing Medical Schools Using Community Hospitals for Clinical Training

Some state legislatures have announced plans to expand the size of their state medical schools by providing the first 2 years of medical education at the main campus while offering clinical instruction in community hospitals at some distance from the main campus. For example, the University of South Carolina School of Medicine in Columbia has proposed a major expansion in enrollment that will be facilitated by having an increased number of students complete their last 2 years of medical school at the Greenville Hospital in Greenville, South Carolina [41]. Students can participate in medical research through the Health Sciences South Carolina Consortium, which includes the University of South Carolina, Clemson University, and the Medical University in Charleston.

The University of North Carolina Board of Governors endorsed a similar plan by the state's two medical schools—the University of North Carolina, Chapel Hill, and the Brody School of Medicine at East Carolina University—to expand their first-year enrollments in phases starting in 2009 [42]. The expansion will be facilitated by having a group of students complete the last 2 years of their medical education in Charlotte, Asheville, or eastern North Carolina. The expansion will be facilitated by the close relationship with the parent programs and a state allocation of $450 million [42]. Finally, the Georgia legislature approved the expansion of the Medical College of Georgia in Augusta and the addition of new campuses in Athens and Savannah; it appropriated $10 million a year for 12 years for operational support and $210 million for capital improvements at the different campuses [43].

The expansion plans for these schools have raised several concerns. For example, the expansion of the Medical College of Georgia was based on a report prepared by a Pittsburgh-based for-profit planning group, Tripp Umbach (a group that had recently completed an economic analysis for the expansion of Kennywood, a popular amusement park in Pittsburgh) [44]. The report suggested that the expansion of the Medical College of Georgia in Augusta would add $350 million to Augusta's economy and account for 3,000 new jobs and $172 million in new tax revenue by 2020 and that the creation of new campuses in Athens and Savannah would generate over a half-billion dollars in economic benefit by 2020 [43].

Some legislators found the report to be "fatally flawed," at least in part, because it had not taken into account opportunities for expanding the existing private medical schools in Georgia, including Emory and Mercer Universities, Morehouse School of Medicine, and the Philadelphia College of Osteopathic Medicare campus in suburban Atlanta. It also did not take into account the fact that the new campus in Savannah was only a short distance from South Carolina's highly rated medical school in Charleston, which was organizing its own plans for substantive growth [43].

The new medical schools that have their third and fourth years separated from the main campuses and the research laboratories must also heed the cautions of Abraham Flexner, who noted [1]:

> The divided school begins by inheriting a serious problem. Its laboratory end, situated at the university, has been recently constituted of modern men; the clinical end, situated in a city at some distance, is usually what is left of the old-fashioned school which the university adopted in taking on its medical department. In course of time these clinical faculties will be reconstituted of men of more modern stamp. But the separation of its clinical branch, with the increasing absorption of the teachers in practice, involves constant danger of fresh alienation. The clinical professor of the university is very apt to be a busy physician; and if so, pedagogical and scientific ideals are all the more easily crowded into a narrow corner, when he does not breathe the bracing atmosphere of adjacent laboratories. In time, a more exacting pedagogical code and increased sensitiveness to real scientific distinction may to some extent correct the tendency. Meanwhile, these institutions, so long as they continue, require much more vigorous administrative supervision than they have anywhere received. A dean, moving freely between the

two branches, and frequent opportunities for social and scientific intercourse between scientific and clinical faculties, may throw a more or less unsteady bridge across the gap. But there is little reason to believe that the divided school will ever function as an organic whole, though it may be tolerable as a halfway stage on the road from the proprietary school to the complete university department.

Thus, even in 1910, it was recognized that all medical schools had to provide the same educational opportunities to ensure that all medical school graduates were equally proficient in the art and science of medicine and that all campuses had to be listed with the scientific foundation found at the main campus.

Developing Free-Standing Medical Schools without Academic Relationships

The creation of new medical schools in Georgia, Florida, and South Carolina is being carried out with substantive state support and in regions of the country with growing populations. However, a new medical school in Scranton, Pennsylvania, appears ill conceived and points out many of the limitations of regulating the creation of a medical school at the state versus federal level [1,45]. The Commonwealth School of Medicine has no affiliation with any of Pennsylvania's existing medical schools or research universities and will utilize a group of small community hospitals for its teaching programs. It is located in a region of the country that is losing rather than gaining population [46,47] and will begin with a one-time subsidy from the state of $35 million—a sum less than 1/10 of the proposed legislative support for the new schools in Florida, Georgia, and North Carolina. The students will be taught by community physicians; however, unlike the new schools in other states, these faculty members will have no ties with existing medical schools.

Furthermore, at a time when rural physicians are experiencing increasing nonclinical workloads, higher patient loads, and diminishing reimbursements, it is difficult to believe that an appropriate number of teachers will be available [21,48]. Although the school's Web site suggests that it will carry on a basic science program, the 19 members of the research faculty have a total of only two independent research awards from the NIH [46,49]. The hope that local businessmen will provide additional support for the school also seems naïve at a time when the United States is facing an economic crisis of enormous proportions [45].

Fewer than 10% of all physicians trained in Pennsylvania remain in the commonwealth because of the extraordinarily high malpractice costs and poor remunerations for primary care physicians. Thus, increasing the number of physicians who stay in the state through tort reform and financial incentives for new graduates might be far more economic and result in a higher quality physician than starting a new rural medical school. Unfortunately, a law that would have provided tuition remission for medical students who remained in Pennsylvania for 10 years was not passed by the Pennsylvania legislature nor was legislation that would have provided much needed caps on malpractice payments.

Another new medical school that raises concerns regarding the quality of its students is the new medical school affiliated with Hofstra University and North Shore-Long Island Jewish Health System on Long Island, New York. Asked in an interview with *The Wall Street Journal* health blog about the cost of starting the new school, Lawrence G. Smith, dean of the soon to be created school, noted [50]:

> There are two real costs to the start up of a medical school. One is the cost of staff and faculty prior to collecting tuition from students. That's in the $15–$20 million range. And then you have to build a medical education center and a living facility. That's the heart and soul of the medical school. Capitalizing both of the buildings together is going to be between $50 and $100 million. Nobody's going to come up with money for that. That's going to be a debt-service issue.

When asked about creation of basic science departments, Dr. Smith commented [50]:

> We are not going to create any of those departments [anatomy, physiology, pharmacology]. I want to link things so if we're learning anatomy and physiology of the heart, we let students get into the operating room and look at open heart surgery to see not the perfect world of the textbook but the real world.

These statements contradict the fundamental principles of medical education that have existed since the time of Flexner: linking the laboratory and the clinical arena.

Another new medical school in the planning stages that raises concerns regarding its potential success is the Virginia Tech Carilion School of Medicine in Roanoke [51]. Unlike other new schools, the school in Roanoke will develop on a very different model patterned after Harvard Medical School's health sciences and technology program and Cleveland Clinic's Lerner College of Medicine [52]. In addition to the traditional medical school curriculum, students will receive training in research methods and all students will be expected to participate in original research and to write a thesis prior to graduation.

In order to fulfill their research obligations, students will graduate in 5 years rather than in 4 years. By enrolling only 40 students in each class, the school will be able to focus on problem-based learning in seminar instructional formats [52]. Key academic infrastructure support will be provided by Virginia Tech, Carilion Clinic and its seven medical residency programs, and 100 full-time faculty physicians as well as what has been described as "a vast array of applicable world-class research underway [at Virginia Tech] in which the students may participate" [52].

Although these goals seem laudatory on paper, a look beneath the promotional information engenders significant concerns. For example, the estimated start-up costs are well below those required to run even an existing medical school. More importantly, the total amount of dollars from research grants to Virginia Tech in 2005 was approximately $10 million—an amount that would have placed the school at number 109 of 123 U.S. medical schools and that ranked them at number 185 of all U.S. institutions funded through the NIH [53]. Furthermore, neither Virginia Tech nor Carilion Clinic received any NIH support for clinical research in 2007 [53]. Thus, it seems inconceivable that the Virginia Tech School of Medicine will be able to achieve its goal of educating physician–scientists and becoming a viable healthcare institution.

Accrediting the New Medical School

The reader would likely assume that regulatory bodies will carefully oversee and accredit all new medical schools. However, the oversight of a new medical school is both complex and confounding. Accreditation is provided by the Liaison Committee on Medical Education. This body "accredits" the "M.D.-granting programs that medical schools offer," rather than the medical school per se [54]. By contrast, accreditation of the medical school as an institution of higher education—and thus its eligibility for student loan guarantees—comes from regional accrediting agencies recognized by the U.S. Department of Education. A developing medical school must proceed through a five-step process to achieve accreditation [55]:

1. applicant school status;
2. candidate school status;
3. preliminary accreditation status;
4. provisional accreditation status; and
5. full accreditation status.

New educational programs do not have to comply immediately with all LCME accreditation standards and do not need to have all of the necessary resources in place to provide 4 years of education for their students. In fact, the school only has to have enough faculty "to deliver the first year of instruction and to make any necessary decisions about student admissions, curriculum design and management, student evaluation and promotion policies, and any other activities that are fundamental to the school's ability to accomplish its mission and goals" [55].

A review of the accreditation standards leaves one to wonder how these new medical schools will fulfill the accreditation requirements of the LCME. For example, LCME guidelines note that "the cost of conducting an accredited program leading to the M.D. degree should be supported from diverse sources, such as income from tuition, endowments, earnings by the faculty, support from the parent university, annual gifts, grants from organizations and individuals and appropriations from government" [20]. The guidelines also note that "clinical resources should be sufficient to ensure breadth and quality of ambulatory and bedside teaching" [54]. In marked contrast with the plans of some of the new medical schools, the guidelines point out [54]:

> [A medical school] should be a component of a university offering other graduate and professional degree programs that contribute to the academic environment of the medical school [and] the program of medical education leading to the M.D. degree must be conducted in an environment that fosters the intellectual challenge and spirit of inquiry appropriate to a community of scholars...[by making] available sufficient opportunities for medical students to participate in research and other scholarly activities of the faculty, and encourage and support student participation.

Finally, the guidelines call for a faculty that has a commitment to "continuing scholarly productivity characteristic of an institution of higher learning"; community physicians appointed to the faculty on a part-time basis or as volunteers "should be effective teachers, serve as role models for students, and provide insight into contemporary methods of providing patient care" [54]. Although it might be assumed that reaching these benchmarks would be a heroic goal for medical schools that have no university association and limited resources, the proposed medical schools in Virginia and New York have received "applicant school" status, the school in Scranton has received "preliminary accreditation" and will begin enrolling students in 2009, and new schools in Orlando, Florida, and El Paso, Texas, have received "preliminary accreditation" [56].

Each new school is unique and raises concerns regarding its ability to achieve educational excellence. Nonetheless, AMC leaders must watch with caution as these new medical schools evolve and recruit students to ensure that they do not create what Flexner's report described as an "over-production of ill trained men due in the main to the existence of a very large number of commercial schools" [1].

International Medical School Graduates and the U.S. Workforce

Although U.S. allopathic (MD) medical schools discontinued their growth in the 1980s and have only increased their size moderately during the present decade, osteopathic (DO) medical schools and international medical schools, including those in the Caribbean Islands, continued to grow. Indeed, the number of Caribbean schools has quadrupled over the past decade [8,14,57]. The increase in the number of U.S. citizens trained at for-profit Caribbean medical schools has generated considerable controversy. Although it is generally accepted that there are a minimum of 29 Caribbean medical schools, the exact number remains undefined [58] because only California makes site visits to the Caribbean schools to evaluate them for licensure purposes [59].

Although students trained at the Caribbean schools receive their preclinical training in the islands, they receive their clinical training at community hospitals in the United States, with no oversight from the Caribbean school, much less from any U.S. governing body. Like U.S.-trained students, students graduating from Caribbean schools must pass standardized U.S. board evaluations prior to being allowed to progress to residency training; however, there is little documentation of the level of their clinical skills and the Caribbean medical schools lack expensive technology for simulation training.

In 2005, Senator Jeff Sessions, a Republican from Alabama, unsuccessfully attempted to cut off federal student loans to students at the Caribbean medical schools [60]. Indeed, strong political pressure in many state legislatures has precluded their ability to regulate these offshore medical schools. In August 2008, it was revealed that New York City's Health and Hospitals Corporation had signed a 10-year, $100 million contract with St. George's Medical School, a profit-making medical school in the Caribbean, to provide clinical training for its students in the city's public hospitals [60]. This led to fears that there would not be enough training sites for students currently enrolled in New York's allopathic medical schools as well as concerns that the New York medical community would be flooded with students of lesser caliber. St. George's admits 1,000 students each year, compared with 160 at the New York University School of Medicine. In addition, Caribbean-trained physicians could, over time, outnumber U.S.-trained physicians.

The implications provided here are that the for-profit Caribbean schools do not have the rigorous clinical training found at U.S. medical schools and can therefore compromise the delivery of excellent patient care. Ironically, this situation is no different from what Flexner found in 1910, when he evaluated the U.S.-based proprietary medical schools that existed before the implementation of state regulations that established uniform standards for U.S. academic medical centers.

The Academic Medical Center's Role in Solving the U.S. Healthcare Workforce Crisis

AMCs have a societal responsibility to ensure that America is training enough physicians to care for the increasing U.S. population, the aging of the population, and the increasing burden of disease. In addition, AMCs must encourage students to pursue careers in academic medicine in order to ensure that the next generation of students will have outstanding teachers to train them as well as opportunities to pursue both clinical and basic science research. The following recommendations provide a guidepost for meeting the important challenges faced by today's AMCs in fulfilling these missions. Together, these recommendations will help ensure that AMCs can meet their primary goal of training a group of students and trainees who can provide outstanding patient care regardless of the population that they serve.

Create a National Task Force on the Workforce Crisis

Although individual AMCs can oversee the quality of education at their own institutions, financial limitations may preclude their ability to succeed across all areas of the educational program. As importantly, the funding for new medical schools and decisions about the structure of existing and new medical schools are regulated in large part at the state level—particularly in the context of state-supported medical schools.

However, state legislatures are ill prepared to take on this responsibility. Individual legislators are often biased by the vision that the establishment of a new medical school in their district could favorably influence the district's economy, are often misinformed as to reasonable solutions to the workforce crisis, and may be influenced by the views of regional constituencies that see the opening of a medical school in their region of the state as a matter of prestige. Academic medicine and its various organizations have also done little to address the workforce issue. As pointed out by Michael Whitcomb [16]:

> The simple fact seems to be that the leaders of the professional organizations that could change the nature of the medical education system in this country are more concerned about the views of their constituents than they are with positions emanating from a group of medical school deans or other leaders in the trenches of academic medicine. Unfortunately, many of their constituents have little understanding of the current situation or have a vested interest in maintaining the status quo.

Thus, the ability of academic medical centers to provide outstanding training for an increased number of students, to recruit underserved minority students to medicine, to attract students to careers in research, and to design and implement new medical schools rationally would be most effectively supported by the creation of a national task force on the physician workforce. This task force should be tasked with looking at all aspects of the workforce issue.

Troyen A. Brennan, chief medical officer of Aetna Health Insurance Company, first pointed out that the federal government should play a key role in developing new methodologies to increase the physician workforce [61]:

> I think the prudent approach would be to have the federal government undertake or sponsor a comprehensive study of the adequacy of the current physician workforce and projected future needs. Policy decisions of this magnitude should be based on the best possible evidence, and one has to be concerned about the existing studies that report shortages, because most of them were undertaken by organizations or individuals with a specific interest in the debate.

Another group that has recognized the need for an authoritative body to address America's healthcare workforce issues is the Association of Academic Health Centers. A white paper coauthored by Daniel Rahn, president of the Medical College of Georgia, and Steven Wartman, president and CEO of the Association of Academic Health Centers [62], noted that a "crucial factor precipitating the healthcare work-force crisis is a lack of comprehensive workforce planning on the parts of academe, government, and the health care professions." The authors asserted that the shortages in the healthcare workforce were not local issues but rather needed input and solutions from state and federal governments.

The national commission on the healthcare workforce they envisioned would be composed of academic clinicians, basic scientists, healthcare providers, and leaders of academic health centers and would serve as an advisory body to Congress but would have no regulatory power [62].

The national task force would have a broader membership and regulatory authority and could be an operational arm of a national commission on AMCs that will be proposed in Chapter 12. The task force should have the opportunity not only to recommend policy but also to effect changes in policy. In addition, it will also be important to ensure that input into the task force's deliberations comes from the leaders of all types of medical schools—state schools, private schools, research-intensive institutions, and those with limited research portfolios—as well as from department chairs, division chiefs, and individuals who spend their time in the trenches of the academic battles.

The task force must also enlist the aid of scholars who focus their research on areas as diverse as organizational psychology, organizational theory, communication, and business structure. In addition, the task force must include leaders from the health insurance industry as well as from the pharmaceutical and device industries in order to bring together a group of highly skilled managers and business leaders who deal with academic medical centers from the outside on a daily basis. Because of its size, it should consist of a steering committee and individual subcommittees, each charged with overseeing specific elements of the overall mission.

Enhance the Public's Recognition of the Healthcare Workforce Crisis

The general public must be made aware of the crisis in the healthcare workforce. Efforts by the Canadian Medical Association to inform the public of the plight of Canada's healthcare workforce might serve as a model for efforts in the United States. As described in the *Ottawa Citizen* in February 2008, downtown Ottawa was "wallpapered with messages about Canada's doctor shortage" [63]. Indeed, the Canadian Medical Association spent approximately $1 million to get its message regarding the doctor shortage into the minds of the public and Canada's governmental leaders. Ads were placed on walls, on local buses, and in newspapers across the country and "help wanted" ads were placed on the doors of emergency rooms and physician offices. The ads linked people to a Web site—moredoctors. ca—where they could fill out a digital postcard that was then transmitted to the appropriate members of Canada's parliament.

With five million Canadians without doctors, the Canadian Medical Association is calling for specific actions on the part of the federal government:

an allocation of $50 million over 3 years that can be used to repatriate Canadian doctors and other health workers who have moved to the United States; acceleration of the rate in which foreign-trained doctors are licensed; and a delay in the requirement for medical students to pay back their loans.

As reported in the article in the *Ottawa Citizen,* it appears that the aggressive public awareness campaign is working. The Web site has received a substantial number of hits and a significant percentage of people who visit the site forward a postcard to their legislative representative [63].

Develop Programs to Encourage Students to Pursue Careers in Medicine

Academic medical centers must make efforts to recruit health professionals more consistent with the increasing ethnic and racial diversity present in the U.S. population who, at the same time, can provide outstanding patient care. One approach is to target recruitment efforts on students in high schools and colleges across the country who show the greatest potential to uphold the standards of care and medical professionalism required to fulfill the societal mission of a physician. To increase the diversity of the workforce, AMCs must search for students who have the aptitude, fortitude, dedication, and interpersonal skills— what could be called the "right stuff."

Such efforts must be broad based and include both secondary schools and colleges that serve a high proportion of underrepresented minorities. Students must be identified early in their educational careers and then nurtured and mentored throughout their educational experience so that they will be able to identify with role models as they progress toward medical school matriculation. Important questions must also be asked as to whether the premedical requirements that now exist in any way reflect an applicant's ability to become an accomplished physician or whether they simply erode the interest of individuals who have the dedication, the interpersonal skills, the academic fortitude, and the intellectual capabilities to become outstanding physicians.

For at least half a century, the barometer by which applicants to U.S. medical schools have been measured has been their performance in inorganic chemistry, organic chemistry, calculus, physics, genetics, and introductory biology and their scores on the Medical College Admission Test (MCAT). It could be argued that the physician of the future might be far better suited to a career in medicine if he or she has taken courses in the liberal arts, psychology, economics, or health policy. In my experience, some of the best students are those that majored in the liberal arts during their 4 years of college and then took all of their premedical training during a postbaccalaureate program.

Many physicians anecdotally note conversations with outstanding young people whose progress toward a career in medicine was derailed by inorganic or organic chemistry. This was validated by a longitudinal study of incoming Stanford University freshmen who indicated that they hoped to become physicians [64]. By the end of their sophomore year, half of the students had experienced a marked decrease in their interest in medicine. The decline in interest was greatest among underrepresented minority students and women but was not associated with scholastic ability as measured by SAT scores.

The principal reason for the students' loss of interest in continuing as premeds was a negative experience in organic or inorganic chemistry. These findings were consistent with another study that found that "most former premed students admitted organic chemistry had played a significant role in the change in their career plans" [65]. These findings are disappointing because virtually every physician will admit that inorganic and organic chemistry had little impact on his or her medical school studies.

Thus, an important step in facilitating our ability to identify students during their undergraduate and high school years and to attract them to the field of medicine will be to design a premedical curriculum in conjunction with U.S. undergraduate institutions that actually prepare an individual for a career in medicine. This effort will require "a multipronged strategy that includes modernizing undergraduate course requirements, revising the content of the admission test, and developing new ways of using course grades and test scores in admission decisions that encourage students to pursue a broad-based education" [66]. We must also develop new ways to assess a student's ability to think independently and creatively, to evaluate his or her moral compass, and to understand the student's potential for professionalism. New programs should be developed to stimulate an interest in science at an early age, such as the use of high-fidelity patient simulators designed to replicate the practice of modern medicine [67].

However, calls for rethinking the structure of the premedical curriculum are not new [68]. The politics of academia—undergraduate and graduate—will assiduously resist change. Here, too, the influence of a governmental task force will have far more sway than the efforts of any single medical school admissions committee.

Address the Enormous Indebtedness of America's Medical Graduates

The ability to continue to attract top students to the field of medicine will only be facilitated by the development of a mechanism to support the costs of undergraduate medical education. No matter how intrigued a student might be in pursuing a career in medicine, the harsh reality of finishing medical school with a level of debt that averages $160,000 that will not be paid off until completion of residency training—and in some cases fellowship training—serves as a major impediment to pursuing a medical career. This financial reality is even harsher for students who have an interest in pursuing a career in the less remunerative areas of medicine including practices in rural and underserved urban areas.

The financial impediments to pursuing a medical career are most onerous in families of lower socioeconomic backgrounds, thereby further limiting the ability of many Hispanic and African-American applicants to pursue a medical degree. The high cost of a medical education and the long period of graduate medical education stand in marked contrast to pre-recession opportunities in the financial or legal sector, where first-year graduates are making six-figure salaries.

The lure to business begins early in the undergraduate years, when summer internship stipends from large Wall Street banks range between $10,000 and $15,000. By contrast, students pursuing summer research projects in academic laboratories often do so without compensation. Despite the fact that many believe that the practice of medicine should be seen as a "calling" rather than as a chosen profession, that call can go unanswered by students who recognize that they will have to practice for many years before they can erode the substantial indebtedness that arises from their medical education.

Several institutions have taken action. For example, the Cleveland Clinic Lerner College of Medicine of Case Western Reserve University provides all of its 32 students per year with full tuition scholarships [69]. Elias Zerhouni, director of the National Institutes of Health, lauded the efforts of the clinic [69]:

> Our nation and the world of medicine suffer from a shortage of physician–scientists who are trained in the methods of science, and willing to devote their careers to the pursuit of knowledge and the advancement of medicine. Efforts such as the full tuition scholarship initiative announced by the Cleveland Clinic are vital and serve as a catalyst for attracting and retaining some of medicine's brightest talent to the vast and growing field of clinical research.

Harvard Medical School has also taken steps by lowering the debt for students whose families have an income of $120,000 or less. As noted by Jules Diesntag, Harvard Medical School's dean for medical education [70]:

> Minimizing debt is also essential for eliminating a potential barrier for students in making career choices. In this way, students will not have to take debt into account or feel pressured to enter into

higher-paying specialties after graduation. They can go into whatever field it is that inspired them to study medicine in the first place.

Unfortunately, it is unlikely that most of the nation's 126 medical schools will be able to provide similar financial support.

Efforts to decrease the high cost of an undergraduate medical education must therefore be undertaken by state or federal governments or private payers so that all medical students have an equal opportunity to receive support. At a time when private payers have billion dollar war chests yet often carry a "nonprofit" status, it is imperative for state and federal agencies that oversee the healthcare industry to see to it that the large profits accumulated by the healthcare insurance industry are used for the greater good and not to continue to support the enormous salaries of the executives of these companies [43]. This type of change can only come about through the efforts of a federal task force possessing both responsibility and authority.

One potential mechanism that should be considered by federal and state governments as well as private payers is the "debt-forgiveness" program. This type of program directs students into areas of societal need and is consistent with recommendations made by the Committee on the Future Health Care Workforce for Older Americans of the Institute of Medicine. The committee recommended that public and private payers provide financial incentives to increase the number of geriatric specialists in all health professions by instituting programs for loan forgiveness, scholarships, and direct financial incentives for students and trainees who become geriatric specialists [71].

The NIH has created a tuition-remission program; however, it only funds loan debt repayment for individuals pursuing clinical research, pediatric research, health disparities research, contraception and infertility research, and clinical research for individuals from disadvantaged backgrounds [72]. The NIH program does not go far enough; funds are only available to support approximately a third of applicants and the funding only covers a part of the student's medical school debt. Furthermore, programs must be developed for clinician–scientists who plan to pursue careers in basic science or translational research projects.

Ensure That All Medical Schools Produce High-Quality Physicians

Consistent with the overall theme of this book, it is critical that AMCs not only provide outstanding care for patients but also train a new generation of students and residents who are imbued with the same focus of providing excellence in patient care. Ensuring quality must be the responsibility of each individual medical school. Although great strides have been made across academic medicine in revising the core curriculum of the first 2 years of medical school, academic medicine must now begin to focus on ensuring that clinical training is equally focused and incorporates both the art and the science of medicine.

Perhaps the most important piece of learning is the relationship that develops between students and trainees and their attending physicians. Thus, quality in education requires that AMCs continue to recruit the best and the brightest faculty—an effort that will rely on many of the recommendations found in the preceding sections.

In addition, the resources necessary for ensuring a high-quality education must come from federal and state governments at a time when AMCs are economically challenged. Thus, the proposed national task force on the healthcare workforce crisis must look at the number of physicians that need to be trained and also assess the most effective way to train physicians who provide federal allocations to see that new medical schools have appropriate levels of support and the appropriate infrastructure to train outstanding physicians. The national task force must oversee the planning, funding, and accreditation of all new medical schools—nonprofit and for profit—to ensure unified quality across the entire healthcare education system.

Clearly, the complex politics of state and local governments, which often look at a medical school as an element of prestige for a community or as a means of increasing the economic strength of a region, must be superseded by a federal agency. This entity can develop a more logical distribution of new medical schools based on patient needs and design a template for the new schools that will ensure that students graduating from these new medical schools are fully prepared to enter the healthcare workforce.

Individual AMCs must also work assiduously to ensure that students receive the same level of clinical education at community affiliates as they do at the quaternary academic center. This requires the presence of dedicated and committed program directors at each affiliated teaching hospital, ongoing evaluations by students, careful assessment of test scores, close interactions between the program directors of each institution, and a willingness to remove physicians from the "teaching service" when they are found to be below the mean in evaluation scores. New or existing medical schools that plan to extend their teaching sites to community facilities should use templates developed at established programs, such as those at Jefferson Medical College, where dedicated community centers have provided outstanding teaching opportunities for half a century.

The national task force could also adjudicate issues regarding the increasing influx of American students from unregulated offshore medical schools.

Individual state licensing agencies and state medical associations have been unable to regulate the flow of students from offshore medical schools because of political pressures; an inability to move toward uniform standards of enforcement across states; and concerns about legal challenges because, in the past, graduates of the foreign schools have gone to court charging state medical establishments with monopolistic interference in their professional rights [73]. American and foreign medical students have every right to expect fair decisions, but only a national task force, free of state politics, will be able to protect the quality of American medical services and ensure consistent quality in the healthcare workforce.

America's healthcare workforce is clearly in trouble. To date, recommendations from authoritative academic bodies have not been heeded and not a single candidate seeking public office has mentioned the workforce issue as being of concern. Therefore, it is imperative that august academic bodies come together to lobby for the initiation of a national task force. By partnering with federal authorities and by defining a mission that focuses not only on increasing the number of practicing physicians but also on ensuring the quality of the workforce, its diversity, and its role in both the community and academic worlds, there is hope that the crisis can be mitigated before the status of the workforce moves from guarded to critical.

References

1. Flexner, A. 1973. Medical education in the United States and Canada: A report to the Carnegie Foundation for the Advancement of Teaching, 346. Bulletin no. 4, New York (reprinted by The Heritage Press, Buffalo, NY).
2. Cooper, R. A. 2004. Weighing the evidence for expanding physician supply. *Annals of Internal Medicine* 141 (9): 705–714.
3. Council on Graduate Medical Education 2000–2020. 2005. Sixteenth report: Physician workforce policy guidelines for the United States. Washington, D.C.: U.S. Department of Health and Human Services, Health Resources and Services Administration.
4. AAMC Center for Workforce Studies. 2005. Recent studies and reports on physician shortages in the U.S. (www.amc.org/meded/cfws/rcntwrkfce.pdf).
5. AAMC Center for Workforce Studies. 2009. HRS data on health professional workforce shortage areas (http://bhpr.hrsa.gov/shortage).
6. Pardes, H. 2000. The perilous state of academic medicine. *Journal of the American Medical Association* 283 (18): 2427–2429.
7. Sheridan, D. J. 2006. Reversing the decline of academic medicine in Europe. *Lancet* 367 (9523): 1698–1701.
8. Cooper, R. A. 2007. It's time to address the problem of physician shortages: Graduate medical education is the key. *Annals of Surgery* 246 (4): 527–534.

9. Cooper, R. A., and Tauber, A. I. 2005. Viewpoint: New physicians for a new century. *Academic Medicine* 80 (12): 1086–1088.

10. Graduate Medical Education National Advisory Committee. 1980. DHHS publication no. HRA 81-651. Washington, D.C.: U.S. Department of Health and Human Services.

11. AAMC. 2008. The physician workforce: Position statement.

12. AAMC. 2005. Analysis in brief. Analysis of medical school expansion plans.

13. AAMC. 2008. Survey of medical schools. Washington, D.C.

14. Salsberg, E., and Grover, A. 2006. Physician workforce shortages: Implications and issues for academic health centers and policymakers. *Academic Medicine* 81 (9): 782–787.

15. American College of Physicians. 1998. The physician workforce and financing of graduate medical education. *Annals of Internal Medicine* 128:142–148.

16. Whitcomb, M. E. 2007. Physician supply revisited. *Academic Medicine* 82 (9): 825–826.

17. Goodman, D. C., and Fisher, E. S. 2008. Physician workforce crisis? Wrong diagnosis, wrong prescription. *New England Journal of Medicine* 358 (16): 1658–1661.

18. Baicker, K., and Chandra, A. 2004. Medicare spending, the physician workforce, and beneficiaries' quality of care. *Health Affairs* (Millwood). Suppl Web exclusives: W184–W197.

19. Starfield, B., Shi, L., Grover, A., and Macinko, J. 2005. The effects of specialist supply on populations' health: Assessing the evidence. *Health Affairs* (Millwood). Suppl Web exclusives: W5-97–W5-107.

20. Starfield, B., Shi, L., Grover, A., and Macinko, J. 2005. Contribution of primary care to health systems and health. *Milbank Quarterly* 83 (3): 457–502.

21. Skeff, K. M., Bowen, J. L., and Irby, D. M. 1997. Protecting time for teaching in the ambulatory care setting. *Academic Medicine* 72 (8): 694–697 (discussion, 693).

22. www.aamc.org/data/aib/start.htm

23. Zisson, S. 2001. Anticipating a clinical investigator shortfall. *CenterWatch* 8 (4): 5–8.39.

24. Zemlo, T. R., Garrison, H. H., Partridge, N. C., and Ley, T. J. 2000. The physician–scientist: Career issues and challenges at the year 2000. *FASEB Journal* 14 (2): 221–230.

25. Nathan, D. G., and Varmus, H. E. 2000. The National Institutes of Health and clinical research: A progress report. *Nature Medicine* 6 (11): 1201–1204.

26. NIH Research Training Opportunities. K30 clinical research curriculum award (http://grants2.nih.gov/training/k30.htm). Accessed March 7, 2008.

27. NIH Clinical Loan Repayment Program (www.lrp.nih.gov/ acc 3/7/08).

28. Egan, L. W., Gallin, E. K., and Sung, N. S. 2002. Debt repayment for trainees. *New England Journal of Medicine* 346 (25): 2013 (author reply, 2014).

29. Pober, J. S., Neuhauser, C. S., and Pober, J. M. 2001. Obstacles facing translational research in academic medical centers. *FASEB Journal* 15 (13): 2303–2313.

30. The Task Force on the Future of Clinician Scientists at the University of California at San Francisco. The future of physician scientists: Initial report and recommendation (www.ucsf.edu/senate/recentreports/clinicianscientistreport.html), February 2001.

31. www.im.org

32. Couzin, J., and Miller, G. 2007. NIH budget. Boom and bust. *Science* 316 (5823): 356–361.

33. Clark, C. 2008. Scripps plans to start new medical school. *The Union-Tribune,* San Diego.

34. Newton, D. A., and Grayson, M. S. 2003. Trends in career choice by U.S. medical school graduates. *Journal of the American Medical Association* 290 (9): 1179–1182.

35. Brotherton, S. E., Rockey, P. H., and Etzel, S. I. 2005. U.S. graduate medical education, 2004–2005: Trends in primary care specialties. *Journal of the American Medical Association* 294 (9): 1075–1082.

36. Mistretta, M. J. 2007. Differential effects of economic factors on specialist and family physician distribution in Illinois: A county-level analysis. *Journal of Rural Health* 23 (3): 215–221.

37. Bethune, C., Hansen, P., Deacon, D., Hurley, K., Kirby, A., and Godwin, M. 2007. Family medicine as a career option: How students' attitudes changed during medical school. *Canadian Family Physician* 53 (5): 881–885, 880.

38. Scott, I., and Gowan, M. 2007. Why medical students switch careers: Changing course during the preclinical years of medical school. *Canadian Family Physician* 53 (1): 94–95.

39. Senf, J. H., Campos-Outcalt, D., Watkins, A. J., Bastacky, S., and Killian, C. 1997. A systematic analysis of how medical school characteristics relate to graduates' choices of primary care specialties. *Academic Medicine* 72 (6): 524–533.

40. Hurt, M. M., and Harris, J. O. 2005. Founding a new college of medicine at Florida State University. *Academic Medicine* 80 (11): 973–979.

41. www.thestate.com/local/v-print/story/337762.html

42. www.newsobserver.com/news/v-print/story/989011.html

43. Snowbeck, C. 2006. Bonuses boost compensation of 10 Highmark executives. *Pittsburgh Post-Gazette,* Nov. 21.

44. www.kennywood.com

45. Tripp Umbach Executive Summary. 2006. A roadmap for medical renewal and economic development in Northeastern Pennsylvania. July 2006.

46. www.thecommonwealthmedical.com/oth/Page.asp?PageID=OTH000034

47. www.census.gov/population/projections/res.tab2.xls www.census.gov/population/projections/res.tab2.xls

48. Vath, B. E., Schneeweiss, R., and Scott, C. S. 2001.Volunteer physician faculty and the changing face of medicine. *Western Journal of Medicine* 174 (4): 242–246.

49. www.nih.gov

50. Goldstein, J. 2008. HealthBlog. *The Wall Street Journal.*

51. Sturgeon, J. 2007. Tech, Carilion outline plan for medical school. *The Roanoke Times,* Jan. 4.

52. www.vtnews.vt.edu/news_print/index.php?relyear=207&itemno=4

53. www.nih.gov

54. Defining the scope of LCME accreditation: Programs, campuses and educational tracks (www.lcme.org).

55. LCME accreditation guidelines for new and developing medical schools (www.lcme.org).

56. www.lcme.org/newschoolprocess.htm, www.lcme.org/newschoolprocess.htm

57. Romano, M. The hazy doc shortage. There's a serious problem, but lack of clarity forestalls solutions (modernhealthcare.com). June 5, 2006.

58. Sheldon, G. F. 2006. Globalization and the health workforce shortage. *Surgery* 140 (3): 354–358.

59. Thomas, C. Y, Hosein, R., and Yan, J. 2005. Assessing the export of nursing services as a diversification option for CARICOM economies. Report prepared for Caribbean Commission on Health and Development.

60. Hartocollis, A. 2008. New York hospitals create outcry in foreign deal. *New York Times,* Aug. 5.

61. Iglehart, J. K. 2008. Grassroots activism and the pursuit of an expanded physician supply. *New England Journal of Medicine* 358 (16): 1741–1749.

62. Rahn, D. W., and Wartman, S. A. 2007. For the healthcare workforce, a critical prognosis. *The Chronicle of Higher Education* 54 (10): B14.

63. Laucius, J. 2008. CMA hopes ad blitz will heal doctor shortage. *The Ottawa Citizen,* Feb. 23.

64. Barr, D. A., Gonzalez, M. E., and Wanat, S. F. 2008. The leaky pipeline: Factors associated with early decline in interest in premedical studies among underrepresented minority undergraduate students. *Academic Medicine* 83 (5): 503–511.

65. Lovecchio, K., and Dundes, L. 2002. Premed survival: Understanding the culling process in premedical undergraduate education. *Academic Medicine* 77 (7): 719–724.

66. Kanter, S. L. 2008. Toward a sound philosophy of premedical education. *Academic Medicine* 83 (5): 423–424.

67. Gordon, J. A., and Oriol, N. E. 2002. Perspective: Fostering biomedical literacy among America's youth: How medical simulation reshapes the strategy. *Academic Medicine* 83 (5): 521–523.

68. Thomas, L. 1978. Notes of a biology-watcher. How to fix the premedical curriculum. *New England Journal of Medicine* 298 (21): 1180–1181.

69. www.clevelandclinic.org

70. Colen, B. D. 2008. Harvard Medical School to reduce student debt burden. *Harvard Science,* March 21.

71. Committee on the Future Health Care Workforce for Older Americans, Institute of Medicine. 2008. *Retooling for America: Building the health care workforce—Executive summary.* Washington, D.C.: Institute of Medicine.

72. www.nih.gov/news/health/Sep2008/08-09.html

73. Hechinger, F. 1985. About education: Medical school quality. *New York Times,* Dec. 17.

Chapter 8

The Changing Demographics of America's AMCs

As a matter of fact, the attainments required by our entire argument are not, as a rule, beyond the reach of the earnest poor boy. He need only take thought in good season, lay in his plans, be prudent, and stick to his purpose. Without these qualities medicine is no calling for him; with them, poverty will rarely block his way.

Abraham Flexner, 1910 [1]

Introduction

At the turn of the century, Abraham Flexner pointed out that a medical education should be available to qualified candidates regardless of their socioeconomic background. However, he admitted that in the 1900s few opportunities were available for what he referred to as the "poor boy" [1]. Medicine at that time was practiced largely by a small segment of society who viewed medicine as a calling as much as a profession or a business. Many, if not most, of the faculty who taught in the nonproprietary medical schools came from the wealthier families of the time. Indeed, in the early parts of the twentieth century, many clinical teachers received little or no reimbursement for their efforts.

Before World War II, admission to medical school was largely restricted to students from upper income families, although demonstrated scholarship and intellectual capacity were clearly required. Medical school admission policies were also restricted by the presence of "outright discrimination against first and second generation immigrants, particularly those from eastern and southern Europe, and against Jews, Catholics, and blacks," as well as a refusal on the part of many schools to admit women [2]. As a result, AMCs evolved to educate specific ethnic and racial groups of students and postgraduate trainees, including the Albert Einstein School of Medicine, the Mount Sinai School of Medicine, the Woman's Medical College of Philadelphia, Howard University, and Meharry College of Medicine. State-supported land-grant universities created their own medical schools and charged substantially lower fees than did private medical schools.

However, after World War II, the financial structure of America's AMCs changed, as did the demographics of the student body and the medical school faculty. Unfortunately, the finances of America's AMCs still require substantive fees from each student, thereby limiting the ability of many students to pursue a medical education. This chapter will describe how the gender, ethnic, racial, and cultural demographics of students and faculty have changed over the past few decades, how these changes have influenced the AMC, and how the AMCs must now respond to these new demographics in order to ensure its ability to continue to provide outstanding patient care.

Demographics of the AMC Student Body Today

Racial, ethnic, and gender diversity began to occur in earnest in America's medical schools in the late 1960s and early 1970s as a result of federal affirmative action programs, expansion of federal and state scholarship and loan programs, and the women's liberation movement [2]. Significant changes in the demographics of the medical school have also occurred over the past 20 years. Two decades ago, 72% of medical students graduating from American medical schools were between 28 and 31 years old, 68% were male, 86% were white, 98% were U.S. citizens, and 76% had received their bachelor's degree shortly before starting medical school [3].

Today, the demographics of the graduating seniors from American medical schools have changed substantially [4]. Although most medical students still matriculate directly from or shortly after completing college, the majority are women (50.2%). Over 11% of graduating seniors are self-described as Asian and 6% as Indian or Pakistani; however, only 6.8% are African American.

Not only have the demographics of America's medical school classes changed, but substantive changes have also occurred in how medical students view the field of medicine and their roles in patient care. In 1986, 25% of students who had defined their career choices had decided to pursue a career in primary care medicine, 17% in family practice, and 8.3% in general internal medicine. Fewer than 2% were planning to pursue dermatology, 3.5% planned to pursue emergency medicine, 5.9% planned to pursue obstetrics and gynecology, 5.4% were interested in general pediatrics, 5.3% were interested in diagnostic radiology, 62% sought a career in general surgery, and 4.2% had decided on a career in ophthalmology. Only 1.7% of graduating seniors planned to pursue a career in cardiovascular disease and only 0.9% were committed to a career in gastroenterology.

Of the graduating seniors, 20% expressed an interest in pursuing research training during their fellowship training, with 41% of those expressing an interest in research believing that they would focus their research training on clinical research. Although 40% of the students thought that they would participate in clinical trials, only 14% expected to dedicate greater than 25% of their career to research. Nonetheless, 27% of students thought that they would have a full-time academic career with a faculty appointment that included responsibilities for teaching and clinical research. Only 1% expected to pursue a full-time academic career focused on teaching and basic science research.

The vast majority of graduates thought that they would likely practice in a group of three or more physicians in a private practice, a large multispecialty group practice, or a state or federal agency. In addition, the majority of respondents planned to practice in a large or moderately sized city or the suburbs (63%); only 1% of graduating seniors expressed an interest in practicing in a rural environment and only 15% planned to practice in a socioeconomically deprived area [3]. Interestingly, in 1986, students raised concerns regarding the future of medical practice—in particular, a loss of practice autonomy and a decrease in financial rewards [5].

By 2006, the goals and aspirations of graduating seniors had changed substantially [4]. Almost 94% said that they would pursue training in either a specialty or subspecialty area. Only 5% expressed an intention to pursue general internal medicine and only 7.7% expressed an interest in family practice. Thus, the number of graduates pursuing a career in primary care medicine had decreased by half over 20 years. The number of students interested in cardiothoracic surgery had decreased from 0.5% in 1986 to 0.2% in 2006. This decrease would not in and of itself seem significant. However, it can be appreciated in the context of the fact that there were only approximately 50 applications for 126 cardiothoracic surgery residency positions in the United States in 2006.

Students graduating in 2006 had a markedly increased interest in anesthesiology, cardiology, and gastroenterology. Interestingly, when asked how important a variety of factors were in determining their specialty of choice, over 70% of respondents noted that the lifestyle associated with the various specialties had a moderate or strong influence on their decision. Over 70% of respondents also credited their mentors and clinical role models for having influenced their decision regarding subspecialty training; however, over 66% attributed the length of the residency training program as a factor in determining their career path. Thus, in 2006, American students chose lifestyle over other reasons as the primary determinant of their area of specialization.

Medical Students' Increased Levels of Debt

An important cultural difference between the classes of 1986 and 2006 was their responses to the indebtedness that they incurred as a result of pursuing a medical education. In 1986, 22.6% of responding seniors had no debt; 37% of students had a debt of greater than $30,000 with the mean debt of all respondents $24,841. By 2006, only 14.9% of students graduated with no debt from their medical school education, and over 55% of all students had debt greater than $100,000. The average medical school debt of all students was $104,674 and the average medical school debt of students who carried a debt was $123,047. Over 37% of these students also had outstanding educational loans for their college or premedical education; the average premedical debt of students in the class of 2006 was approximately $23,000.

This level of indebtedness is not unexpected in view of the marked increase in the cost of a medical education, which doubled between 1996 and 2006. For example, the average fee was $23,980 in 1996 and $39,413 in 2006. Similarly, average cost of tuition and fees for a state resident at a public medical school was $10,011 in 1996 and $20,978 in 2006 [6].

The marked increase in indebtedness of current medical students might be offset if stipends had gone up on the back end of their educational experience (e.g., a marked increase in remuneration for residency positions). Unfortunately, this has not been the case. For example, in 1986, the mean stipend for a first-year resident was $21,994; the mean stipend in 2006 was $43,266. However, if one looks at inflation-adjusted stipends, the mean stipend for a first-year resident was $6,200 in 1968, $6,970 in 1986, and $7,466 in 2006 [7].

In 2004, Di Fang published a study of medical school graduates from 1980 to 1993. Of the 201,688 graduates, only 1% accepted faculty appointments with primary research responsibility; 9% of the graduates accepted faculty appointments with at least 10% of time allotted to research. Dr. Fang was unable to show an association between indebtedness and the pursuit of a career in academic medicine. However, he did find a lower mean level of debt in faculty holding primary research positions who graduated in 1992 and 1993—the point in the survey at which the level of indebtedness began to exceed $40,000 [8].

Thus, one can only imagine the challenge of a family that carries over $100,000 in debt and how that level of indebtedness might direct an individual's career goals over time despite altruistic beliefs at the time of graduation. The resulting burden of indebtedness often results in medical students not choosing a career in academic medicine, but rather choosing a more highly remunerative career in private practice.

Changes in Financial Rewards for the Academic Physician

After World War II, the salaries of the academic faculty did not rival those of physicians in the community; however, the academic faculty often had a very comfortable lifestyle and were able to pursue teaching, research, and patient care. The growing size of the academic faculties provided a relatively large number of physicians, so call schedules were reasonable. Robust funding from the NIH allowed many physicians to care for patients as well as pursue their research activities and generous payments for patient care and high reimbursements for new technology—such as cardiac catheterization, bypass surgery, new surgical procedures for correcting defects of the eye or removing the prostate gland, and new means of treating once life-threatening cancers—provided substantial revenues for the AMC. The academic physician had the pleasure of being the first to hold any new device or to use any new therapy—as well as have the opportunity to teach the new technology to the general practice community—often traveling across the country and around the world. Highly skilled residents and fellows took care of the patients—especially at night.

However, economic changes in the 1990s markedly affected academic scholars and expanded the differences in salaries between private practice and academic physicians. For example, in 2005, the mean salary for an academic anesthesiologist was $243,898, while that of a community physician was $334,400; the mean salary for an academic interventional cardiologist was $276,923, while in the community it was $431,499; the mean salary for an academic family practitioner was $155,542, while that of a community family practitioner was $178,086; and the mean salary of an academic gastroenterologist was $217,631, while that of a community physician was $415,913 [6]. Similarly, an academic internist earned a mean salary of $148,297 compared with the mean of $179,729 for community practitioners, and a general orthopedic surgeon was paid a mean salary of $245,606, while those in private practice had a mean salary of $426,951.

These marked differences in compensation held up whether one assessed the differences at the mean for the entire specialty group, the median, the 25th percentile, or the 75th percentile. Indeed, in many specialties, the gap between physician compensation of an academic faculty member and a physician in private practice was greater when physicians whose compensation was at the 75th or 90th percentile were examined than it was at the median or the mean. When data over a 10-year period are examined, the gap between average compensation for specialists in academic practices and those in private practice is shown to have widened. For example, in 1995, academic physicians had a level of compensation that was approximately 67% of that received by those in the private practice community; in 2003, the gap widened to 60% of that received by the private practice physicians.

The "great lie" of medical economics is that the academic clinician does not work as hard as the physician in a community practice. However, information provided by the Medical Group Management Association (MGMA) demonstrates a very different finding [6]. Using Centers for Medicare and Medicaid Services (CMS) data that come from an analysis of "work" effort as measured by RVUs (relative value units) and analyzed using the resource-based relative value scale (RBRVS) method developed by CMS and tracked by MGMA, it has been demonstrated that the work output of an academic physician equals or exceeds that of his or her private practice colleague.

For example, in 2006, the mean RVUs for an academic interventional cardiologist were 8,790; those for a private practice interventional cardiologist were 9,798. However, the mean RVUs for an academic electrophysiologist were 9,870, while those for an electrophysiologist in private practice were 9,178. Similarly, the work RVUs for a gastroenterologist in an academic practice were 7,801, and those for a gastroenterologist in private practice were 7,791. Finally, the work RVUs for a general surgeon at an AMC were 7,771, while those for a general surgeon in a private practice were 7,223.

Although one might argue that RVUs may not be the most useful measure of "work" in all clinical settings, the data clearly demonstrate that, in 2006, the physician in an academic medical center worked just as hard as a physician in private practice, albeit for a significantly lower salary. The result is that many physicians have left academia and attracting young medical students to careers in academic medicine has become increasingly difficult.

Any discussion of an academic salary is always clouded by the general public's impression that physicians—whether academic or private—are well paid in comparison with other members of society. Indeed, it is difficult to argue with this assertion. However, concerns regarding the remunerations for academic general internists do raise some interesting questions regarding how society values their efforts. For example, the salary of a general internist ($148,297) does not look outrageous compared to the salaries of [9]

- a pharmacist ($93,500);
- a chief executive of a computer and electronics manufacturing company ($169,750);
- a general or operations manager of a company ($128,190);
- a sales manager ($119,880);
- an executive in a clothing manufacturing company ($159,410);
- a manager in a telecommunications carrier ($124,500);
- a public relations manager in a telecommunications carrier ($142,040);
- a human resources manager ($125,330);
- a general manager in the financial investment area ($141,470);
- a sales manager in the commodities area ($138,960); or
- a financial manager ($137,720).

Indeed, one might suggest that the primary physician in charge of overseeing an individual's health should probably make a higher salary.

These comparisons look even more skewed when one realizes that the generalist physician begins his or her productive period a minimum of 7 years after completing a college degree, often begins work life with six-figure debt, and works in a large "company" in which he or she accrues no equity. In addition, it is an interesting but little known fact that U.S. medical residents receive substantially less remuneration than their colleagues in other countries—for a much longer work week.

For example, the AAMC 2007 survey reported that the national mean for U.S. house officers was $24,000 per year for an 80-hour work week, which does not compare favorably with house staff in Austria ($35,000/60-hour work week), Denmark ($35,000/50-hour work week), Germany ($35,000/50-hour work week), the United Kingdom ($30,000/55-hour work week), and Switzerland ($36,000/50-hour work week). These differences are magnified by the fact that the expense of a medical education is far greater in the United States than in Europe. Thus, it is not surprising that it is increasingly difficult to attract students to academic medicine—much less to a career of medicine itself.

Although academic physicians have historically received salaries that were substantially lower than those received by their peers, they have been able to pursue the "Holy Grail" of academia: tenure. Tenure has provided the academic physician with job stability and security, as well as an emotional tethering to the academic institution. Heavily promoted by the American Association of University Professors, tenure was originally designed to protect academic freedom and to bring a "sufficient degree of economic security to make the profession attractive to men and women of ability" [10]. A reasonable clinical workload, the policy of many academic medical centers to support the college tuitions of dependent children, and the opportunity of attaining tenure offered more than enough reasons for the best and brightest of medical school graduates to consider a position in academia.

However, as the healthcare marketplace changed, so too did the view of tenure by most academic medical centers; the uncertainty and volatility of AMC finances simply were no longer compatible with the "security" of tenure [11]. Even at more financially secure institutions, the presence of even a small number of unfunded faculty could abrogate the ability of a particular division or department to recruit and retain young faculty and to pursue growth in new technology in order to remain competitive. Thus, many AMCs have faced the difficult task of restructuring their tenure policies to improve the bottom line; yet, at the same time, they have created a disincentive to pursue an academic career.

Changes in Gender Demographics of the Academic Workforce

Perhaps the largest change to occur in the demographics of American medicine in general and in America's AMCs specifically has been the marked change in the number of women in the AMC workforce. In 1965, 503 women graduated from American medical schools in comparison with 6,906 men [12]. However, by 2005, women represented 50% of the medical school applicant pool, 48% of first-year students, 49% of all medical students, 49% of residents and fellows, and 32% of medical school faculty members [13]. Of women who have pursued careers in academia, 38% are assistant professors, 28% are associate professors, and 16% are full professors. Among women academicians, 19% have attained leadership positions as division chiefs or section chiefs, 10% as department chairs, 43% as assistant deans, 31% as associate and senior associate or vice deans, and 11% as medical school deans.

In the early part of the twentieth century, many medical schools did not accept women as medical students; Harvard did not admit women until 1945 and Jefferson Medical College was the last medical school to accept women in 1960. Thus, the number of women now in academia suggests that, at least in medical school admissions and academic appointments, academic medicine as well as the practice of medicine in general is finally approaching gender equality.

Not surprisingly, this change in gender distribution in the faculty of U.S. medical schools did not occur acutely, but rather as a slow transition over time. In 1965, the ratio of men to women faculty members was 14:1; it was 6.5:1 in 1975, 2.3:1 in 1985, and 1.4:1 in 1995. Importantly, a higher percentage of women than men graduates have joined and remained on the faculty of academic medical centers. It has been proposed that this higher percentage of women recruits to academic faculty appointments may be due to the active recruitment of high-achieving women, the decision of women graduates to seek continued scholarship in medicine and science available in the academic milieu, the expansion of academic opportunities for women, or the ability of a medical-school-based practice to afford a more controllable lifestyle than that found in a private practice setting [14]. However, information is not available to understand definitively the etiology of this change or its impact on the practice of medicine at AMCs.

Unfortunately, it is not clear that women have been treated in the same way as men once they have joined the academic faculties. In a large survey of over 4,000 women in 126 academic departments of pediatrics, it was found that fewer women than men achieved the rank of associate professor or professor [15]. Similar results were obtained when assessing academic success in individuals who graduated from medical school between 1979 and 1993 and joined academic departments in a wide range of specialties [16]. In both male and female pediatricians, higher salaries and higher academic rank were related to greater academic productivity, more hours worked, more institutional support of research, greater overall career satisfaction, and fewer career problems. For both sexes, patient care and teaching activities got in the way of academic productivity.

However, women—especially those at the assistant and associate professor levels—spent more time in clinical care and teaching than did men of the same academic rank; as a result, women were less academically productive. When all factors were adjusted for rank and clinical responsibilities, no differences in the academic rank attained by men and women were found; however, women consistently made less in salary than did men who were in the same job category. In addition, women were less likely to hold positions in highly remunerative specialties such as neurosurgery, cardiology, and gastroenterology.

In a survey undertaken at 24 randomly selected medical schools in the United States, a similar discrepancy was found in faculty salaries of men and women physicians. The investigators also reported that 66% of men and only 47% of women with 15–19 years of seniority were full professors [17]. However, this study was limited by the fact that it did not collect longitudinal data.

Similar results were found in a survey of faculty at the University of Arizona. Investigators found significant differences in faculty salaries, ranks, tracks, leadership positions, resources, and perceptions of the academic culture [18]. For example, women earned 11% less than men when salaries were adjusted for rank, track, degree, specialty, years in rank and administrative positions. Furthermore, a third of men (but only 5% of women) reported being discriminated against; women were significantly more likely to raise concerns about the safety of certain work locations or the times that they were required to work.

The results of the study also showed that men were more likely to receive adequate research space than were women. Interestingly, women were no less likely than men to report conflicts between family responsibilities and work. However, the results of this questionnaire were markedly different from those of previous studies that suggested that concerns with family responsibilities were markedly different between women and men faculty members [19,20].

In fact, in a survey undertaken by the Committee on Women in Medicine and Science at Stanford University School of Medicine, the highest ranking need was a flexible work environment without negative consequences for women with young children; this was followed in importance by needs for a 3-month sabbatical from clinical and administrative duties to concentrate on writing papers and grant applications and better academic mentoring focused on women by departmental leadership [21]. However, the survey did show a decrease in the incidence of sexual harassment, gender discrimination, and gender insensitivity since a previous survey performed 7 years earlier. Thus, despite the marked increase in the number of women in academic medicine, their roles, remuneration, and advancement require careful evaluation to ensure that they receive the same opportunities and rewards as men.

Diversity in the Academic Medical Center

America's medical schools have substantially increased the representation of women over the past two decades; however, they have been far less successful in attracting an increased number of minorities, including African Americans, Hispanics, and Native Americans. Although absolute numbers increased between 1950 and 2004, in 2004 only 6.4% of all graduates were minority students. Studies have clearly demonstrated that diversity supports increased access to healthcare services for the underserved, satisfaction in patient care, and expanded opportunities for patient care [22]. Thus, our failure to increase the numbered minority medical students is troubling.

Numerous programs have been developed to enhance minority enrollment at America's medical schools. For example, in September 2008, Mount Sinai School of Medicine's Center for Multicultural and Community Affairs (CMCA) was awarded a $2.3 million grant to establish a new Northeast Regional Health Career Opportunity Program [23]. In collaboration with Columbia University College of Physicians and Surgeons, UMDNJ-New Jersey Medical School, and the Manhattan Staten Island Area Health Education Center, the program will focus on the recruitment of 200 disadvantaged 7th–12th graders who will take academic enrichment courses during the school year and spend a summer at one of the medical schools to explore healthcare career options.

In addition, medical-school-bound college students will be given the opportunity to take an intensive 4-week course for preparation for the Medical College Admission Test and another group of students will take 6-week science enrichment programs to improve their chances of getting into medical school. This program mirrors similar programs in other states with the common goal of attracting and educating minority students at the earliest possible time during their primary and secondary educational experiences.

Although efforts are ongoing to attract minority students to medical school, an equally important need is to recruit talented minority faculty who can serve as role models and improve the somewhat abysmal record of AMC faculty in terms of diversity. Interestingly, approximately 1% of African American and 0.9% of Hispanic medical students pursue careers in teaching; a similar number pursue careers in biomedical research—a number virtually identical to the number of white students who pursue careers in teaching or research. However, because the absolute number of minority medical students is so small, there is a paucity of minority faculty members in most medical schools and minority students interested in pursuing academic careers are in great demand.

Many medical centers have taken the approach of beginning the faculty recruitment efforts with the recruitment of talented minority medical students, supporting these students through their medical school and residency programs, and then actively recruiting them to faculty positions. Tuition remission programs now established by the NIH that provide tuition remission for minority students who remain in academic medicine are particularly helpful in recruitment efforts; however, now demand is greater than the available funds—a situation that needs to be corrected by federal authorities.

In addition, AMCs must focus their own funds on scholarships and grants wherever possible because an increased number of minority faculty members can have an important impact on the care of patients, particularly those in urban environments or with large patient populations. Indeed, studies have clearly shown that a diverse physician population can help narrow the gap in healthcare disparities that are disproportionately experienced by racial and other minorities.

Lifestyle Changes in the Academic Workplace

Just as the gender demographics of the AMC have changed substantially, so too has the institutional culture. From the 1960s to the 1980s, physicians were known for the long hours that they worked and their overreaching dedication to their careers. The typical physician as depicted on television and in the movies was rarely home and depended on his long-suffering spouse to raise the children and maintain the household. However, sociological studies suggest that members of the so-called Generation X or Generation Y do not desire to work the long hours that physicians in the past worked [24]. Two-career households are far more common; both spouses desire to work but each works shorter hours [25].

Women, who now make up over 50% of graduating medical students and represent a substantial proportion of the physician work force, tend to work fewer hours than their male counterparts even when part-time status is taken into consideration [26]. When a group of dermatologists who had recently graduated from their training programs were surveyed, the women physicians saw patients for an average of 16% fewer hours than did the male physicians [27]. In addition, many Generation X and Generation Y individuals who graduate from medical school never practice medicine. Indeed, from 1997 to 2004 the proportions of graduates planning full-time clinical practice careers decreased from 51.3% to 46.5% as students sought careers in the pharmaceutical industry, basic research, venture capital, private equity, or biotechnology-focused hedge funds [28].

When students have pursued more traditional careers in medicine, their specific career choices tend to be based on their perceptions of which specialties are more "family friendly" and which offer a more "controllable lifestyle" [29]. Thus, recent graduates have not filled in specialties such as internal medicine, pediatrics, and general surgery to the same extent as in previous decades. However, as already noted, finances also play a key role in the decision-making process.

Supporting Changing Demographics of America's Medical Workforce

Recognizing that the demographics of America's medical workforce are markedly different from those of two or three decades ago, it is increasingly important that AMCs change their structure and their culture in order to accommodate young faculty. These individuals face challenges that did not exist 20 years ago and may have goals and aspirations very different from the young faculty members who came before them.

In some ways, the changes that are necessary to accommodate the needs of young faculty might seem simple. However, as has been noted throughout this book, the challenge is to make appropriate changes in the academic workplace while at the same time ensuring that the AMC continues to pursue excellence in patient care. In addition, changes that will create new opportunities for young faculty members cannot be undertaken without recognizing the need to continue to control costs throughout all of the activities of the health center. The following sections provide recommendations as a template for changes that can enhance the ability to deliver outstanding patient care while at the same time supporting the new demographics of the AMC.

Decrease the Debt of Academic Physicians

The increasing indebtedness of the vast majority of students has led to a situation in which academic careers are open only to those who are able to afford medical school without incurring debt. In March 2008, Harvard Medical School announced that it was taking steps to reduce the cost of a 4-year medical education for families with incomes of $120,000 or less. In a letter to the Harvard Medical School faculty, Jeffrey Flier, dean of the Harvard Medical School, said, "It is important that the School not be out of reach to a broad segment of undergraduate students and their families. It is equally imperative to avoid burdening families with a new round of debt shortly after a child has finished college" [30]. As noted by Jules Dienstag, Harvard Medical School dean for medical education [30]:

> Minimizing debt is also essential for eliminating a potential barrier for students in making career choices. This way students will not have to take debt into account or feel pressured to enter into higher paying specialties after graduation. They can go into whatever field it is that inspired them to study medicine in the first place.

By opening Harvard's doors to students of talent regardless of their financial means, the decision to reduce the student debt burden will certainly have an impact on the number of talented students applying to Harvard and, ideally, on the number of Harvard students who pursue careers in academic medicine.

However, the new scholarships provided to students at Harvard raise an important issue. It is generally accepted that students who qualify for prestigious American undergraduate colleges and universities have greater credentials than those accepted by less prestigious institutions and that a very wide range of intellectual capabilities can be found across the students of the nation's thousands of colleges and universities. By contrast, the academic credentials among most first-year medical school students should not and do not differ substantially. Furthermore, it is generally agreed that students in the top 20% of any medical school class have generally equal knowledge bases. All physicians are expected to have similar if not equal abilities to care for the nation's sick by the end of their medical school and residency training.

Thus, it is important that there not be "haves" and "have-nots" in terms of medical education. If some schools begin to attract the best and the brightest by virtue of their ability to support debt-free education for their students, the egalitarian education process will be severely compromised and we could face a two-tiered system of education. Therefore, in an era of physician shortages, efforts must be made to minimize physician debt across all U.S. allopathic medical schools—rather than just schools with robust endowments. This can only be achieved through governmental and state intervention and support of medical education with a goal in which medical schools train students who have the best aptitude for becoming outstanding physicians, rather than those most able to pay the high tuition costs.

Make Academic Medicine More Attractive

In its "Statement of Principles on Family Responsibilities and Academic Work," the American Association of University Professors, the "union" of U.S. academicians, noted that "transforming the academic workplace into one that supports family life requires substantial changes in policy and more significantly changes in academic culture" [31]. Although it is often said that culture trumps strategy, in the case of making an AMC more family friendly, far more than simply a change in culture is needed. As noted earlier, delaying the tenure clock and providing part-time opportunities will certainly go a long way in making the academic workplace more attractive for young physicians with families. However, at a time when the NIH is funding less than 10% of grant applications, it is sheer fantasy to expect that a scientist working 30–40 hours per week can compete with a scientist who is working 70–80 hours per week.

Furthermore, although promotion committees might be willing to promote part-time faculty based on academic success—most often measured in the number of peer-review publications authored, the NIH has no similar mandates. Therefore, funded investigators are expected to accomplish the tasks outlined in their grant applications, and an important criterion in the review of any grant is the reviewer's assessment of the ability of the applicant to complete the proposed experiments. Even if programs could be established to provide half-support from extramural funding agencies for half-effort, there would still be financial considerations at the supporting institution because the space assigned to the part-time investigator would have full-time overhead costs unless the space was shared with another funded part-time investigator. Therefore, federal funding agencies must also establish programs to support part-time investigators.

Intrinsic obstacles also exist for part-time faculty interested in pursuing clinical research or clinical careers in an academic environment. Industry sponsors and clinical research organizations have two fundamental concerns: the quality of the research data accumulated in their clinical trials and the timeliness with which investigators can enroll patients in the trials. Thus, industry sponsors are unwilling to work with investigators who are available to patients only on a part-time basis. To mitigate this problem, AMCs should seek opportunities for "job sharing" so that one physician is always available.

Another external structure that impedes the ability of clinicians to work part time is the fact that many malpractice insurance companies make no accommodations for part-time employees, arguing that part-time physicians have a higher risk of errors. Thus, a part-time physician in a large academic practice plan may have to cover a malpractice overhead cost identical to that of a full-time physician, thereby markedly decreasing his or her financial opportunities or those of the practice group. AMCs must accumulate data to demonstrate that physicians working a 40-hour work week do not have a higher actuarial risk than those working an 80-hour work week.

Job sharing can also obviate problems that arise with physician availability when someone works only part time. By pairing two outstanding physicians in a single job, both patients and referring physicians can view the two as a team rather than as a replacement; they will therefore be far more willing to seek care from this job-sharing team. Academic medical centers must work assiduously to ensure that referring physicians and patients see these clinical partners as a team that brings value and excellence to the care they provide for their patients.

Even for physicians who work full time, AMCs must work to improve the work environment for their faculty. In the most comprehensive study to date, investigators found that the current working environment in AMCs did not affect the physical health or overall life satisfaction of their colleagues. However, they did find that significant numbers of academic faculty acknowledged that work-related strain negatively affected their mental health and job satisfaction. Indeed, high levels of depression, anxiety, and job dissatisfaction were significantly appreciable among younger faculty. General surgeons reported the most depressive symptoms, the highest level of anxiety, the least job satisfaction, and the most work strain; those who identified themselves as orthopedic surgeons appeared to be the least affected by the current academic environment.

These results mirrored earlier specialty-specific studies that pointed out a high level of burnout—especially among younger faculty with administrative responsibilities [32,33]. Such studies become increasingly important when one recognizes that 15% of tenure track surgeons admitted to seriously considering leaving academic practice, many geographical and specialist areas are facing a critical shortage of academic physicians, and residents exhibit a diminishing interest in academic careers [34–37]. AMCs must hire physician extenders and implement new information technology systems so that doctors can spend more time with their patients, spend less time on paperwork and office management, and have adequate numbers of colleagues in order to establish reasonable call schedules. These efforts will not only improve the morale of AMC physicians, but will also help them focus on the core mission of providing excellence in care.

Create an AMC Culture That Recognizes the Diverse Needs and Goals of Women Physicians

AMCs must recognize that their promotion and work policies were designed at a time when most physicians were men and most wives stayed home and raised the children. As pointed out by Dr. Julia Draznin in her article, "The Mommy Tenure Track," the common conundrum faced by a woman physician—in particular, a woman physician–scientist—who has "the curiosity, determination, and desire to challenge herself professionally" is that, at the same time, she is "yearning for a calm and tender life with her family" [38]. This is supported by findings from a study of female graduates of Yale Medical School: 83% of all female graduates over the age of 40 were mothers and 42% of them had their children during their training [39].

In order to provide better opportunities for women in academic medicine, institutions must develop a menu of new opportunities recognizing that each family may choose a different pathway toward the same career goal. In 1983, 70 of the 95 medical schools with fixed probationary periods—the time period when young faculty members needed to demonstrate productivity in order to reach promotion and to retain their positions—had probationary lengths of 7 or less years. At the same time, young faculty members were having children. Thus, novel changes, including lengthening the pretenure probationary period, offering clock-stopping policies during child-rearing periods, and creating new appointment tracks, could obviate the stress arising from conflicts between child-rearing and professional activities.

Although nearly 70% of U.S. medical schools provide the opportunity for faculty to stop the tenure clock because of child-care needs or the need to care for a sick family member, only 1% of men and 1.5% of women at each of 57 AMCs that were surveyed took advantage of these policies [40]. Whether academic faculty fail to take advantage of tenure clock-stopping because of the accompanying decrease in salary support, peer pressure, or institutional culture is unclear and must be clarified by further study. In addition, senior leaders must take courageous steps to eliminate faculty from promotion committees whose mind-set is stuck in earlier decades and replace them with younger and forward-thinking faculty.

Another strategy for supporting the role of women in academic medicine has been the development of part-time work opportunities for both men and women. Women tend to pursue part-time academic opportunities in order to have more time for child-rearing; men opt to take part-time positions in order to increase their salary opportunities by moonlighting or pursuing consultative activities [41]. When a group of pediatricians—a specialty that has traditionally attracted a large number of women faculty—was queried regarding their views of part-time faculty, they were quite supportive and felt that part-time opportunities would improve recruitment, retention, and promotion of female faculty. However, respondents noted that part-time opportunities would only be successful if institutions clearly outlined and modified expectations for clinical productivity for part-time faculty and expanded resources to allow them to optimize their productivity [42].

Even more surprising was the finding that chairmen of departments of medicine—a group generally perceived as hard-core traditionalists who are strongly embedded in the traditions and work ethics of earlier generations—were generally supportive of part-time faculty and were interested in further discussions regarding part-time opportunities [43]. Although part-time employment opportunities might seem an optimal means of fulfilling both family and academic goals, a paucity of men or women faculty have taken advantage of this type of opportunity where it exists [40].

Some of the problems associated with part-time employment have been that the practice of medicine has not lent itself to "shift work" and, as a result, physicians find it difficult to leave the hospital at a prespecified time, particularly when patients are in need of care. Thus, part-time physicians often find that they spend far more than half of their time in the hospital. However, two new types of practices are becoming increasingly prevalent at AMCs and lend themselves well to part-time practice: "hospitalists" and "intensivists."

Many academic hospitals have recognized that clinical care and education can be optimized by a single attending physician caring for a group of hospitalized patients rather than multiple physicians interacting with the house officer and nursing staffs throughout the day. They have also realized that hospital length of stay can be optimized by having the attending physician available in the hospital rather than spending most of his or her time in the outpatient clinic. Thus, these hospitals have developed hospitalist services.

Each geographically distinct group of patients (often with the same disease) are cared for by a single physician and a group of interns and residents—all of whom spend their time in the hospital. Rotating the attending hospitalist every 3 or 4 days results in a physician working a 40-hour week—half-time for an academic physician. A similar algorithm has been used in many academic intensive care units, where physicians work approximately four 10-hour shifts each week. During the remainder of the week, the physicians can pursue research activities or spend time in child-rearing activities. Thus, these "shift-type" hours ensure outstanding patient care because the attending physician is always rested and close to the patient's bedside; at the same time, women (and men) are provided extensive periods of time out of the hospital as well as well-defined hours.

Support Diversity

Although America's medical schools have been able to attract an increasing number of women, their ability to attract students of color has not been nearly as successful. Even more discouraging is the marked inability to recruit minority physicians to AMCs. Many authorities have recognized that the best approach to recruiting minority physicians to medicine—in particular to academic medicine—is to introduce the excitement of science and medicine at the earliest possible time in the educational process. Toward this end, a number of AMCs have developed partnerships with secondary schools and colleges with high proportions of underrepresented minority students to create a pipeline of high school and college students interested in healthcare professions.

In addition, these programs have worked to strengthen the students' educational backgrounds while also working to increase the number of students who enroll in them [44–46]. Although these programs have increased the number of minority students who attend college, it is too early to assess how these partnerships of medical students, faculty, and high school and middle school students result in changes in the number of minority students who eventually enroll in medical school. Other novel approaches have been taken to enhance medical school enrollment of minority students, including MCAT preparatory courses, postbaccalaureate programs focused on underserved minority students, and summer internship programs. These have been undertaken with the goal of enhancing medical school enrollments of well-qualified minority students.

Some AMCs have instituted new instructional programs that have markedly improved academic performance among individuals who had lower board scores and grades prior to matriculation, and preliminary studies suggest that these programs are helpful in student retention [47]. Creating summer fellowships in laboratory science for underrepresented minority applicants can create an increased interest in both research and medicine; however, the summer programs must be ongoing across a number of summers and must be coupled with didactic programs during the intervening school year in order to strengthen the students' academic underpinnings. Unfortunately, the vast majority of these programs are relatively new and their long-term success must be carefully studied in order to develop those that are most effective in reaching their goals.

References

1. Flexner, A. 1973. Medical education in the United States and Canada: A report to the Carnegie Foundation for the Advancement of Teaching, 346. Bulletin no. 4, New York (reprinted by The Heritage Press, Buffalo, NY).
2. Lewis, I. J., and Sheps, C. G. 1983. *The sick citadel,* 263. Cambridge, MA: Oelgeshlager, Gun & Hain, Inc.
3. AAMC. 1986. Medical student graduation questionnaire (www.aamc.org).
4. AAMC. 2006. Medical school graduation questionnaire (www.aamc.org).
5. Hafferty, F. W., and Boulger, J. G. 1986. A look by medical students at medical practice in the future. *Journal of Medical Education* 61 (5): 359–366.
6. MGMA. 2006. Academic practice compensation and production survey for faculty and management (report based on 2005 data), 46–103.
7. AAMC. 2007. AAMC survey of house staff stipends, benefits and funding. Autumn 2006 report.
8. Fang, D. 2004. AAMC. 2004. Analysis in brief 4 (1) (www.aamc.org/data/aib).
9. U.S. Department of Labor, Bureau of Labor Statistics. 2007. Available at www.bls.gov/oes/current/naics3_523000.htm
10. American Association of University Professors. 2001. 1940 Statement of principles on academic freedom and tenure with 1970 interpretive comments. In *AAUP policy documents and reports,* 9th ed. Washington, D.C.: AAUP.
11. Korn, D. 1996. Reengineering academic medical centers: Reengineering academic values? *Academic Medicine* 71 (10): 1033–1043.
12. Magrane, D., and Lang, J. 2005. Women in U.S. Academic Medicare, Statistics and Medicaid School Benchmarking 2005–2006. AAMC. www.aamc.org/members/win/statistics/stats06/stat.htm
13. Magrane, D., and Lang, J. 2006. An overview of women in U.S. academic medicine. Analysis in Brief AAMC 6 (7) 1–2.
14. Magrane, D. 2005. The changing representation of men and women in academic medicine. Analysis in Brief AAMC 5 (2) 1–2.
15. Kaplan, S. H., Sullivan, L. M., Dukes, K. A., Phillips, C. F., Kelch, R. P., and Schaller, J. G. 1996. Sex differences in academic advancement. Results of a national study of pediatricians. *New England Journal of Medicine* 335 (17): 1282–1289.
16. Nonnemaker, L. 2000. Women physicians in academic medicine: New insights from cohort studies. *New England Journal of Medicine* 342 (6): 399–405.
17. Ash, A. S., Carr, P. L., Goldstein, R., and Friedman, R. H. 2004. Compensation and advancement of women in academic medicine: Is there equity? *Annals of Internal Medicine* 141 (3): 238–240.
18. Wright, A. L., Schwindt, L. A., Bassford, T. L., Reyna, V. F., Shisslak, C. M., St. Germain, P. A., and Reed, K. L. 2003. Gender differences in academic advancement: Patterns, causes, and potential solutions in one U.S. college of medicine. *Academic Medicine* 78 (5): 500–508.

19. Fried, L. P., Francomano, C. A., MacDonald, S. M., Wagner, E. M., Stokes, E. J., Carbone, K. M., Bias, W. B., Newman, M. M., and Stobo, J. D. 1998. Career development for women in academic medicine: Multiple interventions in a department of medicine. *Journal of the American Medical Association* 276 (11): 898–905.
20. Carr, P. L., Ash, A. S., Friedman, R. H., Scaramucci, A., Barnett, R. C., Szalacha, L., Palepu, A., and Moskowitz, M. A. 1998. Relation of family responsibilities and gender to the productivity and career satisfaction of medical faculty. *Annals of Internal Medicine* 129 (7): 532–538.
21. McQuire, L. K., Bergen, M. R., and Polan, M. L., 2004. Career advancement for women faculty in a U.S. school of medicine: Perceived needs. *Academic Medicine* 79 (4): 319–325.
22. AAMC. 2006. Diversity in the physician workforce: Facts and figures (www.aamc.org/factsandfigures). Accessed Nov. 4, 2008.
23. Mount Sinai awarded $2.3 million to establish new northeast regional Health Career Opportunity Program alliance. 2008. *Mount Sinai News,* Sept. 11 (www.mountsinai.org).
24. Salsberg, E., and Grover, A. 2006. Physician workforce shortages: Implications and issues for academic health centers and policymakers. *Academic Medicine* 81 (9): 782–787.
25. Jovic, E., Wallace, J. E., and Lemaire, J. 2006.The generation and gender shifts in medicine: An exploratory survey of internal medicine physicians. *BMC Health Service Research* 6:55.
26. Heiliger, P. J., and Hingstman, L. 2000. Career preferences and the work–family balance in medicine: Gender differences among medical specialists. *Social Science Medicine* 50 (9): 1235–1246.
27. Jacobson, C. C., Nguyen, J. C., and Kimball, A. B. 2004. Gender and parenting significantly affect work hours of recent dermatology program graduates. *Archives of Dermatology* 140 (2): 191–196.
28. Jeffe, D. B., Andriole, D. A., Hageman, H. L., and Whelan, A. J. 2007. The changing paradigm of contemporary U.S. allopathic medical school graduates' career paths: Analysis of the 1997–2004 national AAMC graduation questionnaire database. *Academic Medicine* 82 (9): 888–894.
29. Dorsey, E. R., Jarjoura, D., and Rutecki, G. W. 2003. Influence of controllable lifestyle on recent trends in specialty choice by U.S. medical students. *Journal of the American Medical Association* 290 (9): 1173–1178.
30. Colen, B. D. 2008. Harvard Medical School to reduce student debt burden. *Harvard Science,* March 20.
31. American Association of University Professors. 2001. Statement of principles on family responsibilities and academic work (www.aaup.org/statements/REPORTS/ref01fam.htm#7).
32. Gabbe, S. G. Melville, J., Mandel, L., and Walker, E. 2002. Burnout in chairs of obstetrics and gynecology: Diagnosis, treatment, and prevention. *American Journal of Obstetrics and Gynecology* 186 (4): 601–612.

33. Demmy, T. L., Kivlahan, C., Stone, T. T., Teague, L., and Sapienza, P. 2002. Physicians' perceptions of institutional and leadership factors influencing their job satisfaction at one academic medical center. *Academic Medicine* 77 (12 Pt 1): 1235–1240.

34. Schroen, A., Brownstein, M. R., and Sheldon, G. F. 2004. Women in academic general surgery. *Annals of Surgery* 79 (4): 310–318.

35. Bickel, J., and Brown, A. J. 2005. Generation X: Implications for faculty recruitment and development in academic health centers. *Academic Medicine* 80 (3): 205–210.

36. Cain, J. M., Schulkin, J., Parisi, V., Power, M. L., Holzman, G. B., and Williams, S. 2001. Effects of perceptions and mentorship on pursuing a career in academic medicine in obstetrics and gynecology. *Academic Medicine* 76 (6): 628–634.

37. Brotherton, S. E., Rockey, P. H., and Etzel, S. I. 2004. U.S. graduate medical education, 2003–2004. *Journal of the American Medical Association* 292 (9): 1032–1037.

38. Draznin, J. 2004. The "mommy tenure track." *Academic Medicine* 79 (4): 289–290.

39. Potee, R. A., Gerber, A. J., and Ickovics, J. R. 1999. Medicine and motherhood: Shifting trends among female physicians from 1922 to 1999. *Academic Medicine* 74 (8): 911–919.

40. Bunton, S. A., and Mallon, W. T. 2007. The continued evolution of faculty appointment and tenure policies at U.S. medical schools. *Academic Medicine* 82 (3): 281–289.

41. Fox, G., Schwartz, A., and Hart, K. M. 2006. Work–family balance and academic advancement in medical schools. *Academic Psychiatry* 30 (3): 227–234.

42. Kahn, J. A., Degen, S. J. F., Mansour, M. E., Goodman, E., Zeller, M. H., Laor, T., Lanphear, N. E., and Boat, T. F. 2005. Pediatric faculty members' attitudes about part-time faculty positions and policies to support part-time faculty: A study at one medical center. *Academic Medicine* 80 (10): 931–939.

43. Sanfey, H., Savas, J., and Hollands, C. 2006. The view of surgery department chairs on part time faculty in academic practice: Results of a national survey. *American Journal of Surgery* 192 (3): 366–371.

44. Fincher, R. M., Sykes-Brown, W., and Allen-Noble, R. 2002. Health science learning academy: A successful "pipeline" educational program for high school students. *Academic Medicine* 77 (7): 737–738.

45. Rye, J. A., and Chester, A. L. 1999. WVU—Community partnership that provides science and math enrichment for underrepresented high school students. *Academic Medicine* 74 (4): 352–355.

46. Curran-Everett, D., Collins, S., Hubert, J., and Pidick, T. 1999. Science education partnership between the University of Colorado and a Denver high school. *Academic Medicine* 74 (4): 322–325.

47. Lieberman, S. A., Frye, A. W., Thomas, L., Rabek, J. P., and Anderson, G. D. 2008. Comprehensive changes in the learning environment: Subsequent step 1 scores of academically at-risk students. *Academic Medicine* 83 (10 Suppl): S49–52.

Chapter 9

Teaching Medical Professionalism in the AMC

'Tis no idle challenge which we physicians throw out to the world when we claim that our mission is of the highest and of the noblest kind, not alone in curing disease but in educating the people in the laws of health, and in preventing the spread of plagues and pestilence.

William Osler [1]

Introduction

Over the past decade, changes in U.S. healthcare delivery systems and the economic health of many AMCs have led medical scholars to worry that we have lost some of the basic ideals of the profession of medicine that William Osler espoused over a century ago [2]. Indeed, in response to a survey assessing the effects of the new economic and competitive healthcare environment on medical education, the CEO of one AMC remarked, "The implications for teaching frighten me most. The young men and women who come to us for training today are not radically different from their predecessors. But because of the personal and institutional role models we offer them, they may be radically different when they leave" [3].

Fearing that the current competitive financial environment in which physicians work was eroding the basic principles of medical care that had been taught to students for over a century and causing physicians to abandon their commitment to excellence in patient care, leaders of individual medical centers as well as collections of scholars created task forces to reaffirm the fundamental principles of how physicians interact with their patients, their students, and their communities. These efforts have focused on "professionalism"—what Arnold and Stern have defined as the "foundation of clinical competence, communication skill, and ethical and legal understanding, upon which is built the aspiration to and wise application of the principles of professionalism: excellence, humanism, accountability and altruism" [4].

Although one can argue that quality of care and professionalism are synonymous, the term "professionalism" further defines the attributes of a physician who provides outstanding care to his or her patients: honesty, altruism, engagement, and humility. Thus, in the context of professionalism, quality of care is more a metric than a descriptor. This chapter will

review the efforts to develop guidelines for professionalism;
describe obstacles to teaching professionalism;
discuss how some institutions have created novel programs to improve how they teach professionalism;
detail how the cultures of two outstanding AMCs have been sustained through a focused commitment to long-standing traditions of professionalism; and
make recommendations for enhancing the professionalism of AMCs.

Development of Guidelines for Professionalism in the Practice of Medicine

Recognizing that physicians were challenged by competition in the medical marketplace, an overwhelming array of new technologies and new therapeutics, a decrease in patient safety, and an erosion of public trust, the American Board of Internal Medicine Foundation, the American College of Physicians—American Society of Internal Medicine Foundation, and the European Federation of Internal Medicine undertook a collaborative effort to create a charter to reaffirm the ethical underpinning of the practice of medicine and to describe the commitments between physicians and their patients, or medical professionalism [5].

Acknowledging that professionalism is the basis of medicine's contract with society, the charter provided three fundamental principles: the primacy of patient welfare, the principle of patient autonomy, and the principle of social justice. In addition, the charter set forth a set of professional responsibilities to which physicians must commit themselves:

professional competence;
honesty with patients;
patient confidentiality;
maintaining appropriate relations with patients;
improving quality of care;
improving access to care;
just distribution of finite resources;
scientific knowledge;
maintaining trust by managing conflicts of interest; and
maintaining professional responsibilities, including working collaboratively
    to maximize patient care and participation in self-regulation.

As so often happens in medicine, several different groups came up with slightly different definitions of professionalism. For example, the American Association of Medical Colleges defined a medical professional as knowledgeable, skillful, altruistic, and dutiful [6]. The Accreditation Council for Graduate Medical Education defined professionalism as including medical knowledge, practice-based learning and improvement, patient care, systems-based practice, interpersonal and communication skills, and professionalism (respect, compassion, integrity, responsiveness to needs, altruism, accountability, commitment to excellence, sound ethics, and sensitivity to culture, age, gender, and disabilities) [7]. Finally, in a "normative definition" of professionalism, Swick [8] noted that physicians should

subordinate their own interests to those of others;
adhere to high ethical and moral standards;
respond to societal needs;
demonstrate core humanistic values;
exercise accountability;
demonstrate continuing commitment to excellence;
exhibit commitments to scholarship;
deal with complexity and uncertainty; and
reflect on their actions and decisions.

Despite a large number of articles and lecture series that disseminated the findings of these expert panels, a survey of U.S. physicians in 2003 and 2004 found that 24% disagreed that periodic recertification was desirable and 45% admitted that they had not reported impaired or incompetent colleagues. Thus, the challenge faced by today's AMCs is not to define professionalism but rather to develop new means of teaching professionalism to both students and practicing physicians in the United States.

Obstacles to Teaching Quality Effectively and Developing a Culture of Professionalism

The Hidden Curriculum in AMCs

In 2002, while serving as a scholar in residence at the Association of American Medical Colleges, Thomas Inui undertook a project to evaluate professionalism in American medicine. After extensive reading and interviews with key informants, Inui described a group of core observations. Although he found a high degree of congruence across the medical profession's understanding of the attributes of professionalism, he found a gap between what were recognized as elements of professionalism and the actual actions taken by physicians in their daily lives [9]. Inui noted, "We may be unconscious of some of this gap, but even when conscious we are silent or inarticulate about the dissonance and, in our silence, do not assist our students to understand our challenges when attempting to live up to our profession's ideals" [9].

As a result of this silence, students learn a powerful lesson about the profession of medicine: What their professors tell them to do is not what the professors themselves do in caring for their patients. This lesson then results in a continuing process of the development of cynicism on the part of the students and residents whom the professors teach. The marked disparity between what medical school educators say a student should do and what the students witness them doing has been referred to as the "hidden curriculum" [10–12]. This conundrum can only be addressed by ensuring that all of the individuals charged with educating the next generation of physicians understand that this education is "rooted in the daily activities of individuals and groups in academic medical communities" far more than it is in the lessons taught in the lecture hall [9]. Therefore, teachers not only must espouse professionalism, but also must demonstrate it.

The Legal Environment

Just as the hidden curriculum impedes the ability of academic faculty to teach professionalism effectively, another hidden impediment is the threat of litigation that surrounds many attempts at improving quality of care. Today, all

U.S. hospitals are required to conduct peer review by Joint Commission on Accreditation of Healthcare Organizations standard MS.4.90. A common peer-review mechanism utilized historically by AMCs that is an outstanding platform for teaching professionalism is the departmental morbidity and mortality (M&M) conference [13]. Often run by department chairs, academic morbidity and mortality conferences are renowned for examining errors in medical practice responsible for unexpected or unwanted outcomes; they cause young residents and young faculty great angst as their decision-making capabilities or lack thereof are publicly displayed.

Although these sessions have sometimes been criticized for embarrassing "guilty" physicians and not focusing on prevention or identifying system problems as much as individual decision making, they now have been refined and more carefully organized. They can help immeasurably in identifying problem areas that require attention. To guarantee physician participation in quality-assurance programs, the federal government passed the Health Care Quality Improvement Act in 1986, which provided immunity from civil lawsuits for peer-review panels. However, the passage of laws that removed the "privilege" associated with some forms of peer review has made these conferences less effective in some states.

For example, in 2004, Florida voters overwhelmingly approved a constitutional amendment sponsored by the Academy of Florida Trial Lawyers that made previously confidential peer-review meeting notes available to patients [14]. In addition, Massachusetts allows public access to some peer-review committee documents under the Freedom of Information Act, and the Kentucky Supreme Court determined that peer-review laws that protect the confidentiality of committee notes are not constitutional. Without complete confidentially, physicians became hesitant to voice their true feelings at M&M conferences, preferring instead to address mistakes in private meetings—thereby obviating the ability of the case to serve as an effective teaching vehicle for students and residents.

A litigious environment and a court system that generally favors plaintiffs can also inhibit students, nurses, residents, and attending physicians from reporting adverse events, unprofessional behavior, or suspected incompetence. In addition, the threat of litigation can reduce the enthusiasm of AMC leaders to take punitive actions when physicians have acted in an unprofessional manner or have demonstrated a level of competence inconsistent with the norms of the medical center. In situations in which a physician's privileges to practice in a given hospital are restricted or removed, attorneys have filed suit against the hospital or the medical school on the basis that their client's privileges were removed in order to eliminate "competition" from him or her, rather than because their client was in any way lacking in skill or because behavior was inappropriate.

Indeed, numerous individuals I interviewed shared stories with me about how they had removed the privileges of a physician they believed to be incompetent only to have the AMC settle the subsequent lawsuit or reinstate the privileges of the physician with questionable abilities. In both cases—particularly in the latter case—such actions on the part of AMC leadership resulted in the very cynicism that educational programs in professionalism are attempting to eradicate in AMCs.

In one example, a new faculty member who had just completed her training in interventional gastroenterology performed poorly in her first two cases as an attending (both of which were proctored by the chief of the division), as well as in subsequent cases proctored by other members of the division. After several months of continued oversight, the chief of the division informed the young physician that she would not be able to continue to perform interventional procedures, but that she would be able to perform all of the other elements of a gastroenterology practice and that all of the financial components of her contract would be honored.

Within days, the university received notification that the chief of the division, the medical school, and the hospital were being sued for breach of contract and for restraint of trade. Fearing that the cost of litigation would be significant and that the university could possibly lose its case, all parties settled with the plaintiff before trial. Ironically, several years later, the division chief received a phone call from a hospital in another state asking him to testify on its behalf in its efforts to have the same woman's privileges removed because of allegations of incompetence. Of greater concern was the lesson that the case taught to the trainees in the gastroenterology program: Professionalism was taught but not practiced!

The Silo Structure of AMCs

Administrative and economic structures can also impede effective peer review. For example, when the hospital and the medical school are separate organizations, there are often legal impediments to sharing information. Discussions regarding an adverse event that occurs in the hospital may require the hospital's legal counsel to be present, but the university may be absent or have little say in the case. Because the hospital and the university have their own insurance policies, decisions of either group may be self-serving.

For example, interns, residents, and fellows are covered by the hospital's insurance policy, whereas university physicians are covered by their own insurance. Thus, in defending a particular malpractice case, the hospital and the university may be in conflict when decisions must be made as to whether the individual responsible for an adverse event is an attending physician or a resident. This situation creates a wedge between the long-standing relationship between an academic faculty and its trainees.

Because of this silo effect, quality improvement initiatives cannot be effectively carried out when individual departments perform due diligence independently on adverse events that occur in patients cared for by physicians from multiple departments. It is well recognized that the use of interdisciplinary care teams provides a level of excellence in patient care that is absent when patient care is undertaken in the traditional silo structure, and medical students are now taught the importance of interdisciplinary teams in patient care [15,16]. However, peer review has traditionally taken place within individual departments or divisions without cross-departmental collaboration when adverse events occur. Thus, the silo structure of academia not only can impede quality improvement initiatives but also can lead to finger pointing between various departments regarding the cause of an adverse event.

A Culture of Silence

After interviewing numerous physicians from across the country and extensively reviewing the literature on professionalism, Inui noted that many physicians are silent about the disparity between what physicians should do and what they actually do and that this silence causes students to be cynics [9]. However, the unwillingness of physicians to bring unprofessional behavior to the attention of the appropriate authorities is not limited to individual physicians. For example, the American College of Emergency Physicians policy on disclosure of medical errors is silent on the issue of whether a physician should disclose to a patient another physician's error [17]. Furthermore, in a national survey, the vast majority of physicians agreed that there was a need for professional self-regulation and 96% of respondents agreed that physicians should report impaired or incompetent colleagues to the appropriate authority.

However, nearly half of the respondents who had identified impaired colleagues or serious medical errors had not reported them [18]. Interestingly, cardiologists were least likely to report incompetent or impaired physicians and/or serious medical errors. Physicians who practiced in a staff-model health maintenance organization or in a university medical school practice were most likely to report an impaired colleague or a serious medical error.

AMCs themselves may not support a culture of professionalism when the politics of the institution do not make it expedient to do so; they may find it easier to maintain silence than to take action. For example, one colleague I interviewed shared a story about a physician at an AMC who had not seen one of her patients since performing a procedure on him 3 days earlier, despite multiple attempts by the resident to contact the physician. After being informed of the problem by the resident, the department chair called the patient's physician and demanded that she immediately see the patient and communicate a plan of care to the resident.

The patient's physician finally came to see the patient later that day; however, she added notes to the patient's chart for each of the 3 days that she had not seen her patient. Appropriately, the department chairman reported the event to hospital authorities, who in turn delegated the issue to the appropriate hospital committee. Unfortunately, the committee did nothing more than reprimand the physician, leading my colleague to comment, "How can I teach the values of professionalism to my residents when their own hospital does not appear to be willing to take action in cases of inappropriate behavior?"

No Good Deed Goes Unpunished—Risks of Revealing Unprofessional Behavior

Despite the fact that the basic tenets of professionalism call for physicians to bring unprofessional behavior to the attention of the appropriate AMC official, some physicians have found that to do so results in adverse consequences. From a legal standpoint, academic whistle-blowers may not be protected from suits for slander. In most states, a legal precedent called "conditional privilege" allows an employee to report concerns regarding another employee's actions to the employer without incurring a risk of a lawsuit for libel or slander as long as the concerns were raised in good faith and without malice. However, in May 2007, the Supreme Court of the Commonwealth of Pennsylvania eliminated the legal defense of "conditional privilege" [19]. Thus, physicians practicing there can incur significant liability risks by bringing concerns to administrative officers regarding physicians who are impaired or provide a level of care inconsistent with perceived standards.

Some physicians who have reported unprofessional or unethical behavior may receive adverse publicity. For example, in 2000, three longtime Yale University School of Medicine professors accused Yale in a lawsuit of punishing them when they complained that actions implemented by the chairman of the Department of Radiology to decrease costs had led to "unacceptable patient care and safety consequences" [20]. Allegedly, when the faculty members complained that residents with little experience were interpreting x-ray studies in the emergency room, in violation of Medicare laws, the university decreased their salaries and suggested that one of the group "refrain from [your] critical public and private activism" [20].

Similarly, an orthopedic surgeon at the University of California-Davis Medical Center filed a lawsuit alleging that the dean of the medical school had limited his clinical practice in retaliation for a complaint he had made about another physician's billing and scheduling practices [21]. Finally, at Stanford, two surgeons recently sued the university and the Stanford Hospital's chief of staff for libel and defamation after they accused two other Stanford physicians of malpractice and fraud [22]. Thus, in trying to support a culture of professionalism, these professors found that "no good deed goes unpunished" in some AMCs. AMCs must protect rather than punish whistle-blowers who raise concerns about quality of care issues.

AMC Efforts to Teach Professionalism to Medical Students

Over the past several years, a group of highly successful AMCs has undertaken specific activities at their institutions to foster an enhanced culture of professionalism. These activities have focused on specific areas of the AMC or on students, faculty, or the entire population of the AMC. For example, at the University of Pennsylvania School of Medicine, policies and programs were developed to enhance professionalism in the conduct of clinical trials, relations with pharmaceutical manufacturers, and the clinical and teaching environment [23]. In the clinical and teaching arena, Penn developed a "professional symposium" program to bring experts in the field to campus, created a program to deal with physicians who had an unusual number of patient complaints, and organized an "interdisciplinary rounding program" in which all members of the patient care team, including doctors and nurses, round together. Begun in a single department, these programs will eventually encompass the entire medical institution.

Penn also developed a manual for instructing department chairs and division chiefs on how to deal with disruptive physicians and established small groups of residents in which to teach a "resident professionalism curriculum." The school also began a program to train a cadre of physicians in professionalism, established a program to reward individual physicians who best displayed the attributes of professionalism, and formed a "physician professionalism committee" charged with the goals of building an institution-wide culture of professionalism and remediating disruptive physician behavior. Penn set goals for establishing specific guidelines for educating clinical investigators regarding potential conflicts of interest, tracking and disclosing conflicts of interest, and establishing guidelines for relationships with industry, and developed policies that would ensure professionalism in relations with pharmaceutical manufacturers [23].

In 2005, the University of Chicago established an institution-wide "roadmap to professionalism" designed to increase awareness of professionalism issues at the institution [24]. In contrast to the program at Penn, the University of Chicago program focused on "learners." The goal was to understand how the behaviors and attitudes of medical trainees change during their training and how the school's learning environment influenced these changes. The efforts of the Professionalism Steering Committee included a survey of all stakeholders, including medical students, residents, preceptors, and faculty, in order to target future interventions. To engage residents in the process, the group also focused workshops on evaluating relationships between residents and pharmaceutical company representatives, challenges in effectively handling patient-care hand-offs, and development of tools that would allow patients to evaluate the residents who care for them.

The New York University School of Medicine has initiated a program to determine how best to teach professionalism. The unique aspect of this program is the use of a Web-based professional development portfolio to document students' professional development throughout their medical school career [25]. The NYU system includes a training program for mentors, but places the responsibility for professionalism assessment on the student.

The University of Indiana has taken a different approach to the development of institutional professionalism. Fearing that "medicine had become more of a business than a calling that has led directly to a concomitant—and appropriate—decline in esteem of our profession in the eyes of the public," the university implemented a professionalism program by beginning a "cultural overhaul" of the institution in 2000 [26]. Led by the dean of the School of Medicine, the effort began by developing guiding principles and core values. Indiana's efforts focused on seeking enhanced professionalism through faculty recruitment, medical school admission, the medical school curriculum, physician compensation, and development of a relationship-centered care initiative [27].

Vanderbilt University School of Medicine has taken a somewhat different approach to its new program in professionalism. Recognizing the need to develop new ways to teach professionalism, the school's leadership also recognized that culture would not change without "identifying, measuring, and addressing unprofessional behavior" [28]. Unique programs that have been initiated at Vanderbilt include an "academic leadership program" for new department chairs and division chiefs that teaches leadership skills but at the same time focuses on understanding disruptive behavior and ways to address it and the development of an objective process for guiding interventions when disruptive behavior occurs. This includes informal intervention, awareness intervention, authority intervention, and disciplinary intervention. To ensure consistent application of intervention tools, Vanderbilt has also created the Vanderbilt Professional Conduct Policy as well as developed a formal process for reporting physician- and resident-based complaints that includes an electronic database.

Finally, all managers receive training in a protocol called HEART [29]:

*h*ear the person;
*e*mpathize with the concern;
*a*pologize if appropriate;
*r*espond with a plan for assessing the allegation and closing loops; and
*t*hanks for bringing attention to the issue.

Because all of these programs are new, it is still too early to measure their success. However, a common theme is that, although each program must actively involve all members of the AMC, the development of new policies must be "top driven" by physician leaders.

Creating a Culture of Professionalism at Two of America's Oldest and Best AMCs

The importance of professionalism has clearly become a hot topic within academic medicine. In response to mandates from the Accreditation Council for Graduate Medical Education (ACGME), professionalism is now taught to residents at all teaching hospitals as a core competency, and some AMCs have begun to evaluate opportunities to spread professionalism across all elements of the AMC [7]. However, it must be recognized that although the term "professionalism" is new, its intrinsic elements have served as the core of some AMCs for a century.

Two leading examples of institutions that have had a long-standing culture focused on excellence in patient care are the Mayo Clinic and The Johns Hopkins Hospital. It is not surprising that with a century-old history of a culture focused on providing excellence in patient care, these two AMCs have been ranked numbers 1 and 2 among America's hospitals (Hopkins has been number 1 for the past 18 years). Although the Mayo Clinic and the Johns Hopkins Medical Institutions provide didactic programs in professionalism, we will see that the real lessons come from the day-to-day demonstrations of professionalism inextricably embedded in the culture of each institution. Thus, these two institutions, which are very different in structure, serve as templates for creating a culture of professionalism throughout medicine.

The Mayo Clinic

In 1863, Dr. William Worral Mayo, an Englishman, moved to Rochester, Minnesota, to examine new recruits for the Union Army [30]. At the end of the war he remained in Rochester and in 1883 and 1888 he was joined in his practice by his two sons, William J. and Charles H. Mayo, respectively. Also in 1883, the founder of Sisters of St. Francis, Mother Alfred Moes, proposed to build and staff a hospital if Dr. W. W. Mayo would provide the medical care. Their reputation for excellence spread and the Mayo brothers invited others to join them, accepting their first partner in 1892. However, regardless of specialty, each new member of the practice was expected to work as part of a multispecialty medical team—the first such "group practice" in the United States.

In 1910, in a lecture to the medical students at Rush Medical College, Dr. William J. Mayo defined the core mission of the Mayo Clinic when he noted, "The best interest of the patient is the only interest to be considered, and in order that the sick may have the benefit of advancing knowledge, union of forces is necessary" [31]. In this public articulation of the guiding principles of the clinic, Dr. Mayo stated that its primary goal was to establish a covenant between the patient and Mayo's staff such that everyone recognized that the "needs of the patient come first." In addition, in his reference to the "union of forces," he noted the importance of translating scientific discovery rapidly and effectively into improvements in clinical care and the overarching belief that excellence in the delivery of care required teamwork across and within departments [32]. The clinical leaders who followed Dr. Mayo ensured that these philosophies were adhered to over the ensuing 100 years.

In the late 1990s, the clinic's clinical practice committee became concerned that the economic challenges of the times and changes in healthcare financing would threaten the ideals that had guided the clinic's operations for nearly a century [32]. As a result, Mayo appointed a multidisciplinary work group to analyze the elements of an ideal patient care experience. In 2001, the work group publicly reaffirmed the Mayo Clinic's covenant with patients and the expectations for a patient's care experience in a document entitled, "The Mayo Clinic Model of Care" [33]. The document reaffirmed its core-value-based culture and model of care by noting that "the Mayo Clinic will provide high-quality compassionate care in an integrated multispecialty environment with the primary focus of meeting the needs of the patient."

Mayo leadership also took actions to address patient concerns and to support the Mayo Clinic model of care. For example, it established the PLEASE CARE service essential program that outlined the attitudes and behaviors that Mayo staff should exhibit, including [34,35]:

*p*resent—acknowledge the patient;

*l*isten—give each person undivided attention;

*e*mpathize—express compassion;

*a*ction—find the answer;

*s*ummarize—restate key information;

*e*xcite—exceed each person's expectations;

*c*onfidentiality—protect patient privacy;

*a*ttitude—make a positive impression;

*r*espect—adapt to diverse cultures, disabilities, and languages; and

*e*motional intelligence.

The goal of the work was to ensure that all staff recognized that "when you are interacting with a patient, you are the Mayo Clinic."

Mayo leadership also established the clinical practice quality oversight committee to provide direction and oversight to all patient care improvement activities. A Quality Management Services Department was established to consolidate all efforts at improving patient safety and quality of care and a Quality Academy was begun to train individual teams. In 2007, the Mayo Clinic began the "creating the future" strategic plan to improve the institution's ability to meet the needs of each patient by connecting best practices across all departments.

Recognizing that culture trumps strategy, recruitment and hiring practices see to it that physicians who join the Mayo Clinic share in the institution's values and fit with the institutional culture. In addition, all new staff members undergo a thorough orientation program that fully acculturates and assimilates them into the Mayo family. Ongoing programs regularly assess all personnel using patient surveys, 360-degree evaluations, and performance reviews. Finally, in 2001, the Mayo Clinic implemented a comprehensive multilevel career and leadership development program for physicians and scientists to ensure that they are preparing the next generation of Mayo leaders [36].

Thus, as seen in great businesses, Mayo attains its greatness by identifying and committing to the core focus of providing outstanding patient care; managing with committed physician leaders; ensuring that the right people are on the team; making decisions and adapting operations consistent with the core mission; remaining optimistic about achieving success, but continuously evaluating; and addressing potential environmental threats [37]. In addition, the Mayo Clinic does not just develop algorithms and plans; its leadership ensures that the plans are executed [38].

The Johns Hopkins Hospital

Just as the Mayo Clinic was founded on a core mission of providing excellence in patient care, so too were The Johns Hopkins Hospital and its accompanying medical school. In 1873, Johns Hopkins, a Baltimore philanthropist, sent a letter to a group of individuals whom he had designated as the trustees of the new hospital instructing them to erect a hospital on a parcel of land that he had given them in the city of Baltimore [39]. He noted that the hospital "shall, in construction and arrangement, compare favorably with any other institution of like character in this country or in Europe" [39]. In addition, Hopkins instructed the trustees "to secure for the services of the Hospital, surgeons and physicians of the highest character and greatest skill" and to "bear constantly in mind that it is my wish and purpose that the institution shall ultimately form a part of the Medical School of that University for which I have made ample provision by my will."

In order to adhere to Hopkins's dicta, the trustees hired Dr. John S. Billings to build the hospital. As noted by the historian Augusta Tucker, "Excellence was the only thing which Dr. Billings would ever accept out of anybody, be he a carpenter, a bricklayer, a professor, or a Trustee. This Army doctor had intense energy, great decision, utter fairness, and a complete inability to countenance either in men or material mediocre performance" [40]. For the faculty, Dr. Billings hired four men, each of whom shared his belief in the need for excellence in all aspects of the hospital and the school of medicine: the pathologist Dr. William H. Welch; the internist Dr. William Osler, who would serve as physician-in-chief, the surgeon Dr. William Halsted, who would serve as surgeon-in-chief; and D. Howard Kelly, who would serve as gynecologist-in-chief.

Osler, a staunch advocate of good nursing, hygiene, and prevention was instrumental in teaching doctors to prescribe only drugs that had proven efficacy and in establishing the bedside as the major site of teaching for third- and fourth-year students. By their third year, students were taking patient histories, performing physical examinations, and doing laboratory tests instead of sitting in lecture halls [40]. While establishing the concept of a "residency" to further the education of medical school graduates, Osler railed against for-profit medical schools with low standards. His 1892 textbook, *Principles and Practice of Medicine,* became the landmark text of internal medicine and would continue as such for many years after his death.

For nearly two decades, The Johns Hopkins Hospital has led *U.S. News and World Report*'s yearly list of U.S. hospitals, and the medical school has topped the list for NIH funding while making substantive contributions to the treatment of human disease. If one looks carefully at Hopkins, it is easy to point out a number of factors that, from a business standpoint, would be associated with success: an outstanding and highly engaged board who have brought expertise in a variety of areas to the institution; a series of courageous yet modest leaders who have diligently moved the institution forward, afforded long-term stability to the position, and set up their successors for even greater success; and a focus on developing the next generation of physicians [37].

In addition, the hospital's incredible success in fundraising from community leaders and grateful patients has gone a long way in providing at least some of the resources necessary to maintain cutting-edge technology. However, I would argue that what truly sets Hopkins and those like it apart is the culture—in particular, a culture that strives inextricably toward providing excellence in all facets of its mission. This core value of clinical and research excellence was established by the "four horsemen" of Hopkins (Osler, Welch, Halsted, and Kelly). However, it was first given a name in 1950 upon the celebration of Welch's hundredth birthday, when Alan Gregg stated [41]:

> I suggest that something extraordinarily precious comes out of the close but entirely free association of really superior people. To this emergent quality I give the name—the heritage of excellence, mostly because it lasts so long and because it never comes from, nor appeals to, mediocrities....What more do men of superior character and capacity require for their association than freedom, responsibility and expectation? The wisdom of the university is to provide those three—freedom, responsibility and expectation. It is the interaction of such men that attracts great young men, leads to great living and itself lives on long afterwards as a heritage of excellence ready at any time to burst into bloom again.

Importantly, the heritage of excellence at Hopkins begins at the most formative stages: the selection of its medical students. The faculty always joked that to be a Hopkins medical student one not only had to have a straight A average and extraordinarily high board scores, but also had to be proficient in at least one musical instrument, demonstrate leadership capabilities, play a varsity NCAA sport, or pursue research during one's undergraduate education. I was always amazed by the fact that virtually every Hopkins medical student had incredible and unique talents. Thus, there was a self-selection for students who embodied a more universal view of humankind and who collectively displayed a passion for medicine, a love of science and learning, a dedication to service, and a commitment to collegiality [42].

But selection of its medical students was just one step in the pyramidal structure that led to those who would eventually teach the next generation of students. The next process of separating the wheat from the chaff occurred with the selection of the residents. A significant number of Hopkins residents came from Hopkins' own pool of students; others came from other programs around the country. Thus, there was a cultural continuum while at the same time providing opportunities to bring in individuals from different academic backgrounds.

A similar structure existed at the next level of separation: selection of individuals for fellowship training. Here, too, individuals were selected who clearly fit the vision of excellence and were clearly dedicated to the goal of providing the best possible care for patients. Finally, at the top of the selection pyramid was the selection of members of the faculty. Thus, through this pyramidal process, Hopkins has continuously repopulated its clinical, research, and teaching ranks with individuals firmly solidified in the culture of the institution and exemplars of the best of medical professionalism.

Although quality control is always an issue in any hospital, it is far easier to achieve at an institution such as Hopkins because of the homogeneity of the culture. Care that is below the level of "excellence" is simply not tolerated; therefore, horizontal accountability and peer pressure—rather than top-down mandates—facilitate continuous performance improvement. However, when there are lapses in professionalism, the presence of inter- and intradepartmental accountability, the institutional imperative to maintain the Hopkins culture, and courageous leaders able to take actions aimed at doing what is right for patient care ensure that the long-held precepts of always providing outstanding patient care are continuously met.

As the medical environment in the United States has changed, Hopkins has continued to modify its teaching programs in order to ensure that the institution maintains its ability to foster a special environment within which personal and professional growth can occur. Therefore, in 2005, the School of Medicine created a "learning community." A team made up of a large group of stakeholders, including students, faculty physician–teachers, and deans, established a program focused on achieving seven goals [43]:

fostering a welcoming and supportive community for students of diverse backgrounds;
promoting faculty advising and mentoring relationships with all students;
fostering social and cooperative connections between students;
assisting students in building networks within the medical school to meet their personal goals;
assembling a group of clinician role models who best exemplify excellence in humanism, professionalism, and the clinical skills of medicine;

encouraging scholarship and inquiry; and
providing career counseling.

In order to accomplish these goals, the students are separated into four colleges—each of which is named for extraordinary physicians and scientists who have walked the halls of Hopkins. A select group of 24 faculty members is hand-picked to serve as advisors of the various colleges based on the strength of their desire to be part of the program and an appreciation of the institutions' core values. Each advisor has a group of five students from each of the 4 years; he or she meets regularly with these students and teaches them in the "clinical skills" course. Importantly, each of the college faculty receives an additional 20% of his or her salary from the office of the dean in order to ensure that he or she is rewarded for the time spent in advising and teaching the members of the college.

Perhaps no story better describes the ethos of the Hopkins resident—and thus the culture of the institution—as well as an obituary of an Osler medical resident who died suddenly and tragically in March 2008 [44]:

> Beneath Priya's friendly smile was a gritty fighter and advocate. No one was more admirably possessive of their patients, no one more upset if anything interfered with her non-negotiable high standard of patient care. On a handful of occasions, I enjoyed a front row seat to her fierce advocacy. When she felt a new patient had been rushed to the floor without a necessary test, she shared her thoughts with the appropriate staff member in the transferring department, not to castigate but rather to ensure it would never happen again. If she felt a specialist needed to come to the hospital in the middle of the night to see one of her patients, she would make it happen, despite an often reluctant, sleepy consultant on the other end of the phone. It was a joy to watch her in action. She was one of the few who passed what I call the "mom" litmus test. She was the kind of physician, and more importantly the kind of person, I would want taking care of and advocating for my mother were she ever admitted to the hospital.

The attributes of this young resident were the very ones that passed as "an unbroken chain from the very beginning: Osler, Halsted, Welch, Kelly." As noted by a former Hopkins dean, they picked their successors and then they picked their successors and they picked their successors. So all the way, we are seeing the same heritage of excellence—the phrase Tommy Turner likes to use—that the original people had" [45].

Developing a Culture of Professionalism in the AMC

A great deal has been written about how AMCs can most effectively inculcate a culture of professionalism in their trainees and their faculty and in so doing improve society's view of the profession of medicine and improve the care of patients and the treatment of disease. The preceding discussions have illustrated some of the programs that have been carried out at America's top AMCs. However, many of these discussions have avoided some of the politically charged issues that can impede the ability of an AMC to change its culture effectively.

For example, they often presume that both hospital and medical school have the same goals and objectives, that department chairs can regulate the behavior of physicians at all of the institution's teaching facilities, and that there are no legal or political impediments to eradicating the hidden curriculum that obviates the ability to train students and residents appropriately and prevent the cynicism that erodes the professionalism of many healthcare centers. Thus, the recommendations discussed in the remaining sections of this chapter are not commonly discussed in the literature. However, all efforts at improving professionalism in an AMC have a common goal of excellence in patient care—a goal that few could argue with as an effective strategy for an AMC and one that is difficult to politicize.

Educate AMC Leaders Regarding How to Deal with Difficult Professionalism Issues

Because of the complexities involved with adjudicating quality in an AMC, physician leaders should be provided with a handbook and checklists that provide suggestions and strategies for dealing with problems that might arise. The problems that face AMC leaders—especially department chairs and division chiefs—are complex and no two situations are identical. However, AMCs and/ or national organizations can work to produce a handbook that will educate both new and established leaders regarding the potential pitfalls they will face in dealing with lapses in professionalism.

The availability of a checklist is also important because actions taken to protect the safety of patients must be taken expeditiously. The checklist should detail whom to call and what to do. AMC leaders must be fully informed of the potential consequences of their actions and must seek legal counsel before taking any potentially punitive actions. They should also be educated in how to deal with physicians who are impaired, perform at a less than acceptable level, or raise ethical concerns in their treatment of patients or their relationships with peers and staff. Physician leaders must also be intimately familiar with the hospital bylaws that govern physician behavior because these may not adequately list behaviors that are considered inconsistent with continued practice at an individual AMC.

Many actions may appear to warrant dismissal; however, if they are not formally written in the hospital's bylaws, it often becomes difficult to dismiss a staff member for violating them. Therefore, AMC leaders must be fully informed regarding the hospital's bylaws and, when the bylaws and the tenets of professionalism conflict, efforts should be made to change the bylaws before issues arise. Physician leaders must also be aware of the institutional commitments to indemnification because actions against a staff member can often result in litigation against the physician leader. In addition, physician leaders should be informed regarding the rules and regulations of state licensing bureaus, which may provide an alternative to the hospital in dealing with compromised physicians. All of these recommendations should be included in a training program for new academic leaders.

Develop Metrics to Assess Quality of Care and the Professionalism of Individual Caregivers

An important issue that limits the ability of academic physicians to adjudicate issues regarding quality of care and professionalism is their inability to measure "quality" effectively. As pointed out by Michael Porter and Elizabeth Teisberg in their book, *Redefining Health Care,* most of our current measures of quality are focused on process information or methods and on institution-wide measures rather than on the ability of a single physician or group of physicians effectively to treat disease acutely or over the entire life cycle of a patient [46]. For example, quality measures that hospitals routinely collect for patients hospitalized with congestive heart failure include only:

a notation of the patient's ejection fraction;
whether the patient was treated with specific medications, including an angiotensin-converting enzyme inhibitor and a beta blocker;
whether the patient received counseling about smoking cessation; and
whether the patient received educational materials about the disease.

If all of these criteria are met, the patient is assumed to have received excellent care. However, these markers of care are just one small part of the evaluation, diagnosis, and care of a patient with heart failure [47]. Thus, we must identify quality measures that can assess an individual physician's performance [48].

AMCs can also learn valuable lessons from the Cleveland Clinic. Since 1999, the clinic has publicly reported the clinical outcomes of its cardiac and thoracic surgery programs and, more recently, has reported the outcomes for most of its other clinical departments as well [49]. Interestingly, a 2005 survey of hospital administrators found that the vast majority were against public reporting of medical errors because of fears of increased lawsuits and the risk that less than expected results would result in the loss of patient volumes [50]. Thus, hospital leaders must be convinced that their success in the increasingly competitive healthcare environment will come only through their ability to document and market their ability to provide outstanding care [46].

A novel model for enhancing professionalism in medicine is the adoption at Hopkins of an "apology and disclosure program" for physicians and staff. Designed by Dr. Michael A. Williams, the program recognizes that all people are fallible; that, although errors occur, a good-faith effort should be made to avoid them; and that when a major error is made, it should be disclosed to the patient and the family [51]. Unfortunately, not all states preclude "apologies" from being included in medical malpractice cases [52].

Therefore, it is not surprising that many health systems in the United States do not reward, compensate, or encourage physicians who disclose errors. Hospitals often assign risk management to administrative managers rather than to physician managers or physician leaders—leading physicians to suspect that the health system has little or no interest in acknowledging or disclosing medical errors [53]. However, it can be argued that the willingness of the Cleveland Clinic and Hopkins to disclose their faults and their successes publicly is representative of some of the elements that have allowed them to evolve a culture of excellence.

Eliminate the "Hidden Curriculum" in AMCs

One of the largest challenges for AMC leaders—especially those with open staff models or who use affiliated hospitals to train medical students and residents—has been to ensure a homogeneity of excellence across all of the instructional areas and that the hidden curriculum does not negate the didactic instruction the students receive during their first 2 years of medical school. The hidden curriculum results in cynicism in medical students as they begin to recognize that some physicians do not show quality of care or commitment to the medical mission; therefore, it becomes critical that AMCs be able to hand-pick instructors that will serve as role models for students so that professionalism is ubiquitous throughout students' clinical experiences.

To do this, AMC leaders must put aside politics and economics and place the teaching of professionalism—and therefore the future quality of their workforce—as the primary goal of the institution. As the number of medical students at each of the current allopathic medical schools increases and new medical schools are developed using community hospitals as the base for clinical education, AMCs must work assiduously with scholars in the social sciences to develop objective criteria and metrics to identify capable teachers. In addition, AMC leaders must have the courage to exclude physicians from training programs when they fail to demonstrate an appropriate level of professionalism, and external review committees must look carefully at the teaching environment to ensure that a generation of cynical physicians will not be the result of the training.

Develop Multidisciplinary Teams to Evaluate Professionalism

It is important not only that various departments collaborate in the care of the patient, but also that they collaborate in quality improvement initiatives when an adverse event occurs. Too often, quality improvement initiatives exist in individual departments (e.g., M&M conferences), resulting in finger pointing when individuals are unable or unwilling to take responsibility for the adverse event. Even when the cause of the event is clear, the walls of the academic silos often preclude effective communications to ensure that issues of quality or professionalism have been addressed.

Therefore, peer review in today's academic center requires the development of multidisciplinary peer-review teams that parallel the interdisciplinary teams that work collaboratively to provide optimal patient care. Thus, just as information technology, case management, and social support systems must be centered on the patient rather than departments or cost centers, so too should quality of care initiatives be centered on the patient and his or her disease [46].

References

1. Hinohara, S., and Hisae, N., eds. 2001. *Osler's "A Way of Life" and other addresses with commentary and annotations,* 378. Durham, NC: Duke University Press.
2. Larson, E. B. 2007. Physicians should be civic professionals, not just knowledge workers. *American Journal of Medicine* 120 (11): 1005–1009.
3. Davidson, R. J. 1990. Viewpoint: Academic medical centers—It is time for a declaration of values. *Health Care Management Review* 15 (2): 81–85.
4. Stern, A. 2006. What is medical professionalism? In *Measuring medical professionalism,* ed. S. D. Arnold, 19. Oxford, England: Oxford University Press.
5. Sox, H. C. 2002. Medical professionalism in the new millennium: A physician charter. *Annals of Internal Medicine* 136:243.
6. Anderson, P. C. 1999. Mentoring. *Academic Medicine* 74 (1): 4–5.
7. ACGME. 1999. ACGME Outcome Project. General competencies (www.acgme.org/outcome/comp/compFull.asp).

8. Swick, H. M. 2000. Toward a normative definition of medical professionalism. *Academic Medicine* 75 (6): 612–616.
9. Inui, T. S. 2003. A flag in the wind: Educating for professionalism in medicine. AAMC.
10. Hafferty, F. W., and Franks, R. 1994. The hidden curriculum, ethics teaching, and the structure of medical education. *Academic Medicine* 69 (11): 861–871.
11. Goldie, J., Schwartz, L., McConnachie, A., and Morrison, J. 2004. The impact of a modern medical curriculum on students' proposed behavior on meeting ethical dilemmas. *Medical Education* 38 (9): 942–949.
12. Wachtler, C., and Troein, M. 2003. A hidden curriculum: Mapping cultural competency in a medical program. *Medical Education* 37 (10): 861–868.
13. Pierluissi, E., Fischer, M. A., Campbell, A. R., and Landefeld, C. S. 2003. Discussion of medical errors in morbidity and mortality conferences. *Journal of the American Medical Association* 290 (21): 2838–2842.
14. Gladman, M. 2009. The future for peer review. *Trustee Magazine* December.
15. Uhlig, P. 2002. Joint commission. *Journal on Quality Improvement* 12:666–672.
16. Uhlig, P. N., Brown, J., Nason, A. K., Camelio, A., and Kendall, E. 2002. John M. Eisenberg Patient Safety Awards. System innovation: Concord Hospital. *Communications Journal of Quality Improvement* 28 (12): 666–672.
17. American College of Emergency Physicians. 2003. Disclosure of medical errors: Policy statement (www.acep.org/webportal/practiceresources/policystatements/ethics/disclosuremedicalerrors.htm).
18. Campbell, E. G., Regan, S., Gruen, R. L., Ferris, T. G., Sowmya, R. R., Cleary, P. D., and Blumenthal, D. 2007. Professionalism in medicine: Results of a national survey of physicians. *Annals of Internal Medicine* 147 (11): 795–802.
19. Appeal from the Order of the Superior Court entered on March 21, 2005 at no. 1042 EDA 2004. J-33-2006, No. 46 EAP 2005. Decided May 31, 2007. *American Future Systems, Inc. DBA Progressive Business Publication v. Better Business Bureau of Eastern Pennsylvania and Better Business Bureau of Metropolitan Washington.*
20. Zielbauer, P. 2000. Doctors sue Yale, saying cost cuts hurt patients and complaints led to backlash. *New York Times,* April 30.
21. Quizon, D. 2006. Professor files lawsuit. *The California Aggie,* May 8.
22. Geballe, N. 2001. Pair of doctors sue Stanford and hospital chief for libel. *The Stanford Daily,* April 19.
23. Wasserstein, A. G., Brennan, P. J., and Rubenstein, A. 2007. Institutional leadership and faculty response: Fostering professionalism at the University of Pennsylvania School of Medicine, *Academic Medicine* (82): 1049–1056.
24. Humphrey, H. J., Smith, K., Reddy, S., Scott, D., Madara, J. L., and Arora, V. M. 2007. Promoting an environment of professionalism: The University of Chicago "roadmap." *Academic Medicine* 82 (11): 1098–1107.
25. Kalet, A. L., Sanger, J., Chase, J., and Keller, A. 2007. Promoting professionalism through an online professional development portfolio: Successes, joys, and frustrations. *Academic Medicine* 82 (11): 1065–1072.
26. Brater, D. C. 2007. Viewpoint: Infusing professionalism into a school of medicine: Perspectives from the dean. *Academic Medicine* 82 (11): 1094–1097.

27. Litzelman, D. K., and Cottingham, A. H. 2007. The new formal competency-based curriculum and informal curriculum at Indiana University School of Medicine: Overview and five-year analysis. *Academic Medicine* 82 (4): 410–421.
28. Hickson, G. B., Pichert, J. W., Webb, L. E., and Gabbe, S. G. 2007. A complementary approach to promoting professionalism: Identifying, measuring, and addressing unprofessional behaviors. *Academic Medicine* 82 (11): 1040–1048.
29. Govern, P. 2005. Plan turns complaints into opportunities. *Reporter,* Vanderbilt Medical Center, Sept. 16.
30. History of Mayo Clinic (www.diavlos.gr/orto96/ortowww/historym.htm).
31. Mayo, W. 2000. The necessity of cooperation in medicine. *Mayo Clinic Proceedings* 75:553–536.
32. Viggiano, T. R., Pawlina, W., Lindor, K. D., Olsen, K. D., and Cortese, D. A. 2007. Putting the needs of the patient first: Mayo Clinic's core value, institutional culture, and professionalism covenant. *Academic Medicine* 82 (11): 1089–1093.
33. Costopoulos, M. G., Mikhail, M. A., Wennberg, P. W., Rooke, T. W., and Moutlon, L. L. 2002. A new hospital patient care model for the new millennium: Preliminary Mayo Clinic experience. *Archives of Internal Medicine* 162:716–718.
34. Berry, L., and Seltman, K. D. 2007. *Building a strong service brand: Lessons from Mayo Clinic.* Cambridge, MA: Harvard Business Publishing.
35. Bendapudi, N., Berry, L. L., Frey, G. A., Parish, J. T., and Rayburn, W. L. 2006. Patients' perspectives on ideal physician behaviors. *Mayo Clinic Proceedings* 81 (3): 338–344.
36. Berry, L. L., and Seltman, K. D. 2008. *Management lessons from Mayo Clinic: Inside one of the world's most advanced service organizations.* New York: McGraw–Hill Companies, 256 pp.
37. Collins, J. 2001. *Good to great,* 300. New York: Harper Collins Publishers Inc.
38. Bossidy, L., and Charan, R. 2002. *Execution—The discipline of getting things done,* 269. New York: Crown Publishing Group.
39. Folsom, N., Jones, J., Morris, C., and Smith, S. 1875. Letter of Johns Hopkins to the trustees. In *Hospital plans,* 353. New York: William Wood & Co.
40. Tucker, A. 1973. *It happened at Hopkins—A teaching hospital,* 283. Baltimore, MD: The Johns Hopkins Hospital on behalf of the *Johns Hopkins Medical Journal.*
41. Greg, A. 1950. Dr. Welch's influence on medical education. Johns Hopkins Hospital Supplement 87:28.
42. www.hopkinsmedcine.org/admissions/chooses.html
43. Stewart, R. 2007. The new and improved learning community at Johns Hopkins University resembles that at Hogwart's School of Witchcraft and Wizardry. *Medical Teacher* 29:353–357.
44. Munoz, D. 2008. Remembering Priya. *Hopkins Medicine* Spring–summer: 59.
45. Warren, M. 2000. *Johns Hopkins, knowledge for the world: 1876–2001.* Baltimore, MD: the Johns Hopkins University Press.
46. Porter, M. E., and Teisberg, E. O. 2006. *Redefining health care: Creating value-based competition on results.* Boston: Harvard Business School Press, 506 pp.

47. Hunt, S. A. 2005. ACC/AHA 2005 guideline update for the diagnosis and management of chronic heart failure in the adult: A report of the American College of Cardiology/American Heart Association Task Force on Practice Guidelines (writing committee to update the 2001 guidelines for the evaluation and management of heart failure). *Journal of the American College of Cardiologists* 46 (6): e1–82.

48. Kassirer, J. P. 1994. The use and abuse of practice profiles. *New England Journal of Medicine* 330 (9): 634–636.

49. Cleveland Clinic—Heart & Vascular Institute. 2008. Outcomes 2007. Cleveland, OH: the Cleveland Clinic Foundation.

50. Weissman, J. S., Annas, C. L., Epstein, A. M., Schneider, E. C., Clarridge, B., Kirle, L., Gatsonis, C., Feibelmann, S., and Ridley, N. 2005. Error reporting and disclosure systems: Views from hospital leaders. *Journal of the American Medical Association* 293 (11): 1359–1366.

51. Avitzur, O. 2006. Why an apology goes a long way when medical errors occur. *Neurology Today* 6:16–19.

52. Dresser, R. 2008. The limits of apology law. *Hastings Center Report* 38:6–7.

53. Moskop, J. C., Geiderman, J. M., Hobgood, C. D., and Larkin, G. L. 2006. Emergency physicians and disclosure of medical errors. *Annals of Emergency Medicine* 48 (5): 523–531.

SPHERE OF ACTION: BUSINESS

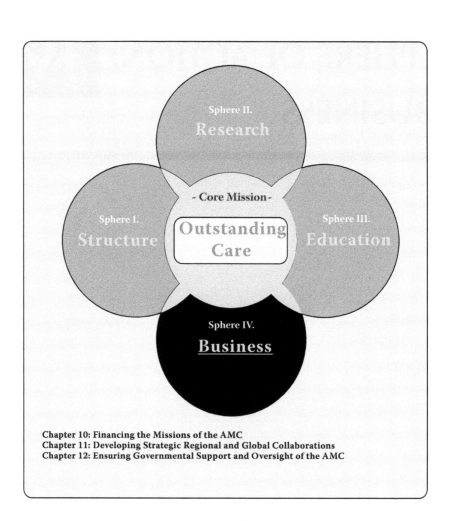

- Core Mission -

Outstanding Care

Sphere II.
Research

Sphere I.
Structure

Sphere III.
Education

Sphere IV.
Business

Chapter 10

Financing the Missions of the AMC

> In these schools an annual balance to the good is obtained for distribution by slighting general equipment, by overworking laboratory teachers, by wholly omitting certain branches, by leaving certain departments relatively underdeveloped or by resisting any decided elevation of standards.
>
> **Abraham Flexner, 1910** [1]

Introduction

In his landmark study of America's medical schools, Abraham Flexner found a relationship between finances and the quality of education. Indeed, he noted that "as it is clear that there is no justification just now for the existence of medical schools that are incapable of greatly bettering the type, it follows that schools unable or indisposed to spend the requisite sums lack a valid reason for being" [1]. Today, many AMCs are financially challenged due to marked changes in the healthcare marketplace, including decreased reimbursements for clinical care, increased competition from community hospitals, and decreased NIH funding [2–4]. In some cases, financial crises have threatened the very existence of AMCs. As a result, AMCs must focus not only on their academic missions but also on the "business of medicine" because "without a margin there can be no mission."

That AMCs were significantly challenged by their financial environment first came to public attention in 1998 when the Allegheny Health, Education, and Research Foundation (AHERF), owner of the Medical College of Pennsylvania-Hahnemann University (MCPH), declared bankruptcy—the first AMC in the history of the United States to do so [5]. The AHERF bankruptcy was just one of many pieces of evidence supporting the tenuous financial situation of AMCs. For example, from 2002 to 2003, 20 U.S. medical schools self-reported a decrease in total revenues, nearly half reported a decrease in practice plan revenues, and over half reported a decrease in support from their affiliated hospitals [6]. Financial shortfalls have occurred at academic hospitals in geographic locales as diverse as Texas, Boston, and New York [7–11].

Fearing that losses in their hospitals would affect their endowments, the University of Minnesota, George Washington University, Tulane University, Georgetown University, St. Louis University, the University of Southern California, the University of Oklahoma, and others sold their hospitals to for-profit entities. Jefferson Medical College, Medical College of Georgia, University of Indiana, University of Kansas, University of Nebraska, University of Oregon, and the University of Wisconsin changed the teaching hospital governance from common university ownership to a private nonprofit or independent authority [12].

In 2008, decreases in funding from the Detroit Medical Center resulted in Wayne State laying off both doctors and staff and threatened the very existence of the medical school [13]. The University of Tennessee Health Science Center in Memphis was described as "sick, suffering from aging infrastructure, an inability to pull in top job candidates and dwindling state funds" [14]. Needing a modern teaching hospital to replace its outdated 224-bed John Dempsey Hospital, the University of Connecticut Health Center reported that it would likely close the fiscal year with a $22 million deficit [15]. The University of Medicine and Dentistry of New Jersey announced that it would not renew the contracts of 18 pediatricians due to a "fiscal crisis" arising from a "large budget deficit" [16].

Reacting to these financial changes, Moody's and Standard & Poor's lowered the credit rating of many academic hospitals and healthcare systems, making it more difficult for them to borrow money [12]. Indeed, these many financial difficulties led some experts to suggest that AMCs "cut back on expensive research, teaching activities, and clinical innovations, or face growing deficits and in some cases, extinction" [17]. The financial meltdown in the fall of 2008 also negatively affected the finances of almost all AMCs as endowment payouts fell precipitously, the number of uninsured patients increased, and patients deferred elective procedures. Indeed, virtually every major AMC announced efforts to decrease expenditures, including staff layoffs, salary freezes, and hiring freezes.

This chapter will review the challenges to evaluating the financial health of an individual AMC, describe the traditional revenue sources of the AMC and how they have changed in recent times, illustrate how some AMCs have developed novel entrepreneurial strategies to build new financial opportunities, and provide recommendations about how AMCs can improve their financial health.

Challenges to Evaluating the Financial Health of an AMC

Unlike public companies, the financial performance of an academic health center is rarely transparent. As a result, understanding the financial health of any given AMC can be challenging if not problematic. Funds often flow among the medical school, the hospital, and the faculty practice plan in a nontransparent fashion. In addition, some AMCs have a diverse array of nonmedical businesses, which can include health insurance companies, real estate firms, sports training facilities, assisted living and retirement communities, and biotechnology incubators or research parks. These businesses may cross-subsidize losses in the clinical operations of the hospital or in the medical school, although this is not obvious on the balance sheet.

Analyzing the financial structure of a single AMC or comparing the financial health of different AMCs is also made difficult because there are no common reporting structures [18]. AMC financial reporting can fall into three categories: the minimalist approach, the intermediate approach, and the comprehensive approach [18]. Even though comprehensive reporting provides the most detailed assessment of the overall financial health of an AMC, it provides no information about the performance of the various parts of the organization. For example, between 1997 and 1999, the hospital division of the University of Pittsburgh Medical Center reported cumulative operating profits of approximately $88 million. However, losses in the nonhospital divisions—physician practices, insurance products, and their various operations, including nursing homes, strategic businesses, and a sports complex—resulted in an overall operating loss for the system [19].

It is also important to note that no AMC falls directly into a specific reporting structure and that the various components of a given AMC may have different ways of reporting their financial performance. This is particularly true when the hospital and the medical school are not integrated, as well as when parts of the academic hospital are "owned" by outside interests.

The ability to understand the financial underpinnings of AMCs is also compromised because, as nonprofit institutions, they are not responsible for public disclosure of financial information [20]. The major sources of financial information are Medicare cost reports, surveys by the American Hospital Association and the Association of American Medical Colleges, IRS form 990, and audited financial statements. Each source is focused on the hospital rather than the medical school and all have limitations:

- Medicare cost reports do not provide enough information to allow investigators to adjust for differences in reporting practices and do not include information about investment income, commercial properties, or partnering hospitals [20].
- The American Hospital Association and the Association of American Medical Colleges provide important data on the average finances at AMCs; however, they do not provide information to the public regarding individual hospitals or individual medical schools and the information is self-reported.
- IRS form 990, the annual report to the Internal Revenue Service, can be obtained by the public at www.gidestar.org; however, the reports generally relate to the organization with the tax identification number—usually a single hospital or hospital affiliate.
- Audited financial statements are produced by all private nonprofit hospitals and most publicly owned hospitals; however, only some states require these statements to be publicly accessible, they are filed by the hospital alone, and the data are only available after a substantial lag time.

Thus, it is very difficult for economists to study AMC finances and to create new strategies to improve the economics of healthcare at an AMC.

Traditional Sources of AMC Revenue

To understand the financial health of America's AMCs, it is important to understand the major sources of their financial support. In fiscal year 2005, the LCME 1-A annual financial questionnaire showed that the 124 reporting medical schools received 37% of their revenues from their faculty practice plan, 24% from federal grants and contracts, 12% from their associated hospital and medical school programs, 8% from nonfederal grants and contracts, 6% from state and local appropriations, 4% from gifts and endowments, 3% from tuitions and fees, and 6% from miscellaneous sources [21].

For the 75 of the 124 medical schools that were publicly supported, 34% of their revenues came from the faculty practice plan, 23% from federal grants and contracts, 12% from the hospital and medical school programs, 7% from nonfederal grants and contracts, 12% from state and local appropriations, 3% from gifts and endowments, 3% from tuition and fees, and 6% from miscellaneous sources. By contrast, the 49 private medical schools received 41% of their revenues from the faculty practice plan. Thus, returns on patient care make up the most significant source of revenue for an AMC. By looking at the following areas of revenue support, we can learn more about the financial condition of an AMC and see where the most obvious problems and challenges exist.

Reimbursements for Clinical Care

Like community hospitals and physician practice groups, AMCs receive reimbursement for the care they provide from private health insurers, the government, state health insurance programs for the care of children, and direct payments from patients. A comprehensive discussion of healthcare financing is outside the scope of this book; comprehensive reviews can be found in several excellent texts, as well as in government reports [22–25]. However, it is relevant to understand the different types of reimbursements for care and how each has changed over the past decade.

Private Health Insurance

Most Americans pay for their healthcare using some form of private health insurance. The majority of private health insurance is obtained through employer-sponsored plans because private health insurance for an individual is extremely expensive and difficult to obtain when preexisting medical problems are present. There are two types of private health coverage: state-licensed health insurance organizations and self-funded employee health benefit plans [26]. State-licensed health insuring organizations include:

commercial health insurers, which are usually publicly traded companies or mutual insurance companies by the policy holders;

Blue Cross and Blue Shield plans, which were originally organized as not-for-profit organizations under state laws but more recently have begun to shift toward a for-profit model; and

health maintenance organizations (HMOs), which operate as both insurers and healthcare providers.

Prominent examples of state-licensed HMOs include Kaiser Permanente and Harvard Pilgrim [26]. By contrast with state-licensed health insuring organizations, self-funded employee health benefit plans operate under federal law and are sponsored by employers, employee organizations, or a combination of the two. These plans often contract with third parties to administer the plans, including health insurers or HMOs. Private health insurers negotiate reimbursements with individual AMCs; very different reimbursement rates are found in different states and even among different AMCs in the same city. For example, a colleague from a large Midwestern AMC noted that his group received reimbursements from its Blue Cross Blue Shield carrier that were 180% of Medicare, whereas another colleague noted his institution received reimbursements at only 120% of Medicare. Unfortunately, these differences are only recognized through conversations with leaders at other institutions; they are difficult to document and therefore create confusion about how AMCs are actually reimbursed.

Managed Care Organizations

Healthcare in the latter part of the twentieth century was marked by the entry of "managed care" into the health insurance market place. Managed care has been defined as a "system that uses financial incentives and management controls to direct patients to providers who are responsible for giving appropriate, cost-effective care.…Managed care systems are intended to control the cost of healthcare by emphasizing prevention, early intervention and outpatient care" [27]. A somewhat simpler definition was provided by Barton: "In managed care, both patient utilization and provider practices are managed by an entity that has fiduciary interest in the interaction between them" [28].

Over the past years, a variety of managed care organizations has arisen in the United States [22,29]. Each has a different organizational structure and has both disadvantages and advantages; however, defining the category into which an individual managed care plan falls is often difficult. As of 2006, 93% of working Americans who were not on Medicare and had health insurance were enrolled in some type of managed care plan—a finding in marked contrast to 1988, when only 3% of workers with health insurance were enrolled in managed care [22]. Managed care seeks aggressively to control costs, so patients enrolled in managed care plans are often directed to community hospitals because the plans are unwilling to reimburse at the higher cost levels found at AMCs.

Self-Pay, Medicare, and Medicaid

When patients pay for medical care themselves, the fees they pay are referred to as "out-of-pocket expenditures." These expenditures may cover the entire cost of the service or a part of the service, or they may represent a fixed "deductible," which is an out-of-pocket expense that must be paid for any health services rendered over a specific period of time. When hospitals or doctors provide care without reimbursement, the care is referred to as "charity care" or "forgiven debts." If healthcare costs are paid for by an entity other than the patient or the provider of the care, the entity paying for the care is referred to as the "third-party payer."

Government spending for healthcare comes in the form of Medicare and Medicaid. Medicare, the first national social insurance program, was established by Congress in 1965 as part of President Lyndon Johnson's "Great Society" program [25]. Originally, individuals who were 65 years of age or older were eligible for Medicare; however, coverage was later broadened to include the permanently disabled and their dependents as well as persons with end-stage renal disease. Medicare has four parts: Part A provides hospital insurance; Part B covers physician and other professional services; Part C permits Medicare beneficiaries to enroll in managed care organizations; and Part D provides prescription drug coverage. Hospitals are reimbursed from Medicare on an episode-of-care basis; the amount of each payment is determined by a formula based on the so-called "diagnosis-related group" (DRG) [22].

Authorized by Title XIX of the Social Security Act, Medicaid was also begun in 1965 with the goal of providing healthcare services for some of the country's poor; eligibility is determined by the individual's level of income [30]. Medicaid, unlike Medicare, is administered by the states and is supported by federal and state tax dollars. In many states, a combination of strict eligibility requirements and low fees paid to providers has limited the role of Medicaid. In 2003, Medicaid covered 17% of all personal healthcare spending and 55 million people received some level of Medicaid coverage. However, the group of patients who have too much income to be eligible for Medicaid but not enough income to pay for private health insurance makes up the bulk of the nearly 50 million individuals in the United States who have no healthcare coverage and receive much of their healthcare from AMCs [22].

Decreasing Reimbursements for Clinical Care

Increased Number of Patients without Insurance

The 2006 census demonstrated that over 47 million Americans, representing 16% of the U.S. population, had no health insurance [31]. It has been estimated that the 126 AMCs care for between 40% and 60% of the nation's uninsured [32]. The effect of the increasing number of uninsured patients can be seen by looking at the finances of the AMCs in Chicago. Northwestern, University of

Chicago, and Rush University Medical Center had net profits in 2007 of $142 million, $140 million, and $120 million, respectively; the Loyola University Medical Center, University of Illinois Medical Center, and the John H. Strogen, Jr., Hospital of Cook County reported net profits of $31 million, $3.1 million, and $19.1 million, respectively [33].

The marked disparity in revenues accrued by these academic medical centers was due, at least in part, to the level of charity care that they provided. In 2006 Northwestern Memorial spent $20.8 million on charity care—less than 2% of its revenues and a fraction of what it received in tax breaks as a nonprofit hospital [34]. By contrast, Chicago's Cook County Hospital, a teaching affiliate of Rush Medical School, spent 14% of its revenues on charity care. Thus, as a result of these differences in payer mix, "some nonprofit hospitals, particularly ones in inner cities that handle large numbers of uninsured patients, remain under financial strain and are struggling to keep their doors open" [34]. The disparity could threaten the ability of AMCs with smaller margins to provide outstanding patient care in all clinical areas and represents another case of the presence of haves and have-nots among the various AMCs.

Cuts in Medicare Funding

Since the Balanced Budget Act of 1997, there have been continuous refinements and further cuts in Medicare spending—all of which have in one way or another harmed the AMC and resulted in negative operating margins at a substantial number of teaching hospitals [35]. Whether the cuts in Medicare affect AMCs differently when compared with community hospitals has been a contentious question. However, careful analysis demonstrates that the revenues of an AMC are affected to a greater degree by Medicare reductions than are those of community hospitals [36]. Because AMCs often have a lower percentage of Medicare patients than do community hospitals, the balance sheet looks the same for both types of institutions. However, if the AMC has a proportion of Medicare patients greater than or equal to that of a community hospital, its operating margins would be substantially less.

Nonetheless, continued cuts and threatened cuts in Medicare reimbursements make AMCs more vulnerable to financial changes. Indeed, the 10.6% cuts in reimbursements that were only reversed at the last minute by congressional actions in the fall of 2008 would have had an enormous negative impact on AMCs. Academic medical centers have also raised concerns about the fact that reimbursements vary considerably across different states.

Perhaps the most important difference between physicians in community practices and AMC physicians is that academic clinicians cannot decline to provide care to Medicare patients, whereas physicians in private practice can do so without recrimination [37]. Thus, although the effects of Medicare reductions are thought to be similar for major teaching hospitals and nonteaching hospitals, the decreases have further exacerbated ongoing financial strains at the academic health centers [36].

Cuts in Medicaid Reimbursements

The government has substantially cut not only Medicare funding but also the budget for Medicaid. These cuts in Medicaid have been especially painful for safety net hospitals, many of which are associated with AMCs. Public hospitals have closed in Los Angeles, Washington, D.C., St. Louis, and Milwaukee; those in Miami, Memphis, and Chicago have been challenged by increasing financial woes. In March 2008, a coalition led by the National Association of Public Hospitals and Health Systems, the American Hospital Association, and the Association of American Medical Colleges filed suit in federal court to prevent the Bush administration from implementing a proposed Medicaid regulation that would cut $5 billion in funding to so called safety net hospitals [38].

Although viewed as a health insurance plan for the poor, Medicaid also funds highly specialized programs, including trauma centers, burn units, and emergency preparedness programs. As noted by Darrell G. Kirch, president and CEO of the AAMC [38]:

> Many public hospitals provide critical services that support both local and regional communities. The loss of Medicaid funds may threaten this critical infrastructure. Whether it's a bus crash, a fire or a terrorist incident, without these Medicaid funds, public hospitals will be less able to help people when they most need our highly specialized services.

Many if not most of these public hospitals serve as teaching sites for AMCs (Bellevue Hospital in Manhattan, Boston City Hospital, Charity Hospital in New Orleans, and Cook County Hospital in Chicago). Thus, federal cuts in Medicaid spending also adversely affect the AMC with which the hospitals are affiliated because faculty salaries often are supported by public hospitals, which serve as important training sites for students and residents.

The plight of Grady Memorial Hospital in Atlanta, an old and venerable teaching hospital staffed by physicians from Emory University School of Medicine and Morehouse School of Medicine, is representative of the problems faced by safety net hospitals. Grady has faced imminent closure as a result of increasing costs of medical care and the constant threat of cuts in federal support [39]. With 675 beds, 16 operating rooms, one of the country's largest AIDS clinics, a dialysis unit, and a 24-hour emergency center for sickle cell anemia, Grady supports over 850,000 outpatient visits a year and admits more than 30,000 inpatients [39].

A third of Grady's patients have Medicaid, a third have no insurance at all, and many come from the growing illegal immigrant population of Atlanta. Fulton County had to cut its subsidy to the Grady emergency medical service, the only emergency ambulance fleet in Atlanta. With the 2008 budget gap projected to be $52 million and an accumulated debt of $71 million, Grady was ready to close until it was rescued by $24 million from the state to support the trauma program for 1 year, an increase in Medicaid reimbursement rates from the state, and, most importantly, a $200 million gift from the Woodruff Foundation, the largest gift on record to a single public hospital [40]. Thus, philanthropy and state support allowed Grady to continue to care for Atlanta's poor.

Federal Disproportionate Share Payments

AMCs in underserved areas receive disproportionate share payments (DSH) intended to offset the increased number of uninsured patients for which AMCs care. However, few data are available to identify whether the DSH is adequate or inadequate to support the costs of care in the AMC. Interpreting the data is difficult because some hospitals include only direct costs for patient care in their assessment of "costs," whereas others include everything from depreciation to malpractice insurance and the expenses for the hospital gift shop.

The University of Michigan Health System performed a cost-per-case calculation for the fiscal year 1997 and found that its average cost per case was $565 more than the average cost per case for comparable academic teaching hospitals in the United States and $1,630 more than average cost per case for nonteaching hospitals in southeast Michigan [41]. One explanation for the disparity was that 15% of the patients at Michigan had been transferred from another hospital for advanced treatment at the AMC.

DSH payments also vary from year to year based on the whims of federal funding [42]; they also vary from state to state [43]. Average costs per primary care resident ranged from $43,707 in North Dakota to $93,072 in New York. Indeed, the difference in dollars from the highest to the lowest amount per primary care resident within each of 11 states was greater than $100,000. In California, one teaching hospital reported costs that were more than 12 times those of another teaching hospital.

Of even greater concern was the fact that there was no relationship between the costs and the number of primary care health personnel shortage areas (PCHPSAs) in a given region. Thus, states with an overabundance of physicians could receive more support than states with a lack of primary care physicians. Taken together, these findings suggest that AMCs receive no incentive for training physicians for a practice in underserved areas and that there is a financial incentive to train residents to practice in areas that have relatively less need for their services [43].

Federal Support for Research

Because at least a quarter of the dollars that support the overhead of American medical schools comes from federal grants and contracts, the recent cutbacks in NIH funding have had an enormous impact on AMC finances. As was pointed out in an earlier chapter, NIH funding for research increased twofold in absolute dollars between 1998 and 2003—from over $9 billion in 1998 to over $16 billion in 2002 [44]. However, when analyzed based on the value of a dollar, the increase in dollars was only 5%. Since 2003, the NIH budget has remained flat. As a result, when adjusted for inflation and the value of the dollar, NIH funding has actually decreased over the period from 2003 to 2008 [45].

The decrease in NIH funding has been especially troublesome for AMCs that began to increase their laboratory space with new construction during the boom years between 1998 and 2003 but were unable to support construction costs through increased indirect cost revenues when NIH funding flattened beginning in 2003 [45,46]. For private medical schools that depend on either operating expenses or endowments (versus state support) to cover the debt service on new buildings, the consequences of overbuilding were potentially enormous, particularly because the slowdown in NIH funding shows no signs of abating.

When NIH funding first flattened 5 years ago, the group that suffered the most was composed of medical schools that had smaller research portfolios and fewer alternative resources for research funding—including endowments, lucrative for-profit entities, substantial health system margins, or income streams from patent royalties. The elite institutions were also better able to cope with a downturn because many of the applications submitted by their scientists had historically received priority scores that placed them in the top 10th percentile. However, as the NIH downturn has continued for nearly 6 years, even universities with large NIH portfolios have begun to suffer because young investigators tend to score lower on their initial grant applications, all investigators are submitting more grants even within a single funding period, and the general economic environment has also suffered a downturn.

At Duke, an institution ranked second in NIH funding, the medical school has responded to funding shortfalls by creating a bridge funding program that provides up to $100,000 to support researchers whose grant proposals are not approved [47]. However, even at Duke, individual faculty members have been adversely affected by the downturn [47]. Thus, the flat funding at the NIH is having an adverse affect on all AMCs—an effect that doubling the NIH budget over the next 10 years (as proposed by the Democratic platform for the November 2008 election) will not mitigate. The recent allocation of $10 billion from the Congressional Stimulus Package to the NIH will also have a positive impact in the short term. However, it is unclear how the NIH budget will change once the 2-year window of stimulus package support has ended.

Hospital/Health System Support to the Medical School

Some, but not all, academic medical centers receive support from the hospital or hospitals with which they are affiliated. Unfortunately, these data are proprietary and, of the data that do exist, much is anecdotal. In the past year, it has been reported through the press as well as through personal communication that some hospitals have provided substantive support for their academic mission. For example, the University of Pittsburgh Medical Center Health System contributed approximately $167 million to the academic missions of the University of Pittsburgh School of Medicine in 2007, and the Duke Health System gave a gift of $30 million per year to the School of Medicine over a period of 10 years. Some hospitals, including the Barnes-Jewish in St. Louis, share positive margins with the academic physician group that provides care in the hospital.

No information is available about medical schools that receive no support for research and other academic missions from their affiliated hospitals, although one would assume that support for the academic mission is far less prevalent among hospitals and medical schools that are not administratively or economically linked. For these hospitals, a combination of the Stark law, anti-kickback laws, and other legal impediments makes it very difficult to transfer funds from the hospital to the academic missions of the medical school. Obviously, the many AMC hospitals that do not have substantial operating margins also find it problematic to support the academic missions of the AMC—again giving rise to the AMC haves and have-nots.

AMC Support from State and Local Entities

For state-supported AMCs, financial revenue comes from state and local resources. Like other financial resources, enormous variations can be seen across different institutions and different states. Intuitively, one might assume that it would be easier to follow the flow of state dollars to the AMC than dollars from other sources; however, like most of the financial underpinnings of the AMC, the funds flow pathway is often opaque. In November 2006, the state of Connecticut commissioned a study to assess the general fund appropriations for operating expenses to AMCs from seven other states that, like Connecticut, supported centers owned and governed by the state university: Virginia, Pennsylvania, Missouri, Iowa, Arkansas, New Jersey, and Texas [48]. State appropriations to these different institutions varied widely:

University of Virginia Medical Center: $0;
Penn State Medical Center: $0.80 million;
University of Missouri, Columbia: $13.135 million (education and research costs included in university operating budget);
University of Iowa Hospitals and Clinic: $27.29 million (hospital and clinics only);
University of Connecticut Health Center: $76.92 million;
University of Arkansas Medical Sciences: $87.80 million;
New Jersey Medical and Dental University: $233.38 million (state also paid $159.8 million in fringe benefits for faculty and staff); and
University of Texas, Galveston: $297.95 million.

The marked disparities in state funding to public medical centers were further illustrated by the fact that only three states—Minnesota, Texas, and Louisiana—dedicated funds from a specific source to their AMCs:

Minnesota dedicates 6.5 cents of its 48 cent per pack cigarette tax to the University of Minnesota. In fiscal year 2007, Minnesota tax statutes credited $22.25 million per year to a special revenue fund and appropriated that amount to the university's regents for the benefit of the AMC. Minnesota also dedicated money to a medical education and research costs fund to compensate hospitals and clinics, including the University of Minnesota School of Medicine, for part of their clinical education costs. These funds came from a combination of general fund appropriations, Medicaid funds, and tobacco settlement money.
Texas also uses its tobacco settlement revenue to capitalize endowment funds. For example, it dedicated $595 million to establish 13 endowment funds for medical schools. In fiscal year 2005, the Texas legislature appropriated $9 million of these funds to the University of Texas Health Center in San Antonio, $4.5 million to the M. D. Anderson Cancer Center in Houston, and $2.250 million to the UT Southwestern Medical Center in Dallas.
Louisiana dedicates 12 cents from its 36 cent per pack cigarette tax to a tobacco tax healthcare fund with 48.2% going to the cancer research center at the Louisiana State University Health Sciences Center in New

Orleans and 28% to the cancer center at the Louisiana State University Health Sciences Center in Shreveport.

Pennsylvania dedicates dollars from the tobacco settlement to support research; however, these dollars do not support AMCs exclusively and are tied to the total number of NIH dollars for each state institution. Thus, in Pennsylvania, medical centers already rich in NIH support benefit to a much greater degree than do institutions with smaller NIH portfolios.

Federal Support for Graduate Medical Education (Residents and Fellows)

Another important source of income for AMCs is the dollars that flow to them in support of graduate medical education (GME). Support for GME began in 1965 when the federal government recognized the importance of GME in providing high quality of care for Medicare beneficiaries [49]. These payments have been divided into two portions: the direct medical education (DME) payment and the indirect medical education (IME) adjustment. DME payment covers salaries and fringe benefits of residents, salaries and overhead costs of supervising faculty, the costs of administering the GME program, and institutional overhead costs.

In 1985, the Consolidated Omnibus Budget Reconciliation Act established a payment scale for GME based on a base-year expense from the hospital's cost report from either FY 1985 or FY 1986. Payments remained largely the same, with the exception of adjustments for the consumer price index, until 1999, when the Balanced Budget Refinement Act substantially changed the payment structure for DME by establishing a weighted national average per resident DME payment [50].

Other congressional legislation has had dramatic effects on GME funding. For example, in 1985, the Consolidated Omnibus Budget Reconciliation Act limited payments to the length of training necessary to achieve primary board certification in the chosen field of study, with subsequent subspecialty training being financed at a 50% rate. The Omnibus Budget Reconciliation Act of 1993 (PL 103-66) eliminated payment increases to account for inflation in fiscal years 1994 and 1995 in all specialties, with the exception of primary care. Finally, the Balanced Budget Act of 1997 (PL 105-33) placed a "cap" on the number of residents in training on December 31, 1996, or from the hospital's cost report for the previous fiscal year. Thus, with reimbursement based on the number of residents at a hospital at the end of 1996, it has become increasingly difficult for AMCs to adjust their resident staff to changing needs or demographics.

A part of GME funding is allocated to support the efforts of the physicians who oversee the activities of the trainees. These activities were not well regulated in the 1980s and early 1990s; however, Medicare published strict criteria in 1996. They stipulated that, to receive payment for teaching, a teaching physician must have no other clinical or administrative responsibilities while supervising residents, be responsible for the management of the patients and assure that all actions are appropriate, review the resident's plan at the time of the patient visit, and document his or her role in providing care to the patient [51].

In addition, for the care of complex patients, the teaching physician must be present, must participate in the delivery of care, and must document this participation. The ACGME, the organization that oversees and accredits all training programs, mandated an increase in the number of teaching physicians who must oversee each group of medical residents, effective July 2009; however, GME funding did not increase, resulting in the hospital or the medical school supporting the increased cost.

Despite the fact that federal funding for GME has been reduced substantially over the past few years, AMCs still receive nearly $6 billion annually from Medicare alone for the support of residency and fellowship programs; however, these funds are provided to the teaching hospital and not to the physicians instructing the students and residents [49]. Therefore, medical schools or, in some cases, individual departments must negotiate with their individual teaching hospitals for their share of these GME dollars—an often complex task, especially when the teaching hospital and the medical school are not administratively or economically linked.

Negotiations are often complicated because little information has been available regarding the actual costs of educating a resident or subspecialty fellow and whether these costs fall on the side of the hospital or on the side of the physician–teachers and the practice plan. Furthermore, the calculations on which GME dollars are based and the actual costs faced by the teaching faculty have no relationship. Therefore, the hospital may not provide the teaching faculty with enough revenues to enable the mission of teaching to continue unabated.

In an effort better to understand the actual cost of teaching a medical resident or subspecialty fellow, three different groups independently assessed the educational costs to departments. A study by Zeidel et al. [52] derived total costs by including administrative costs for program staff as well as overhead for office space and materials. The study used guidelines established by the Residency Review Committee for Internal Medicine to identify the support needed for physician staff in each training program [53] and time studies to assess the costs for bedside inpatient teaching as well as for outpatient teaching [52].

Nasca and colleagues took a similar approach using a different data set [54]. However, they assigned no costs to the clinical departments for bedside teaching, arguing that by providing faculty members with help in performing their inpatient duties, the residents actually pay for themselves. The Hunter Group, a healthcare consulting group, used a blended approach that took the training schedule for the residents and divided it into primary care time and specialty care time for both inpatient and outpatient services.

Interestingly, each of these techniques came up with a similar cost of training: approximately $35,000 per year for each resident and approximately $30,000 per year for each subspecialty trainee [52]. If one multiplies the cost of training by the number of trainees in the United States, the dollars allocated for GME are far less that the amount needed. As a result, AMCs spend more on teaching than they receive, causing financial stress on the medical school.

AMC Endowments and Fundraising Activities

Another key financial support for some AMCs is the yearly interest from university or medical school endowments. These revenues can be used for capital projects or operating expenses. Marked differences in the values of the endowments of different AMCs are often representative of the long-standing tradition of giving at the various institutions, the sophistication of their development offices, and the active collaboration of faculty in fundraising efforts.

Although the size of an AMC's endowment is rarely published, some information can be gleaned by studying the capital campaign status published each year by the *Chronicle of Higher Education.* In a recent report, it noted that Duke University had completed a $2.3 billion fundraising drive in 2003, Johns Hopkins had completed a $1.46 billion fundraising campaign in 2000 and had raised $3.05 billion of a goal of $3.2 billion in 2008, and New York University completed a $2.4 billion fundraising campaign in 2007; the University of Pennsylvania has already received $1.63 billion toward a final goal of $3.5 billion targeted for completion by 2012. Although these development activities will not be allocated only to the medical school, a large proportion of the dollars at many of these schools goes to the medical school and parallel development activities are often undertaken on the part of the affiliated or owned hospitals.

By contrast, many academic medical centers have raised far more modest amounts of development funds over the same period of time and thus have fewer options for investing in the types of new technology and personnel necessary to keep academic medical centers competitive in the healthcare environment. Paying for a new research building or new hospital structure with development dollars rather than by taking on new debt has had an enormous impact on the ability of many AMCs to stay on the cutting edge. Unfortunately, regardless of size, all university endowments have decreased in size as a result of the

2008–2009 collapse of the financial markets, resulting in decreased funds flow across all sectors of the university and medical school.

A growing list of America's academic medical centers increased their endowment portfolios by changing their names in exchange for a transformational gift from a grateful patient, a trustee, or a member of the community. These include:

the University of Southern California School of Medicine, which was renamed the Keck School of Medicine of the University of Southern California after receiving a $110 million gift from the W. M. Keck Foundation in 1999;

the Brown University School of Medicine, which was renamed the Warren Alpert Medical School of Brown University after receiving a $100 million gift from the Warren Alpert Foundation;

the Cornell Medical College, which was renamed the Joan and Sanford I. Weill Medical College and Graduate School of Medical Science of Cornell University after receiving a $100 million gift from the Weill family;

the New York University Medical Center, was renamed the New York University Elaine A. and Kenneth G. Langone Medical Center in honor of their unrestricted gift of $200 million, the largest in the history of the medical center [55]; and

the University of South Dakota in Sioux Falls, which was renamed the Sanford School of Medicine of the University of South Dakota after a gift of $20 million [56].

Florida International University's new school of medicine had intended to rename the medical school for Herbert Wertheim after his donation of $20 million. However, both the gift and the naming were put on hold because of concerns that the gift should have been larger to warrant "naming" rights [57]. Thus, even in selling naming rights, there are haves and have-nots among the different American medical schools.

Revenues from Entrepreneurial Activities

Academic medical centers have also sought opportunities to develop new revenue streams within the nonprofit sector utilizing resources that are already in hand. One such example is the formation of a new school of pharmacy at Thomas Jefferson University in Philadelphia. This came about from a group of unique opportunities: a need for pharmacists in both rural and urban areas of Pennsylvania, starting salaries for pharmacists that were near and sometimes higher than the starting salary for a general internist, and a limited number of positions in the nation's pharmacy schools. It was recognized that construction of a new teaching building for the medical school would free up classroom space and that many of the pharmacy school courses could be taught by existing faculty in the university's basic science departments. Therefore, it was clear that opening a new pharmacy school would be a good business opportunity. Indeed, the pharmacy school has become a superb opportunity to increase resources for both the university and the school of medicine.

Other AMCs have increased their yearly revenues by pursuing ventures outside the nonprofit sector. Investments have included assisted-living facilities, health plans, nursing homes, information technology services, physician billing services, creation of biotechnology incubators, residences for students and faculty, sports training facilities, rehabilitation hospitals, and healthcare consulting organizations. These for-profit ventures can bring new sources of revenue to the academic health center, support new buildings and infrastructure, and extend the financial risk of the AMC over a broader number of enterprises.

Perhaps no AMC has invested more in entrepreneurial ventures than the University of Pittsburgh Medical Center (UPMC) by investing heavily in what it perceives as the future of medicine and healthcare. For example, in April 2003, UPMC invested in a Virginia-based biotechnology firm whose parent company was involved in producing the cloned sheep Dolly [58]. In the same year, it also purchased a large bioterrorism research group from Johns Hopkins University, appropriately believing that bioterrorism research grants would be plentiful in times ahead.

UPMC also took every opportunity to partner with for-profit businesses for the benefits of the university and the faculty. For example, through a partnership with GE, the cardiology programs at both UPMC-Presbyterian and UPMC-Shadyside became demonstration sites for new technology in cardiovascular imaging. They were able to install state-of-the-art equipment at a cost that was a fraction of that of other hospitals—particularly those that were only building a single new lab. To date, UPMC participates in some way in over 100 partnerships or joint ventures, including pre- and postacute care facilities, international businesses, health plans, information technology companies, and real estate ventures. These investments provide income and spread risk over a larger number of entities.

AMC Finances during a Capital Market Crisis

The capital market crisis and volatility in national markets in 2008–2009 has and will continue to have a major impact on the finances of AMCs. "Virtually all new healthcare bond issues have been postponed," investors have lost confidence in bonds regardless of their insurance profile, and AMCs have had little access in the capital markets [59]. For AMCs with large endowment portfolios that depend on the income for operating expenses and those that have financed debt with variable-rate bonds, the turbulence in the financial markets will be especially challenging [60].

For example, Stanford University saw variable rates on a $186 million auction note increase to 8%. This increase cost the university nearly $180,000 and resulted in Stanford converting auction-rate securities into less risky investments, albeit ones with lower yields. However, the economic slowdown may also result in cuts in Medicaid reimbursements as states face massive budget shortfalls. With an increase in the number of uninsured as unemployment increases, a decline in philanthropy, and continued changes in Medicare reimbursements, many hospitals will be adversely affected by the market crisis.

The volatility in the stock market has been responsible for a significant drop in net income reported by UPMC. With a $3.3 billion portfolio being managed by 114 external investment experts (including 20 hedge fund managers and 61 private equity managers), UPMC reported total investment gains of $206 million in 2006 and $403 million in 2007, but only $3 million in the first 6 months of fiscal 2008 [61]. Although the value of UPMC's investment portfolio dropped $321 million to $2.8 billion from July through September 2008, the health system reported a cash flow of $513 million in fiscal year 2008 [62]. UPMC laid off 500 employees, fewer than 1% of its total work force; however, its robust operating revenues have allowed it to continue to invest in providing outstanding patient care [61].

For AMCs with narrower profit margins, the inability to borrow money through traditional bond offerings may have severe consequences [63]. For example, Rush University Medical Center in Chicago just broke ground on a new, 14-floor building, hoping to pay for it through a bond offering that has not yet materialized [63]. Thus, as a result of the credit crisis, "freestanding institutions and small health systems with weaker balance sheets and limited access to capital may need to partner with stronger players or sell in an environment of declining value" [59]. Reliance on the capital markets in the past provided an opportunity for AMCs to invest discretionary dollars in new technology and people. However, the current financial crisis can threaten the very existence of AMCs that have relied too heavily on investment income. Ideally, AMCs that rely on their investment portfolios for operational expenses have contingency plans in case of market downturns.

When Business Trumps the Core Mission of Excellence in Patient Care

Although AMCs must develop a business-like approach, they must ensure that all of their business decisions are consistent with the core mission of providing outstanding patient care. Thus, the core mission provides a compass for all decision making. As pointed out by Porter and Teisberg, AMCs that do not focus on providing excellence in patient care will not be able to compete in the increasingly competitive healthcare marketplace. More importantly, AMCs that lose their focus on providing excellence in patient care and make decisions based on what is best for their "business" risk compromising patient care and losing the trust of the society that they serve.

An example of how making decisions based on what is best for the business rather than on what is best for the patient can compromise patient care was recently detailed by John Carreyrou in an article appearing on the front page of *The Wall Street Journal* [64]. In 1981, UPMC recruited Dr. Thomas Starzl, the first surgeon successfully to transplant a human liver, from the University of Colorado. Within a short period of time, UPMC became the leading transplant center in the world, performing nearly 600 liver transplants each year. The charge for a liver transplant is between $400,000 and $500,000, so UPMC reaped enormous financial rewards and gained great prestige.

UPMC leaders parlayed the profits from liver transplants into the development of one of the nation's largest and most financially successful nonprofit hospital systems, with operations in Pennsylvania, Sicily, Ireland, and Qatar. With three-quarters of its $7 billion in annual revenues exempt from federal and local taxes, UPMC has been criticized for having many of the trappings of a for-profit company: Its chief executive earns $4 million per year, 13 other employees earn between $1 million and $2 million, and executives travel on a corporate jet. However, these business excesses were often ignored because the academic missions had clearly profited from the largesse of the health system.

Over the two decades after the perfection of liver transplantation, Dr. Starzl and his team trained the world's transplant surgeons to perform the complex procedure. As a result, by 2001, the number of transplants at UPMC had decreased to approximately 130 per year. Seeking to restore the luster and the financial performance of the liver transplant program, UPMC recruited Dr. Amadeo Marcos, "a dashing Venezuelan…with a taste for Ferraris and Porches, who specialized in the emerging field of transplants from living donors" [64]. Although the use of living related donor livers was highly controversial—particularly after the deaths of both donors and recipients occurred in New York—Dr. Marcos promised to use the technique to double the liver transplant volume in his first year. Nonetheless, the recruitment was not reviewed favorably by the academic physicians.

Dr. Marcos came with baggage: a complaint for sexual assault that had resulted in his being pressured to resign from the Virginia Commonwealth University School of Medicine and charges levied against the University of Rochester Medical Center for circumventing state organ allocation rules between 2000 and 2003, when Dr. Marcos had been in charge of the program [64]. At a time when a shortage of unrelated liver donors limits the number of liver transplants, the development of a program based on using living, related donors would markedly increase the ability of the hospital to perform these highly reimbursed procedures. Thus, hiring Dr. Marcos was a reasonable decision from a business standpoint—but not necessarily from a patient safety standpoint.

Within a year, Dr. Marcos had doubled the hospital's liver transplant volumes. However, as noted in Carreyrou's report, significant concerns were raised about the program. The average age of deceased liver donors increased from 41 when Dr. Marcos joined the program to 47—9 years above the national average. Thirty liver recipients died within 2 days of surgery and 35% of liver transplants over a 6-year period (441 transplants) were performed on patients who did not have a level of disease consistent with requiring a transplant. Taken together, these results suggested that liver recipients were being put at risk to increase the total number of transplants performed. Indeed, according to Dr. Howard Doyle, who worked in UPMC's transplant intensive-care unit before leaving for a position in New York, "For the first time in years, we had people dying on the operating table or in the ICU" [64].

Although Dr. Marcos reported that no donors experienced serious complications and that only 34% of a subset of transplant recipients suffered a serious complication, a subsequent review by Dr. Starzl found that the rate of life-threatening complications was actually 60% [64]. When Dr. Starzl brought his concerns to UPMC's chief executive officer, other officials, and the chair of the Department of Surgery, "a tense six-month standoff ensued" [64]. Worried that the results would be covered up, Dr. Starzl submitted his results to a medical journal, but the journal was not able to publish the findings after receiving a call from UPMC's chairman of surgery informing them that Dr. Starzl had not received patient authorization to collect the data.

Ironically, the married Dr. Marcos was only asked to resign from UPMC after his arrest during an altercation with a female co-worker with whom he was having an affair was reported in the *Pittsburgh Post-Gazette* and a complaint was filed by a second UPMC worker with whom he was also reported to be having an affair [64,65]. Thus, although good business practices are important for supporting the core mission of providing excellence in patient care, making business decisions without the constant internal compass of the core mission can lead to making the wrong decision. A century ago, Osler raised the same concerns when he noted that "the practice of medicine is an art, not a trade; a calling, not a business; a calling in which your heart will be exercised equally with your head" [66].

Improving the Finances of the AMC to Support the Core Mission

At a time when AMCs are financially challenged because of decreased reimbursements from payers, decreased funding for research, increased numbers of uninsured patients, declines in investment revenues, and increased competition from community hospitals, the AMC must identify opportunities to increase its revenues while at the same time decreasing expenditures. The most important target should be improving patient care because improvement in care delivery can increase revenues while at the same time lowering costs. However, AMCs must take additional steps to ensure that flow of funds is effective and timely and that the organizational structure can effectively support the missions of the AMC. Recommendations to fulfill these goals are made in the following sections.

Ensure Delivery of Outstanding Patient Care

Consistent with the primary thesis of this book, the most effective means of increasing AMC revenues is to ensure the delivery of outstanding patient care. This view is consistent with dicta that have been espoused by Porter and Teisberg in their recent text, *Redefining Health Care.* They propose that the ability of an academic or community hospital to be competitive in the future will be determined by its ability to increase revenues and decrease costs by pursuing what the authors refer to as "value-based competition" [67], which encompasses eight fundamental principles:

1. The focus should be on value for patients, not just lowering costs.
2. Competition must be based on results.
3. Competition should center on medical conditions over the full cycle of care.
4. High-quality care should be less costly.
5. Value must be driven by provider experience, scale, and learning at the medical condition level.
6. Competition should be regional and national, not just local.
7. Results information to support value-based competition must be widely available.
8. Innovations that increase value must be strongly rewarded.

Many of the recommendations contained in Porter and Teisberg's report have been described in earlier chapters of this book and have been incorporated into new strategic initiatives or novel organizational platforms at a few of the nation's best AMCs. For example, value-based care requires a team approach with coordination of care and joint accountability for outcomes and cost over the full cycle of care. The development of a team approach to patient care is a fundamental objective of the creation of clinical service lines—a new strategy for AMC organizations that was described in Chapters 1 and 2. AMCs that have an integrated structure across the hospital and the medical school, a closed-staff model in the hospital, and an integrated physician practice plan have a structure that can serve as an optimal platform for providing and quantifying outstanding results across the full cycle of patient care. This objective is much more difficult when the hospital and the medical school are not integrated.

As we have seen in earlier chapters, AMCs are moving toward more coordinated approaches to patient care through the development of service lines—an objective that provides enhanced capabilities for coordinated approaches of care over the full cycle of disease. The principle that value is driven by provider experience, scale, and learning in medical conditions should be easy to achieve in an AMC: Academic specialists and subspecialists concentrate their efforts, innovate rapidly, develop dedicated teams rather than relying on part-time practitioners, have dedicated facilities, and have multiple colleagues in the same practice with whom to discuss difficult cases. In addition, AMCs also participate in clinical trials—a factor that has been shown to be associated with improved outcomes for specific procedures [67]. Coordinated care across the full cycle of disease is therefore far easier to accomplish in an integrated AMC than in a community hospital or in a nonintegrated AMC with an open-staff model.

An important aspect of improving patient care will be to invigorate and financially support the ability of AMC physicians to create innovative models of care as well as innovative treatments for disease. As noted by Porter and Teisberg, "Innovation will reduce the costs of medical care far faster than the current efforts to control medical practice" as well as improving patient care [67]. However, AMCs must develop innovative metrics to assess the efficacy of new processes and organizational strategies on outcomes and costs, rather than focusing exclusively on typical clinical trials that assess changes in clinical endpoints with new drugs or devices. Even at America's top AMCs, "the best clinicians have always learned by looking for what is associated with good results, [but] there is the opportunity to make the process much more systematic and rigorous" [67].

Perhaps the greatest challenge that Porter and Teisberg put before the AMC is that "value in health care delivery is created by doing a few things well, not by trying to do everything" [67]. Meeting this goal is often a challenge for AMCs because it is also assumed that an AMC must do everything in order to fulfill its educational mission. As will be discussed in greater detail in Chapter 11, smaller AMCs must learn to eliminate clinical programs in which they cannot provide outstanding care.

Develop a Rational System for Allocating Funds

Little in the scholarly or professional literature has addressed how funds are best allocated across the many missions of an academic health center. By contrast, scholars in academic business and finance have developed rational processes for allocating resources across the components of a successful business [68]. In successful businesses, the budget process is used to allocate funds toward activities that support the core mission while eliminating funding for functions that do not support the core goals. Thus, the purpose of budgeting is not to decide how many resources each activity gets, but rather to facilitate the growth of key business opportunities.

Furthermore, when revenues decrease unexpectedly, successful businesses decrease expenses by making selective cuts based on an understanding of the long-term value of specific parts of the organization to the ability to fulfill the core goal. Importantly, budget cuts are not simply short-term fixes to get through another budget year, but rather are efforts to maintain a focus on the core goals. AMCs have failed to follow the business paradigm and, as a result, funding decisions are often made based on politics and on who yells the loudest—a methodology that has been referred to as the "charity" model [69].

Historically, AMCs have used revenues or "taxes" from profitable areas to subsidize areas that are not profitable because of low reimbursements or poor performance. Because under optimal conditions 12–13% of an institution's research costs cannot be supported by direct or indirect payments from extramural funding agencies, research efforts have also been cross-subsidized from well-performing clinical centers [69]. This cross-subsidization usually occurs at the level of the dean of the medical school and is often not done in a transparent fashion. Dr. Samuel Wilson described the flow of funds of an individual surgeon at the University of California, Irvine, during a presentation at the 76th Annual Meeting of the Pacific Coast Surgical Association [70]:

> Now take into account the disappearing clinical dollar—1 million dollars in annual charges, with a 36% gross collection rate, less 10% billing costs, 10% dean's tax, 7% department tax, and 20% overhead, is quickly reduced to roughly $190,000 for salary and benefits, leaving little time or resources for research and education.

Referred to as the "dean's tax" by the faculty and as the "academic contribution" by most deans, this tax ranges from 2% of gross clinical revenues to as high as 15% of clinical revenues. Although the dean's tax is necessary to allow the medical school to support its academic missions and to begin new and innovative programs, the use of these funds must be transparent and consistent with the strategic goals of the institution.

Because money is a zero sum game, spending more on one area of the academic medical center means that less will be available for other areas, leading to a vicious cycle that eventually depletes the capabilities of all sectors, weakens institutional finances, results in faculty dissatisfaction, and diminishes the core mission of outstanding patient care [71,72]. Particularly at a time of financial stress, AMCs must use comprehensive strategic planning and restructuring to develop templates for transparent resource allocation that are based on supporting the core mission of the institution [73]. A plan for rational resource allocation was recently developed at the University of Pennsylvania based on five basic principles [74]:

1. align the fund-flow allocation system with the institution's strategic plan;
2. be fair and transparent in funds flow allocation by clearly defining the purpose of the funds, defining performance expectations and support duration, and making decisions based on data;
3. match revenue with expenses;
4. provide appropriate incentives by linking faculty compensation with productivity while at the same time providing opportunities for gain sharing; and
5. measure performance in an ongoing fashion.

Clinical support was categorized as follows: new program start-up; purchased services, including administrative salaries; support for programs, including those important to the mission of the institution that lose money because of market conditions; incentive pay through gain sharing around financial improvements; and pass-through payments from third-party contract payments where global payment is received by the health system and then allocated to hospital and physician practices [74]. Although the Penn system may not work for everyone, it can form a starting point for discussion.

Develop a Data Bank for Academic Healthcare

AMCs hide behind the shield of the "nonprofit" institution; as a result no federal or state statutes regulate their disclosure of financial information. However, unlike most nonprofit organizations, AMCs fulfill a critically important societal need. They train the next generation of physicians, are the homes of seminal discoveries that lead to transformational changes in our ability to treat a wide array of human diseases, and provide outstanding care for complex and high-acuity diseases. In addition, even smaller AMCs in urban locales contribute substantially to the economics of their regions. One need only look at Pittsburgh, Pennsylvania—a city that transitioned from an economy that evolved around the steel industry to one that is now dependent on the healthcare industry in general and specifically the University of Pittsburgh Medical Center.

As a result of their enormous impact on the cities in which they are located and the patients for which they care, AMCs must provide the requisite financial information that will allow healthcare economists and scholars in business and management to evaluate their financial health. It is unlikely that disclosure will come voluntarily because the robust database that is presently reported to the AAMC has never been open in such a way that investigators can assess the finances of individual institutions. Therefore, it is likely that federal or state legislation will be needed to establish standardized reporting templates and regulations regarding the ability of investigators to access data. Indeed, the AMC should be held to the same level of accountability as publicly traded companies because the bankruptcy or failure of an AMC has a societal impact that is no different from the failure of a large, publicly traded company.

Improve Hospital Efficiency and Throughput in Order to Increase Capacity and Revenue

At a time when the capital markets are in crisis and economic slowdowns are threatening the viability of AMCs, the responsibility for "aggressive management of the balance sheet and adherence to a rigorous capital allocation methodology can help improve operating performance and access to capital" [75]. In most respects, this type of commercial management is carried out through the efforts of the chief financial officer and the university president or dean, who must manage relationships with banks, investors, and rating agencies while exploring methods of acquiring increased dollars for capital projects. Other opportunities include restructuring long-term debt and unwinding risky investment strategies.

However, there are also untapped opportunities for hospitals and health systems to accrue additional cash by improving bed utilization through improved patient throughput in the inpatient and outpatient arenas. This is especially true for hospitals that have increased demand for their services by providing outstanding patient care and by demonstrating their success throughout the continuum of disease states from prevention to acute treatment to palliative care. Even a half-day improvement in length of stay can result in millions of dollars of savings by providing opportunities for additional patients to be treated. AMCs should also improve efficiency by rationalizing the use of expensive drugs and equipment, standardizing ordering practices, and developing strategic relationships with vendors to decrease costs and provide access to new and investigational technology.

References

1. Flexner, A. 1973. Medical education in the United States and Canada: A report to the Carnegie Foundation for the Advancement of Teaching, 346. Bulletin no. 4, New York (reprinted by The Heritage Press, Buffalo, NY).
2. Kassirer, J. P. 1994. Academic medical centers under siege. *New England Journal of Medicine* 1331 (20): 1370–1371.
3. Carey, R. M., and Engelhard, C. L. 1996. Academic medicine meets managed care: A high-impact collision. *Academic Medicine* 71 (8): 839–845.
4. Berns, K. I. 1996. Preventing the academic medical center from becoming an oxymoron. *Academic Medicine* 71 (2): 117–120.
5. Birmingham, K. 1999. Can research survive at MCPHU—The new Allegheny? *Nature Medicine* 5 (2): 130–131.
6. AAMC. 2004. LCME Part I-A. Annual financial questionnaire.
7. Greene, J. 2000. Faculty cuts weighed at Texas med school. *American Medical News.* Apr. 24, 9, 11.
8. Goldberg, C. 1999. Teaching hospitals say Medicare cuts have them bleeding red ink. *New York Times on the Web,* May 5.
9. Pham, A. 1999. In unusual move, Beth Israel to cut 8 management jobs. *Boston Globe,* Dec. 8, F1.
10. Kowalczyk, L. 2000. Beth Israel begins layoffs to counter 1999 losses. *Boston Globe,* Feb. 3, D7.
11. Kennedy, R. 1999. New York hospitals braced for cuts. *New York Times,* May 6.
12. http://chronicle.com/weekly/v45/i37/37a03801.htm
13. www.freep.com/apps/pbcs.dll/artlice?AID=/20080305/BUSINESS06/803050426-101
14. Sledge, C. 2008. Money woes beset medical school at UT-Memphis. *Tennessean,* Mar. 21.
15. Waldman, H. 2008. Health center deal urged. March 19 (www.courant.com/news/local/hc).
16. Stewart, A. 2008. Pediatrics staff takes major cut at UMDNJ. *Newark Star-Ledger,* March 17.
17. Thier, S., and Keohane, N. 1998. Point of view: How can we assure the survival of academic health centers? *The Chronicle of Higher Education,* March 13, A64.
18. Kane, N. 2001. The financial health of academic medical centers. In *The future of academic medical centers,* ed. H. Aaron, 101. Washington, D.C.: Brookings Institute Press.
19. Gaynor, P. 2000. Investing a lot in medicine. *Pittsburgh Post-Gazette,* July 2.
20. Kane, N. M., and Magnus, S. 2001. The Medicare cost report and the limits of hospital accountability: Improving financial accounting data. *Journal of Health Policy, Politics and Law* 26 (1): 83–107.

21. www.aamc.org

22. Jonas, S., Goldsteen, R., and Goldsteen, K., eds. 2007. *An introduction to the U.S. health care system,* 6th ed., 308. New York: Springer Publishing Company.

23. Medical Payment Advisory Commission to the U.S. Congress (www.medpac.gov).

24. Blue Cross Blue Shield Association. 2007. History of Blue Cross Blue Shield (www.bcbs.com/about/history).

25. Moon, M. 2001. Health policy 2001: Medicare. *New England Journal of Medicine* 344:928.

26. Claxon, G. 2008. *How private insurance works: A primer.* Washington, D.C.: Kaiser Family Foundation.

27. Austrin, M. 1999. *Managed health care simplified: A glossary of terms.* Albany, NY: Delmar Cengage Learning.

28. Barton, P. 1999. The health services delivery system: Managed care. In *Managed care essentials: A book of readings,* ed. J. A. Russell. Chicago: Health Administration Press.

29. Shouldice, R. 1991. *Introduction to managed care.* Arlington, VA: Information Resource Press.

30. Rosenbaum, S. 2002. Medicaid. *New England Journal of Medicine* 346 (8): 635–640.

31. DeNavas, W., Proctor, B. D., and Smith, J. 2007. Income, poverty, and health insurance coverage in the United States 2006. U.S. Census Bureau (http://www.census.gov/prod/2007pubs/p60-233.pdf).

32. http://www.pbs.org/newshour/bb/health/july-dec00/amc.html

33. www.chicagobusiness.com/cgi-bin/businessList.pl

34. Carreyrou, J., and Martinez, B. 2008. Nonprofit hospitals, once for the poor, strike it rich. *The Wall Street Journal,* Apr. 4, A1.

35. Phillips, R. L., Jr., Fryer, G. E., Chen, F. M., Morgan, S. E., Green, L. A., Valente, E., and Miyoshi, T. J. 2004. The Balanced Budget Act of 1997 and the financial health of teaching hospitals. *Annals of Family Medicine* 2:71–78.

36. Konetzka, R. T., Zhu, J., and Volpp, K. G. 2005. Did recent changes in Medicare reimbursement hit teaching hospitals harder? *Academic Medicine* 80 (11): 1069–1074.

37. Plested, G. 2006. AMA, stop impending Medicare cuts. *The Wall Street Journal,* Sept. 9.

38. NAPH, AAMC, NACH, hospitals file lawsuit against federal government to stop Medicaid cuts (http://www.aha.org/content/2008/pdf/080311-alameda-v-leavitt.pdf).

39. Dewan, S., and Sack, K. 2008. A safety-net hospital falls into financial crisis. *New York Times,* Jan. 8.

40. Dewan, S. 2008. Charity hospital on brink, gets a $200 million gift. *New York Times,* Apr. 8, 2–9.

41. Pobojewski, S. 1998. Why academic medical centers cost more. *The University Record,* Dec. 14.

42. Henderson, T. 1999. Funding of graduate medical education by state Medicaid programs. Association of American Medical Colleges.

43. Fryer, G. E., Jr., Green, L. A., Dovey, S., and Phillips, R. L., Jr. 2001. Direct graduate medical education payments to teaching hospitals by Medicare: Unexplained variation and public policy contradictions. *Academic Medicine* 76 (5): 439–445.
44. http://grants.nih.gov/grants/award/research
45. Couzin, J., and Miller, G. 2007. NIH budget. Boom and bust. *Science* 316 (5823): 356–361.
46. Kaiser, J. 2007. U.S. research policy. Med schools add labs despite budget crunch. *Science* 317 (5843): 1309–1310.
47. Johnson, M. 2008. Research fund pool runs dry. *Duke Chronicle*, Apr. 8.
48. Spigel, S. 2006. Academic health center financing. OLR research report, Nov. 22.
49. Centers for Medicare and Medicaid Services. Hospital cost report. 2007.
50. Fitzgibbon, J. 2005. Financing graduate medical education. In *A toolkit for internal medicine education programs,* 8th ed., eds. M. D. Henderson, R. F. Ficalora, and V. L. Huebner. Washington, D.C.: Association of Program Directors in Internal Medicine.
51. Bazell, C., and Salsberg, E. 1998. The impact of graduate medical education financing—Policies on pediatric residency training pediatrics. *Pediatrics* 101 (4): 785–794.
52. Zeidel, M. L., Kroboth, F., McDermott, S., Mehalic, M., Clayton, C. P., Rich, E. C., and Kinsey, M. D. 2005. Estimating the cost to departments of medicine of training residents and fellows: A collaborative analysis. *American Journal of Medicine* 118 (5): 557–564.
53. Accreditation Council for Graduate Medical Education (www.acgme.org).
54. Nasca, T. J., Veloski, J. J., Monnier, J. A., Cunningham, J. P., Valerio, S., Lewis, T. J., and Gonnella, J. S. 2001. Minimum instructional and program-specific administrative costs of educating residents in internal medicine. *Archives of Internal Medicine* 161 (5): 760–766.
55. NYU Medical Center changes name honor chairman of board & wife (http://communications.med.nyu.edu/news/2008/nyu-medical-center-changes-name-honor-chairman-board-wife), Apr. 16, 2008.
56. www.sdbor.edu/pulbicatons/documents/122705medicalschool.pdf
57. Florida university loses $20M gift, plus $20M match after donor felt insulted by school president. *USA Today,* Nov. 10, 2006.
58. Levin, S. 2005. Empire building: Expansion and departures. *Pittsburgh Post-Gazette,* Dec. 29.
59. Levin, S. A., and Dickey, K. 2008. The impact of capital markets crisis and economic slowdown on hospitals and health systems (www.chartis.com).
60. Wolverton, B. 2008. With the collapse of variable-rate markets, some colleges face staggering debt costs. *The Chronicle of Higher Education.* March 6, 2008.
61. Fitzpatrick, D. 2008. UPMC net profit declines. *Pittsburgh Post-Gazette,* Feb. 14.
62. Twedt, S. 2008. UPMC posts strong revenue. *Pittsburgh Post-Gazette,* Oct. 25.
63. Abelson, R. 2008. Disappearing credit forces hospitals to delay improvements. *The New York Times,* Oct. 15.
64. Carreyrou, J. 2008. Doing a volume business in liver transplants. *The Wall Street Journal,* Nov. 21, A1.

65. Fitzpatrick, D., Fahy, J., and Fuoco, M. A. 2008. Transplant chief quitting not related to patient issues. *Pittsburgh Post-Gazette,* Mar. 5.
66. www.oslerbooks.com/otherpages/oslerpages/vh.osler.html
67. Porter, M. E., and Teisberg, E. O. 2006. *Redefining health care: Creating value-based competition on results,* 506. Boston: Harvard Business School Press.
68. Mariotti, J. 2003. *Allocating corporate capital fairly. Best practice.* Cambridge, MA: Perseus Publishing
69. Mallon, W. T. 2006. The financial management of research centers and institutes at U.S. medical schools: Findings from six institutions. *Academic Medicine* 81 (6): 513–519.
70. Wilson, S. 2005. The academic department of surgery: Between Scylla and Charybdis. *Archives of Surgery* 140 (8): 719–723.
71. Porter, M. E., and Teisberg, E. O. 2004. Redefining competition in health care. *Harvard Business Review* 82 (6): 64–76, 136.
72. Roy, A. 2001. Why orthopedic surgeons leave full-time academic positions for private practice. *Journal of Bone and Joint Surgery* 83-A:456–460.
73. Niven, P. 2003. *Balanced scorecard—Step by step for government and nonprofit agencies.* Hoboken, NJ: John Wiley & Sons Inc.
74. Kennedy, D. W., Johnston, E., and Arnold, E. 2007. Aligning academic and clinical missions through an integrated funds-flow allocation process. *Academic Medicine* 82 (12): 1172–1177.
75. Chartis Group (www.chartis.com).

Chapter 11

Developing Strategic Regional and Global Collaborations

> You will ask, "How are these facilities and advantages to be procured in a small town or in the country?" The answer is, by cooperation. Every little center must have its laboratory for special examinations. The country physician must be allied with a group of associated workers and no longer thrown upon his own resources. By means of the rural free delivery, telephone, automobile, trolley, and steamlines, quick communication will aid the new order of things and help make possible such association.
>
> **Dr. William J. Mayo** [1]

Introduction

In the early 1900s, Dr. William J. Mayo, one of the founders of the Mayo Clinic, pointed out the need for AMCs such as the Mayo Clinic to support the delivery of outstanding clinical care in regions that were a distance from the AMC. However, at that time it was also pointed out that AMCs needed to collaborate with each other in order to optimize the delivery of care within individual communities or regions. As AMCs have become increasingly challenged to survive in highly competitive markets, they have begun to export their expertise in their own geographic regions, across the country, and around the world. By providing increased access to knowledge, modern technology, and healthcare, U.S. academic medical centers can work collaboratively to improve the health of the global community. Indeed, in some areas, the progress that comes from improved healthcare can lead to economic growth and modernization, which can serve as a platform for development of peace.

Globalization of healthcare can also serve more pragmatic needs of AMCs because the expansion of their care delivery systems to other regions can open new markets and in so doing improve the economic performance of an AMC—particularly in situations where the AMC has already captured a significant portion of its home market. This chapter will examine the efforts of some AMCs to expand their business internationally, nationally, and locally; present some guidelines for effectively expanding the geographic base of an academic practice; and offer recommendations on how some AMCs can achieve improved performance by collaborating with AMCs located within the same or different geographic locales.

Globalization of Healthcare

Recently, an increasing number of academic medical centers have begun to work on strategies to develop business opportunities outside their historic geographic regions. Porter and Teisberg were the first scholars in healthcare economics to suggest that geographic expansion could benefit AMCs. They noted [2]:

> Geographic expansion in particular medical conditions offers a huge untapped growth opportunity for healthcare providers. Excellent providers in a practice unit can grow regionally, nationally, and even internationally. In the process, they will leverage scale, expertise, care delivery methods, staff training, measurement systems, and reputation to serve more patients. A rising number of patients in the practice unit feed economies of scale, the sub-specialization of teams, and more efficient division of labor across locations. Ultimately, the best providers in a practice unit can operate nationally through extensive networks of dedicated facilities. While this possibility seems radical today, the main barriers are attitudinal and artificial (e.g., state licensing requirements and archaic corporate practice of medicine laws).

We will see that the success of geographic expansion does not come from merging stand-alone, broad-line institutions but rather from selecting areas of high quality. It also comes from integrating the geographic sites by establishing common performance measurements and standards, shared training of physicians and staff, integration of the management structure, and publication of quality results to demonstrate an equivalent level of care across all of the care delivery locations.

Improving the World's Healthcare

Historically, some academic medical centers have received payments from individual patients who were foreign nationals and therefore paid a substantially higher fee than did governmental or private insurers. These payments were often in return for high-end surgical interventions, including solid-organ transplantation and cardiothoracic surgery. More recently, an increasing number of academic medical centers have begun to expand their operations internationally, thus bringing their patient care missions to the very regions of the world from where they recruited patients in years past. In his presidential address in 2007, Steven Wartman, president of the Association of Academic Health Centers, noted [3]:

> This is the moment when academic health centers collectively can point the way toward positive change around the world, including increasing access to knowledge, modern technology and health care. We can and must join together to form international alliances and partnerships, to develop programs that enhance health and well-being, and to advance the concept of a global community.

Wartman put forward a vision for global health that was both collaborative and altruistic. Although he recognized the international alliances that have already been formed by various academic health centers, he viewed them as [3]

> first steps towards overarching models and networks that join together multiple academic health centers in the United States with our neighbors overseas. As we continue to rethink our traditional assumptions about the organization and management of academic health centers, we must consider as a priority the work that they can do in the new global context.

Many of the earliest efforts by America's AMCs to improve global health have been driven more through the auspices of schools of public health than through the entrepreneurial activities of the clinical centers of the academic medical center. For example, in 2006, the deans of the schools of Medicine, Public Health and Nursing at Hopkins created the Johns Hopkins Center for Global Health [4]. The mission of the center was to "facilitate and focus the extensive expertise and resources of the Johns Hopkins Institutions together with global collaborators—governments, nongovernmental organizations, universities, and communities—to effectively address and ameliorate the world's most pressing health issues" [4]. Although projects are often focused on research, there is also a strong commitment to education, healthcare delivery, and the development of a new generation of global health leaders [4].

Other schools have followed similar paradigms to improve the health of the world's populations through education, training, and research as well as preparing the United States for emerging global health threats. These include institutions as diverse as New York University, Wright State University School of Medicine, and Harvard Medical International, a self-supporting, not-for-profit subsidiary of Harvard Medical School [5–7].

Duke recently opened the Duke-National University of Singapore (NUS) Graduate Medical School in Singapore [8]. As noted by Dr. R. Sanders Williams, dean of the school, it is committed "to educate superbly skilled physicians who will take their place alongside the many fine doctors who practice in hospitals and clinics of Singapore today." However, the school will also be committed "to be a pioneer in basic biomedical research, in clinical and translational investigations in health services research and health policy, and in the biomedical industries" [9].

The creation of the Duke-NUS Graduate Medical School's research mission was facilitated by a gift of $80 million from the estate of Tan Sri Khoo Teck Puat to support biomedical research initiatives. With a matching gift from the Singapore government, the funds will be used to support groundbreaking research in the school's four core programs: infectious diseases, cancer and stem cell biology, neurobehavioral disorders, and cardiovascular and metabolic disorders.

The Duke–NUS partnership is clearly a win–win situation for both institutions. For Duke, the partnership extends its brand to another part of the world, helps differentiate Duke from other outstanding AMCs through the quality and scale of its international missions, and facilitates some of its outstanding research in global health [10]. In addition, Duke has used the opportunity to experiment with institutional structures. For example, rather than creating traditional departments, the new medical school consists of an organizational paradigm that groups faculty around an "educational team" and "signature research programs" in major disease areas [10]. Lessons learned in AMC structure in Singapore can be effectively imported to the main campus in Durham, North Carolina. For NUS, the school provides new knowledge in healthcare and an opportunity to expand its work force of physicians, physician–scientists, and physician entrepreneurs, and creates a prestigious AMC in Singapore.

Some AMCs have taken more modest approaches to globalization. Noted for its expertise in infectious diseases, the University of Rochester has partnered with the Gates Foundation to create training networks for prevention of HIV as well as programs to design how vaccinations and immunizations could be carried out in the case of epidemic outbreaks [10]. In addition, the University of Rochester nursing school helps train and certify healthcare providers in other countries in the area of clinical trial management. At the University of Texas-Houston Health Science Center, international educational activities have been driven by individual faculty members and facilitated by less formal agreements of cooperation as well as formal written program agreements [10].

New York–Presbyterian Hospital, Weill Cornell Medical College, Columbia College of Physicians and Surgeons, and Hallym University Medical Center in Seoul, Korea, entered into an affiliation agreement to begin an international collaboration aimed at enhancing patient care, clinical and biomedical research, medical education, and training [11]. The central focus on the United States–South Korea affiliation is the opportunity for physicians and scientists from Hallym to train in New York and for New York physicians to take advantage of unique opportunities to train in Korea and to participate in collaborative research projects.

Meanwhile, other institutions have looked at global health and ongoing threats to the health of the world's population as a new science that requires the development of university-wide transdisciplinary initiatives. Indeed, the University of California, San Francisco, began a program of global health sciences that was focused on bringing together biologists, clinicians, population biologists, and scholars in the social and behavioral sciences from all 10 University of California campuses. They will develop an integrated program for education and research as well as initiate collaborations with academic centers in low- and middle-income countries in order to address neglected global health issues [12].

Although AMCs have worked assiduously for many years to improve international health, many AMCs have found that collaborative global efforts can provide substantial new revenue opportunities—especially when they have optimized their financial opportunities within their own regions, facilitate the development of international reputations and brand, provide new outlets for clinical research, and increase access to foreign patients who may require high-end quaternary care. One of the first AMCs to demonstrate the potential financial benefits of a global strategy was the University of Pittsburgh Medical Center (UPMC).

In the mid-1990s, UPMC recognized that its signature program, solid organ transplantation, was threatened by increasing competition from many new programs in the United States, which were largely staffed by physicians trained at UPMC; a scarcity of organs; and a local market that had little room for growth [13]. Furthermore, UPMC needed new sources of revenue to balance the financial shortfalls from Medicare cutbacks, the increasing power of the dominant private payer in western Pennsylvania, and the fact that, despite having approximately $5.7 billion in revenues, the western Pennsylvania market was limited in growth because of its small size.

Thus, in 1996, UPMC began negotiations to build a hospital in Palermo, Sicily, that would be focused on solid-organ transplantation. Opened in 2004, the 70-bed, $58 million Mediterranean Institute for Transplantation and Advanced Specialized Therapies (ISMETT) has the potential to make $10 million to $20 million in profits each year according to those familiar with the project [14]. Michele McKenney, the UPMC executive who oversaw the project, noted in 2004 that "serving patients where they live rather than having them leave homes is our priority." However, the rationale for UPMC's venture into Palermo was likely more consistent with comments made by David Blumenthal, director of the Institute for Health Policy at Massachusetts General Hospital, when he noted: "It's about money and reputation…They wouldn't be doing it if they were losing money" [14]. UPMC could potentially have expanded in the United States. However, the expansion to Palermo allowed it to reach new markets with its most recognizable brand—one in which it had clearly demonstrated excellence—without having to decrease the prices that it charged for a transplant.

UPMC's efforts to gain new global markets have not stopped with its construction of its transplant hospital in Palermo. With continuing emphasis on exporting its products, UPMC announced in February 2006 that it was developing partnerships with hospitals in the United States and Ireland that lacked the capital to provide intensity-modulated radiation therapy, a new form of cancer treatment [15]. UPMC also signed an agreement to provide education, training, and some hands-on services to the emergency medical system in Qatar in return for $100 million over a period of 4.5 years [16]. It has also partnered with hospitals in Ireland and with the Irish government to build three more hospitals on public hospital grounds in Dublin, Cork, and Limerick.

Once these hospitals are completed, UPMC will become the country's largest operator of private hospitals [17]. The center has been careful to pick partnering countries that seek state-of-the-art tertiary and quaternary care, have the necessary financial resources, have a viable location from the standpoint of competition, and can sustain a financial commitment [10]. Although UPMC's international and commercial division lost $4 million in the first 6 months of its

2008 fiscal year, the UPMC Health System generated $52 million in profit from its 19 area hospitals and $52 million in profit from its insurance arm. Although UPMC has worked to build an international consortium, it has also worked to expand its brand across a wider geographic area—spending nearly a million dollars each year running full-page advertisements in the local and national issues of the *New York Times*.

Expanding Educational and Clinical Excellence to the Persian Gulf

Academic medical centers have also looked to the Persian Gulf for new opportunities in global health. Flush with billions of dollars from their rich supplies of oil, three of the emirates have aggressively worked to recruit American universities to build a world-class educational program to join the explosion of luxury hotels, first-class airlines, high-tech weaponry, and palace-like homes that dot these tiny but wealthy desert countries [18].

The Qatar Foundation, a multibillion-dollar endowment established in 1995 by the country's ruler, Sheikh Hamad bin Khalifa Al-Thani, promised $750 million over 11 years to Weill Cornell Medical College for the creation of a medical school that would replicate the quality and standards of Cornell University. Some faculty are recruited to be in residence in Qatar; others spend short periods of time there. Distance learning provides opportunities for some faculty to teach from New York, and some clinicians are chosen from regional healthcare providers. However, all faculty members are appointed by administrators in New York and the Cornell admissions committee chooses all students for the Qatar program. The completion of a research facility and a new teaching hospital will lead to further expansion of the current program [10].

Dubai, a country with less oil wealth than nearby Qatar, established Knowledge Village in 2003. Composed of a group of second-tier institutions, Knowledge Village offers 100% repatriation of assets and profits tax free and is set up as a profit-making enterprise [18]. In addition, the educational programs are focused, at least in part, on the large expatriate community that accounts for 90% of the emirate's population. Recently, Harvard Medical International, a nonprofit arm of Harvard Medical School, established Harvard Medical School Dubai in Dubai Health Care City—a $1.8 billion complex that will contain private hospitals, pharmaceutical companies, research centers, five-star hotels, and a residential community [18].

Abu Dhabi, the capital of the United Arab Emirates, has an estimated 10% of the world's oil reserves. It is building a comprehensive liberal arts university for

New York University on Saadiyat Island—a $28 billion effort that will include a branch of the Louvre, a Guggenheim museum, a performing arts center that will be managed by the Lincoln Center, and a branch of the graduate program in the public health school of Johns Hopkins [18]. In addition, Johns Hopkins Medical International recently began managing a large tertiary hospital, Tawam Hospital, in Abu Dhabi [19].

Johns Hopkins Medical International had expanded its efforts through education collaborations with Children's Hospital of Fudan University in China, a strategic alliance with India's largest private hospital group, hospital affiliations in Ireland and Panama, and an academic division in Singapore. However, the management contract with a large hospital is a first for Hopkins—one that will hopefully lead to development of centers of excellence in a variety of specialties [19]. In addition, in 2010, the Cleveland Clinic plans to open Cleveland Clinic Abu Dhabi, which will include a multispecialty tertiary center and adjacent clinic [20]. The physician-led medical center will include world-class physicians who will receive continuing medical training directly from the Cleveland Clinic.

The efforts to build medical schools and hospitals in the Persian Gulf emirates are interesting from the standpoint of opening new revenue opportunities for America's academic medical centers. However, they are also interesting from a geopolitical standpoint because they represent a historic shift in the long-standing prominence of Cairo, Baghdad, and Beirut in Middle Eastern academics [21].

However, the Persian Gulf is not the only area of focus for global ventures on the part of academic health centers. After the Cultural Revolution, China's medical education system was shut down and not reestablished until the late 1970s. Thus, both rural and urban areas have great need of physicians. Unfortunately, the Chinese medical education system is hindered by outdated teaching models, insufficient funding, and confusion due to a variety of educational programs and degrees. China's need of a redesigned educational system provides an excellent opportunity for American AMCs to open new markets in the Far East [10]. This is particularly relevant now because China appears to have been less affected by the collapse of the global economy.

Development of Regional Collaborations in Clinical Care

To date, regional collaborations in care and regional rationalization of services have come about when AMCs have purchased community hospitals. An example of this is the development of the University of Pittsburgh Medical Center

(UPMC) Health System. In 1973, the University Health Center of Pittsburgh, as it was then called, consisted of a loosely incorporated network of Presbyterian-University Hospital, Falk Clinic (an outpatient clinic), Western Psychiatric Institute and Clinic, and Magee-Women's Hospital. However, the medical center began a growth surge between 1986 and 1992. During that time period [14],

> Presbyterian University Hospital announced a $230 million renovation and expansion project to allow expansion of its transplant center and the new Pittsburgh Cancer Institute;
> the Montefiore Hospital was purchased for $140 million and merged with Presbyterian University Hospital to become part of the newly named University of Pittsburgh Medical Center; and
> revenues increased from $85 million to $518 million.

In the face of growing competition from the Allegheny Health System and fearing that a for-profit health system could come into the western Pennsylvania region and purchase one of the larger quaternary care community hospitals and effectively compete for the region's healthcare business, UPMC began a focused effort to coalesce the region's physicians and hospitals under the umbrella of the UPMC Health System. If it were big enough, UPMC could also dominate the insurance market and mitigate any efforts to decrease reimbursements from providers. By 2002, the UPMC Health System had over 5,000 physicians, 18 hospitals, a 40% market share of patients in Allegheny County, and a nearly 26% market share in the 29-county western Pennsylvania region. Market share allowed UPMC to forge favorable relationships with some third-party payers as well as to benefit from economies of scale in purchasing and other financial activities [22].

Regional and National Collaborations to Enhance Medical Education

AMCs have also developed affiliation agreements with regional health centers as part of expanded educational initiatives. For example, the University of Wisconsin School of Medicine announced the formation of regional campuses at the Marshfield Clinic in Marshfield and the Gundersen Lutheran Medical Center in La Crosse [23]. Similarly, the University of Kansas School of Medicine-Wichita formed a partnership in 1999 with the Kansas Department of Health and Environment as a result of the planning activities of the Kansas Public Health Workforce Development Committee.

The development of academic-practice partnerships that draw upon a network of health organizations provided an effective way to build the community health infrastructure that could overcome inherent impediments to successful care delivery; improve training of healthcare workers, including nurses; and expand the opportunities for practice-based research as well as for the sharing of scare resources between integrated projects [24]. Although these efforts provide excellent training opportunities for medical students and link community outpatient and inpatient facilities with the quality assurance programs of the academic medical center, their financial benefits in terms of increased funds flow to the academic medical center have not been demonstrated.

An even longer distance affiliation agreement that focused on education was the one announced in June 2004 between the Methodist Hospital in Houston, Texas, and the Weill Medical College of Cornell University and New York–Presbyterian Hospital—a transcontinental alliance between major not-for-profit academic health centers in the United States unique in its size, scope, and geographic separation [25]. Because of the geographic separation, the parties were not competitors in providing clinical care and therefore hypothesized that collaborations in education, research, quality improvement, information technology, and international program development could benefit all three institutions.

By developing a common clinical research infrastructure, master templates for clinical trial agreements, mutual efforts to improve clinical care by sharing best practices, quality methods, and clinical databases—as well as sharing the graduate medical education structure of New York–Presbyterian with Methodist Hospital—it was hoped that the alliance could help meet some of the challenges facing academic medical centers [26]. As pointed out by Dirk Sostman of the Methodist Hospital: "Since many consider that AHCs are in a state of economic and cultural crisis, it seemed that such an exploration could have importance beyond the collective interests of the three institutions" [25].

However, in fairness, it must be pointed out that one of the drivers for Methodist Hospital to affiliate with a hospital and medical school 1,600 miles away was that Methodist lost its affiliation with its neighbor, the Baylor College of Medicine, when the two had a falling out over Baylor's decision to build its own outpatient clinic [27]. Thus, it is unclear whether the Methodist Hospital–Weill Medical School affiliation will influence the financial health of either institution.

Development of National Markets

An example in which an academic medical center has taken a "lead" product into new national markets is the establishment of management contracts by which the Cleveland Clinic operates the cardiac surgery programs at the Rochester General Hospital in Rochester, New York, and the Chester County Hospital in West Chester, Pennsylvania. Surgeons from both Rochester and West Chester participate in clinical protocols, research studies, educational conferences, and all of the quality improvement activities in Cleveland [28]. They spend time in Cleveland learning new techniques, serve as members of the Cleveland Clinic staff, and their results are reported as part of the surgical outcomes database widely published by the clinic on a biannual basis. They bring to their communities the strategies of the number 1 ranked cardiovascular program in the country.

A similar and new affiliation has been forged between Columbia-Presbyterian's cardiology program in New York and that of Mt. Sinai Hospital in Florida—a collaboration that will link Columbia's cutting-edge technology with Mt. Sinai's long-standing reputation for patient care. The affiliation brings cutting-edge research studies to Mt. Sinai, helps Mt. Sinai to differentiate its program from competing hospitals, and facilitates the recruitment of individuals with training and expertise in state-of-the-art technology. Mt. Sinai faculty have the opportunity to obtain continual training through visits to New York as well as through joint conferences using telecommunications. Mt. Sinai faculty are jointly recruited by Columbia and Mt. Sinai, and Mt. Sinai faculty have academic appointments at Columbia.

Collaborations and Affiliations in the Local Marketplace

Due to price competition in the healthcare market, increasing financial pressures due to reductions in public subsidies, increased competition from community hospitals, and "variability in institutional reputation and financial resources," a series of highly publicized mergers took place among America's AMCs in the mid- to late 1990s [29]. These were driven at least in part by the large number of mergers and acquisitions that had swept through the U.S. business community and literature suggesting that consolidation through organized healthcare delivery systems would benefit AMCs [30,31]. In 1994, there were 30 mergers of nonprofit hospitals, as opposed to 153 in 1997 [32]. In academic medicine, a group of highly publicized mergers included

> the Medical College of Pennsylvania and Hahnemann School of Medicine;
> the teaching hospitals of Stanford University and the University of California, San Francisco;

the Massachusetts General and Brigham and Women's Hospitals;

the University of Cincinnati University Hospital and the Health Alliance of Greater Cincinnati;

the University of Massachusetts Medical Center and Memorial Health Care; and

the Penn State University Hershey Medical Center and Geisinger Health System.

However, by the late 1990s, many of these mergers had failed. A study by the consulting firm McKinsey & Co. reported that when looking at for-profit and nonprofit hospitals, 300 of 750 mergers had failed [32]. In addition, the literature became filled with articles touting the folly of teaching-hospital mergers [33].

At the turn of the century, many of the healthcare economists who had recommended mergers just a few years earlier were trying to dissect the errors that had led to the failure of these many academic mergers. One study found that the most common reasons for an alliance to end were the incompatibility of corporate cultures or personalities, a clash of managerial personalities, differing project personalities, and varying levels of project priority to each alliance partner [34]. Others suggested that some alliances had failed because of a failure to address the interplay of specific factors, including environmental and organizational characteristics, alliance formation features, and attributes of strategic relationships including commitment, collaboration, communication, trust, and conflict resolution [35]. However, I would argue that the reason many of these mergers failed was because the underlying rationale was incorrect: improving revenues rather than improving patient care.

An example of a failed merger that was undertaken for the wrong reasons was the merger of the Penn State University Hershey Medical Center and Geisinger Health System in Danville, Pennsylvania, into one large clinical enterprise. Announced in 1997, the basic premise was that the new entity—the Penn State Geisinger Health System—would provide an opportunity to enter the insurance business, operate an independent health maintenance organization, and generate revenue on the premium dollar. The positive margin expected from the merger would provide revenue to support the academic activities of the school of medicine [36].

However, by November 1999, the dissolution of the merger was announced by the board of trustees. The failure of the merger was thought by some to be the development of a structure under which academic and clinical affairs no longer had the same reporting structure after the merger; the dean was entrusted with only the academic missions of the medical school and the overall economics of the clinical enterprise were overseen by the chief executive officer of the Health

System and the board of directors to which the CEO reported [36]. Others have blamed the failure of the Penn State–Geisinger model on dysfunctional leadership, distrust among board members, and different organizational cultures [37]. However, nowhere in the merger documents was it mentioned that the merger would improve care for the patients of central Pennsylvania.

Another highly publicized merger that failed was the merger of Stanford University Hospital, Lucile Salter Packard Children's Hospital, and the associated faculty practice plans of both Stanford University and the equivalent clinical enterprise of the University of California, San Francisco (UCSF). The respective schools of medicine remained separate [38]. Both hospitals had been disadvantaged by residing in an area with one of the highest managed care penetrations in the nation. Capitation rates were so low that UCSF Stanford Health Care was losing money when treating HMO or MediCal patients. The merger was designed to [38]

enable the two centers to increase their market share of complex care (a 2% increase in market share would bring the enterprise an additional $100 million of revenue);

enable Stanford and UCSF to differentiate themselves more effectively from community competitors;

establish a strong market position for each of the medical centers' pediatric programs;

reduce administrative overhead; and

increase organizational purchasing power through economies of scale, administrative streamlining, and a decrease in the cost of technology by avoiding duplication.

However, within 2 years, the merger fell apart as the system incurred an $86 million operational loss and a $73 million net overall loss [39]. The failure of the merger was attributed to the difficulties inherent in merging complex organizations with different structures and cultures, the challenges of merging a public and private institution, and the failure of faculty to establish loyalties to the new institution [40]. However, the fact that institutions' hospitals were placed under a separate and independent corporate umbrella also raised serious concerns regarding the merger's effects on the quality of education and clinical research [41]. As with the failed merger of Hershey Medical Center and Geisinger, the Stanford–UCSF merger was not structured or undertaken to improve patient care but rather to enhance revenues.

AMCs Can Achieve the Primary Goal of Providing Outstanding Patient Care by Developing Novel Collaborations

Based on experiences to date with mergers among America's AMCs, it would appear that mergers should be guided and driven by what will most likely improve or maintain outstanding patient care rather than simply for financial reasons. Thus, in the evolving healthcare marketplace and in the face of a global economic crisis, AMCs must think "out of the box" by developing new strategies to provide outstanding patient care for their own patient population as well as for patients who have historically resided in different geographic regions. These strategies may include the three described in the next sections.

Development of Global Initiatives to Provide Outstanding Care to the World's Populations

All AMCs should explore the potential for providing outstanding care for the world's underserved populations and, if possible, provide those services. As we have seen, a number of AMCs have recently developed initiatives in the Far East, the Arab Emirates, and Europe. The downside of these ventures has been that they require an investment in money, time, and personnel in order to ensure success. However, the upside is enormous. In some cases, the upside is a marked improvement in healthcare delivery, education, or research in an underserved country. In other cases, there is a substantial financial reward for the U.S. academic medical center. Unfortunately, because of the investment needed to make these efforts successful and sustainable, the global opportunities are only available to the academic "haves" but not the academic "have-nots."

Collaborations in Healthcare Delivery That Cross State Boundaries

A radical approach to transcontinental collaborations has been the partnering between programs of excellence at an AMC and either community hospitals or large teaching hospitals that have resulted in improvements in patient care. A model for this approach has been the Cleveland Clinic Heart & Vascular Institute, the top-ranked cardiology and cardiac surgery program in the United States. For the past 13 years, the clinic has partnered with small community hospitals, such as the Chester County Hospital in West Chester, Pennsylvania, as well as with large teaching hospitals, including Rochester General Hospital in Rochester, New York, to bring Cleveland Clinic physicians, protocols, and training to these affiliate programs.

As described earlier, the clinic publishes its patient outcomes and volumes for many of its surgical and interventional procedures and provides them each year to referring physicians across the country as well as making them available online. The collaboration with multiple sites also allows patients to be diverted for care to the optimum facility. For example, patients requiring highly specialized surgical procedures such as heart transplantation are rapidly triaged from affiliated programs to Cleveland. Although this type of collaboration has not yet occurred between two AMCs, there are no obstacles other than ego. In the model put forth by Porter and Teisberg, institutions will only be financially viable if they can provide a level of care in a particular disease that can be demonstrated to be outstanding. As such, AMCs that cannot provide outstanding care in all areas might be better served by improving care by partnering than by eliminating areas of specializations.

Development of Partnering Opportunities within Local Markets

History would suggest that mergers of academic institutions are complex, difficult to carry out, and, in most situations, do not work [42]. However, I would argue that the reason why many mergers have failed is that they were undertaken for the wrong reasons: financial gain, market protection, spreading the risk, or increasing patient flow. By contrast, mergers and affiliations among different AMCs should work if their basic premise, as well as their composition and structure, is based on fulfilling the core mission of outstanding patient care. Although this hypothesis seems radical, the business literature and the experience of several AMCs support this concept.

As I have noted earlier in this book, Jim Collins points out in *Good to Great* that organizations move from good to great by adhering to "a single organizing idea, a basic principle, or concept that unifies and guides everything" [43]. This single focus encompasses that at which one can be the best in the world, that which drives one's economic engine, and that about which one is deeply passionate. When comparing the good companies and the great companies, Collins noted that "not one of the good-to-great companies focused obsessively on growth" but instead focused on quality [43]. Thus, the AMCs that merged in order to increase size and as a result to have a larger impact in the marketplace were clearly misguided because the quality of the product, rather than size, is what matters.

One might argue that a single AMC should be able to survive in its own market if it can provide excellence in patient care in all areas. This is true; however, only a relatively small group of AMCs can claim excellence in each area of clinical medicine. In most cases, these are long-standing institutions or newer institutions that have emerged through a unique structure that provides an exceptional level of financial support. Indeed, looking at the majority of hospitals, Porter and Teisberg note [2]:

> The current structure in which many local providers operate at modest scale in their home region is an artifact of history and has little logic in terms of patient value. Even if most services are provided locally, services in each practice unit can be managed or supported by premier integrated national organizations.

Again, it is important to note that Porter and Teisberg based their assessment on the hospitals' ability to provide outstanding patient care rather than on the financial aspects of the hospitals. Indeed, three "local mergers" that have successfully taken place include Massachusetts General Hospital and the Brigham and Women's Hospital, Beth Israel Hospital and Deaconess Hospital, and New York Hospital and Columbia Presbyterian Hospital. However, each of these six hospitals had very similar cultures: Massachusetts General, the Brigham and Women's, Beth Israel, and the Deaconess were all historic teaching hospitals of Harvard Medical School and most were among the "haves" of AMCs in terms of endowments, research support, and annual fundraising efforts.

The hypothesis that local affiliations can work when they are based on the core principle of providing outstanding patient care is supported by the success of the partnership between Meharry Medical College and Vanderbilt University Medical Center [44]. The alliance encompassed three very different institutions—all of which had existed in Nashville since the late 1800s:

Meharry Medical College was established for the distinct purpose of training African American physicians in 1876 and remains the largest private, comprehensive, historically African American institution for educating health professionals and scientists in the United States. Meharry operated Hubbard Hospital, which provided healthcare for the majority of Nashville's African American population.

Established in 1874, Vanderbilt University Medical Center is a research-intensive AMC whose hospital was ranked number 16 and whose medical school was ranked number 15 by *U.S. News and World Report* in 2008 [45].

Nashville General Hospital opened in 1890 to provide care for the city's indigent population. Vanderbilt had maintained an exclusive contract with

Nashville General until 1985, when Meharry also gained a clinical affiliation with the hospital.

In 1992, Hubbard Hospital and Nashville General Hospital faced major needs for renovation or replacement at a time when the introduction of TennCare and other managed care plans in Nashville had lessened the need for two hospitals that primarily served the poor and uninsured. As a result, the Metro Council of Nashville-Davidson County elected to merge Nashville General and Hubbard Hospital. As part of the agreement, Meharry would assume all responsibility for professional staffing at Nashville General, an ambulatory clinic would remain at Nashville General's historic site, Meharry would assume the cost for renovating Hubbard Hospital, and the county would lease the Hubbard facility from Meharry for a period of 30 years. As a result of the agreement, Vanderbilt was not administratively responsible for the professional staffing of Nashville General for the first time since it opened.

Both academic centers were stressed by the decision. Although Vanderbilt no longer had the obligation to staff Nashville General, it lost a valuable training site for its fellows, residents, and students. By contrast, Meharry gained a renovated and up-to-date clinical facility on its own campus, but it did not have enough staff to assume responsibility for full clinical coverage at Nashville General. As a result, the two institutions formed an alliance with the goal being to:

improve the educational experience of students and house staff of both institutions;
increase joint research and training grants;
enhance the quality and quantity of services for the patients of Nashville General; and
jointly provide new ways of maintaining the health of the community [46].

Thus, by taking advantage of the strengths of each institution, the alliance between Vanderbilt and Meharry would result in meeting the fundamental core mission of providing outstanding patient care for all of the patients served by Nashville General Hospital.

Implementing the Meharry–Vanderbilt alliance was not easy. The creation of a successful alliance required real resources, a buy-in from all stakeholders, the creation of mechanisms to ensure good communication and trust, federal support for collaborative research, sensitivity to the cultural aspects of each partner institution, and willingness to use the strengths of each of the partners. Indeed, the success of the program was seen in the ability of the departments of surgery to form a joint department while at the same time preserving the integrity of each institution. Faculty appointments, including the appointment of a new chief of surgery at Meharry, were made jointly by both institutions; economies of scale were met by sharing resources, facilities, and faculty for medical education; and Meharry gained a surgical residency program.

The alliance has led to expansion of all educational programs, growth in research and research funding, the awarding of a clinical and translational science award that incorporates investigators at both institutions, and an increase in surgical volume. As noted by the chairs of surgery at Meharry and Vanderbilt, "Nothing that has transpired would have occurred without the commitment to excellence and mission displayed by the individuals who have been recruited to work in this alliance" [47].

Other cities can learn important lessons from the experience in Nashville—in particular, that AMCs within the same geographic region but with historically different cultures can find important ways in which collaboration can make both institutions stronger and better able to fulfill their societal missions. The AMC demographics in Philadelphia provide an ideal case study for the potential development of intercity collaboration. Because the state reports volumes and outcomes for cardiovascular procedures, this discussion will focus on cardiovascular services, although the same logic could be applied to other services as well.

Today, Philadelphia has four allopathic medical schools and their affiliated hospitals with cardiac programs: the University of Pennsylvania (Hospital of the University of Pennsylvania, Penn Presbyterian Medical Center, Pennsylvania Hospital), Drexel University School of Medicine (Hahnemann University Hospital), Thomas Jefferson University (Thomas Jefferson University Hospital), and Temple University (Temple University Hospital). In 2007, the Hospital of the University of Pennsylvania accounted for 1,297 cardiovascular surgery discharges, Penn Presbyterian Medical Center had 569, Thomas Jefferson University Hospital had 360, Pennsylvania Hospital had 271, Hahnemann University Hospital had 260, and Temple University Hospital had 241 [48].

Although the relationship between patient outcome and volume is controversial [49–51], after careful review of the literature, the Leapfrog Group (a coalition of more than 150 large public and private healthcare purchasers that represents over 40 million people) recommended that individual hospitals performing more than 450 cardiac surgery cases per year be Leapfrog Group compliant (with the exception of New York, New Jersey, Pennsylvania, and California, which base their standards on being in the lowest quartile of mortality rates in the state) [52].

Similarly, in Michigan, a hospital cannot initiate a new open heart surgery program without having a consulting agreement with a hospital that has an existing open heart surgery program that performs a minimum of 400 open heart surgical cases per year for 3 consecutive years. The new program must perform a minimum of 300 operations. Leapfrog Group standards also require a minimum of 400 percutaneous coronary interventions each year. This standard is met at only a few of the Philadelphia AMCs, although it is met by a number of community hospitals.

Not only do Jefferson's, Hahnemann's, and Temple's cardiac surgery programs not meet Leapfrog Group standards, but the low volumes preclude these programs' participation in clinical trials of some of the most innovative new technologies in the field of cardiovascular medicine. For example, because of its large patient volumes, Penn participates in the study of new technologies, including percutaneous mitral valve repair and aortic valve replacement—procedures that can replace or repair a cardiac valve without the need for open heart surgery.

However, the other academic medical centers are precluded from participating in these studies because they lack the requisite clinical volumes. Sponsors for the new devices require that participating centers have hybrid catheterization laboratories that can accommodate both cardiologists and surgeons, interventional cardiologists who perform large volumes of complex procedures, and a large volume of aortic valve surgery. The requisite large hospital volumes are not because of the need to enroll a large number of patients but rather because these complex procedures have a steep learning curve; therefore, physicians need to do cases on a regular basis in order to maintain their technical skills.

A similar lack of appropriate volumes is seen when cardiac transplantation volumes among the Philadelphia academic hospitals are examined. Between January 1, 2008, and September 30, 2008, Penn performed 34 heart transplants, Jefferson performed 11, and Hahnemann and Temple both performed 6. Although the U.S. Centers for Medicare and Medicaid Services recently lowered the number of yearly transplants needed to qualify for federal reimbursement from 12 to 10, a recent study from Johns Hopkins suggested that the standards to designate hospitals that are best at performing heart transplants needed to be increased to at least 14 procedures per year [53]. The study showed that death rates at 1 month and 1 year after transplant increased steadily at hospitals that performed fewer than 14 heart transplants per year. At least two of Philadelphia's four transplant programs are unlikely to meet the federal requirements and certainly did not meet the Hopkins requirements in 2008.

With the cardiac surgery programs at Hahnemann, Temple, and Jefferson not meeting optimal volume standards, some experts, including Porter and Teisberg, would suggest that these programs will not survive in a quality-guided market. Although extremely radical, the current situation facing the cardiothoracic surgery program at these three long-standing institutions could be solved by development of a collaborative program in cardiothoracic surgery. By combining the three programs,

> their total case volume would be nearly 800 cardiac procedures per year;
> they would perform 23 heart transplants per year;

the program would have access to exciting new investigational tools and techniques;

opportunities for residency training in cardiothoracic surgery would be re-invigorated; and

most importantly, patient care would be improved.

As a result, the combined program would become a leading referral site for regional cardiac care. The structure of a collaborative program would have to overcome the many cultural differences among the three competing AMCs, would have to supersede the egos of the staffs of various institutions, and would not be easily accomplished. However, the focus on improving care would be innovative and exciting.

A merger or alliance with other local programs may not be politically, legally, or economically expedient, other "global" strategies might be useful. For example, any or all of these programs might also benefit by "partnering" in some way with a nationally recognized cardiovascular program that is outside of their market area. This would allow them to bring world-class credentials in cardiovascular disease to the local marketplace and take advantage of the spin-offs from national name recognition while at the same time providing their cardiologists and cardiovascular surgeons with ready access to new and innovative technology (recognizing that some select disease states would travel to the "home base" for care). By folding their statistics into the overall statistics of the "partnering" program, they would also provide both payers and patients with a significant level of confidence in the quality of the program while at the same time meeting all Leapfrog-type benchmarks. This type of arrangement would not be substantially different than the efforts described earlier between Columbia-Presbyterian and Mt. Sinai Hospital of Florida but would represent one of the first alliances in a single product line between two academic medical centers.

Finally, it must be recognized that any of these three hospitals could take a more traditional approach to increasing their procedural volumes in cardiovascular disease—investing heavily in the recruitment of individuals who could bring with them the latest new technology by virtue of their positions as the national leaders in these new areas. The ability to attract these types of individuals would in all likelihood also require the recruitment of the basic science programs that may underpin these new clinical arenas. For example, the recruitment of an interventional cardiologist or cardiothoracic surgeon who is implanting autologous stem cells in the hearts of patients who are days or weeks status-post a myocardial infarction would likely require the establishment of a sophisticated stem cell research laboratory to complement their clinical needs. Similarly, individuals who are injecting DNA that is driven by viral vectors might require a core lab for preparation of viruses under appropriate FDA standards.

This approach would be more palatable from a political standpoint but would require that substantial funds be tasked in a single clinical area. Regardless of whether an AMC takes a more "out of the box" approach such as a local or transcontinental alliance or the more traditional approach of a targeted investment, it must be recognized that in today's highly competitive health care environment, accepting the status quo is not a viable option.

References

1. Mayo, W. 2000. The necessity of cooperation in medicine. *Mayo Clinic Proceedings* 75:553–536.
2. Porter, M. E., and Teisberg, T. O. 2006. *Redefining health care: Creating value-based competition on results.* Boston: Harvard Business School Press.
3. Wartman, S. 2007. Presidential address. Spring dialogues. Association of Academic Health Centers, Mar. 26, 2007. Washington, D.C.
4. Dunning, R. 2007. Johns Hopkins: Global involvement of a Maryland institution. *Maryland Medicine* Summer.
5. Boonshoft School of Medicine, Wright State University (www.med.wright.edu/hsm/aboutus.html).
6. NYU Center for Global Health (http://globalhealth/med/nyu.edu).
7. www.hmi.hms.harvard.edu
8. Williams, R. From the dean (www.gms.edu.sg/index.php?Corporate).
9. Duke in Singapore: An update on the Duke-NUS Graduate Medical School (http://dukemedmag.duke.edu/article.php?id+16760#16763).
10. A voyage of discovery: Building academic health center infrastructure worldwide. Association of Academic Health Centers (www.aahcdc.org/policy/meetinghighlights/spring08/pg4.php).
11. U.S.–South Korea four-way medical affiliation. 2005. Unique international collaboration to enhance patient care, research and medical education. Press release, Jan. 24, Columbia University Medical School (http://nyp.org/news/hospital/us-korea-affiliation.html).
12. Macfarlane, S. B., Agabian, N., Novotny, T. E., Rutherford, G. W., Stewart, C. C., and Debas, H. T. 2008. Think globally, act locally, and collaborate internationally: Global health sciences at the University of California, San Francisco. *Academic Medicine* 83 (2): 173–179.
13. Fabregas, L. 2004. UPMC gives hope, draws fire from Italy. *Pittsburgh Tribune,* Oct. 17.
14. Levin, S. 2005. Empire building: Consolidation and controversy at UPMC. *Pittsburgh Post-Gazette,* Dec. 27, A1.
15. Snowbeck, C. 2006. UPMC setting up Irish cancer centers using local venture's radiation services. *Pittsburgh Post-Gazette,* Feb. 8.
16. Snowbeck, C. 2006. UPMC expands its reach in Qatar. *Pittsburgh Post-Gazette,* June 13.

17. Fitzpatrick, D. 2008. UPMC to manage hospital in Ireland as continuation of expansion strategy. *Pittsburgh Post-Gazette,* Feb. 26.
18. Krieger, Z. 2008. An academic building boom transforms the Persian Gulf. *The Chronicle of Higher Education,* Mar. 26.
19. Johns Hopkins International. Hopkins around the world (http://www.jhintl.net/forphysicians/default.aspx?id=3368).
20. Work begins on Cleveland Clinic Abu Dhabi. 2008. *The Cleveland Leader,* Jan. 28.
21. Krieger, Z. 2008. Desert bloom. *The Chronicle of Higher Education,* Mar. 28.
22. Levin, S. 2005. Empire building: Clash of titans. *Pittsburgh Post-Gazette,* Dec. 28.
23. Golden, R. N. 2007. Academic campuses extend the school's reach to all corners of the state. *Wisconsin Medical Journal* 106 (4): 231.
24. Hawley, S. R., Molgaard, C. A., Ablah, E., Orr, S. A., Oler-Manske, J. E., and St. Romain, T. 2007. Academic-practice partnerships for community health workforce development. *Journal of Community Health Nursing* 24 (3): 155–165.
25. Sostman, H. D., Forese, L. L., Boom, M. L., and Schroth, L. 2005. Building a transcontinental affiliation: A new model for academic health centers. *Academic Medicine* 80 (11): 1046–1053.
26. Krauss, K., and Smith, J. 1997. Rejecting conventional wisdom: How academic medical centers can regain their leadership positions. *Academic Medicine* 72 (7): 571–575.
27. Greene, J. 2007. From the ground up. *Modern Healthcare* 37:64.
28. West Chester, PA, hospital enters heart surgery affiliation with Cleveland Clinic, Cleveland Clinic Miller Family Heart and Vascular Institute, April 19, 2006 (http://my.clevelandclinic.org/heart/news).
29. Blumenthal, D., and Meyer, G. S. 1996. Academic health centers in a changing environment. *Health Affairs* (Millwood) 15 (2): 200–215.
30. Shortell, S. M., Gillies, R. R., and Anderson, D. A. 1994. The new world of managed care: Creating organized delivery systems. *Health Affairs* (Millwood) 13 (5): 46–64.
31. Kleinke, J. 1998. *Bleeding edge: The business of health care in the new century.* Gaithersburg, MD: Aspen Publishers.
32. Todd, J. 1999. The trouble with mergers: Why are so many nonprofit hospital partnerships crumbling? *Health Care Business* September/October: 82–101.
33. Andreopoulos, S. 1997. The folly of teaching-hospital mergers. *New England Journal of Medicine* 336 (1): 61–64.
34. Longest, B., Rakch, J., and Darr, K. 2000. *Managing health service organizations and systems.* Baltimore, MD: Health Professions Press.
35. Zaman, M., and Mavondo, F. 2001. Measuring strategic alliance success: A conceptual framework. Australian New Zealand Management Association, Sydney, Australia (http://130.195.95.71:8081/WWW.ANZMAC2001/home.htm). Accessed 10/30/08.
36. Pellegrini, V. 2001. Mergers involving academic health centers: A formidable challenge. *Clinical Orthopedic Related Research* 391:288–296.
37. Mallon, W. T. 2003. The alchemists: A case study of a failed merger in academic medicine. *Academic Medicine* 78 (11): 1090–1104.

38. VanEtten, P. 1999. Camelot or common sense? The logic behind the UCSF/ Stanford merger. *Health Affairs* March/April: 143–148.
39. Kirchheimer, B. 2000. Merger now a total split. *Modern Healthcare* 30 (7): 12–13.
40. Richter, R. 1999. Stanford, UCSF to end merger of med centers. *Stanford Report* online, Nov. 3 (http://news-service.stanford.edu/news/1999/november3/merger-113.html).
41. http://www.paloaltoonline.com/weekly/morgue/news/1997Jan_24.ARTICLE.html
42. Segil, L. 2001. Creating alliances that work. CEO Refresher.
43. Collins, J. 2001. *Good to great,* 300. New York: Harper Collins Publishers Inc.
44. Chatman, V. S., Buford, J. F., and Plant, B. 2003. The building and sustaining of a health care partnership: The Meharry–Vanderbilt alliance. *Academic Medicine* 78 (11): 1105–1113.
45. *U.S. News and World Report.* July 10, 2008. Best hospitals honor roll (http://health.usnews.com/articles/health/best-hospitals/2008/07/10/best-hospitals-honor-roll.html).
46. Maupin, J. E., and Jacobsen, H. R. 1998. A memorandum of understanding between Meharry Medical College and Vanderbilt University Medical Center. Nashville, TN.
47. O'Neill, J. A., Jr., and Stain, S. C. 2001. An effective merger of academic surgical programs. *Archives of Surgery* 136 (2): 172–175.
48. Pennsylvania Health Care Cost Containment Council in DRGs 104-111, 525, and 547-500 for the periods July 2006 to June 2007.
49. Welke, K. F., Barnett, M. J., Vaughan Sarrazin, M. S., and Rosenthal, G. E. 2005. Limitations of hospital volume as a measure of quality of care for coronary artery bypass graft surgery. *Annals of Thoracic Surgery* 80 (6): 2114–2119.
50. Rathore, S. S., Epstein, A. J., Volpp, K. G. M., and Krumholz, H. M. 2004. Hospital coronary artery bypass graft surgery volume and patient mortality, 1998–2000. *Annals of Surgery* 239 (1): 110–117.
51. Vaughan Sarrazin, M. S., Hanna, E. L., Gormley, C. J., and Rosenthal, G. E. 2002. Mortality in Medicare beneficiaries following coronary artery bypass graft surgery in states with and without certificate of need regulation. *Journal of the American Medical Association* 288 (15): 1859–1866.
52. Birkmeyer, J. D., and Dimick, J. B. 2004. Potential benefits of the new Leapfrog standards: Effect of process and outcomes measures. *Surgery* 135 (6): 569–575.
53. Heart transplants: Do more or do none, Johns Hopkins study suggests. 2008. Press release, Jan. 29 (http://www.hopkinsmedicine.org/Press_releases/2008/01_29_08.html).

Chapter 12

Ensuring Governmental Support and Oversight of the AMC

> In the future the medical profession will also become closely associated with the government, and with a far more important function—that which deals with the life and health of the people. It appears to me that the laity will soon appreciate the necessity of this work, possibly before the medical profession is ready to undertake it.
>
> **William Mayo, 1910** [1]

Introduction

Although Dr. William Mayo had the foresight nearly a century ago to recognize the importance of government in supporting and regulating the practice of medicine, federal agencies have rarely exerted oversight of AMCs despite the fact that they should be viewed as a public trust. AMCs are entrusted with the tripartite mission of providing outstanding patient care, teaching the next generation of clinicians, and discovering the next generation of therapies. Most organizations in the United States whose activities have significant effects on the safety, health, or financial well-being of the American populace are carefully regulated by federal agencies. For example, the Federal Aviation Administration is charged with ensuring that our airlines are safe and that pilots and crews fly with appropriate levels of sleep, and the Security and Exchange Commission was established to ensure that banking and investment groups follow rules to ensure the confidence of the American populace in investment instruments. The Food and Drug Administration oversees the safety of our supply of food, drugs and devices, the Federal Communications Commission oversees the country's communications outlets, and the Federal Maritime Commission regulates ocean-borne transportation.

When these agencies fail to fulfill their missions, there are public outcries. Indeed, the perception that government failed in its obligation to oversee the banking and investment community led in large part to the ouster of many Republican candidates in the 2008 elections and to the election of Barack Obama as the 44th president of the United States. However, despite the fact that AMCs are a "public trust," no federal agency oversees or regulates their activities other than licensing groups that ensure the adequacy of medical education (LCME) or the Joint Commission on Hospital Accreditation, which evaluates all of the nation's hospitals. This chapter looks at the historic relationship between government and AMCs, medical advocacy groups and their effectiveness in supporting the missions of the AMCs, and efforts to create and the need to develop a national commission to provide federal support for AMCs.

The Historic Relationship between Federal and State Governments and AMCs

The first governmental intervention in America's system for medical education occurred in 1910 after Abraham Flexner's expose showed that many of America's medical schools were graduating poorly trained doctors. State legislatures passed legislation that was largely responsible for the demise of proprietary medical schools in the United States. However, it would take almost 20 years for all of the state legislatures to implement needed reform. A second example of government regulations that modified the structure of many AMCs was the National Cancer Act of 1971, which mandated that federally designated "cancer centers" of excellence have a level of administrative and financial independence that separated them from the structure of traditional clinical departments. This allowed cancer centers to grow and flourish unencumbered by the traditional hierarchical structure of the AMC described in Chapters 1 and 2.

The federal government also has an enormous impact on AMCs by virtue of its allocation of funds to the National Institutes of Health and the Medicare and Medicaid programs during each budget cycle and its financing of graduate medical education. The allocation of these funds has been guided more by budget limitations than by a concerted effort by Congress to recognize, understand, and support the various missions of the AMC. As noted in Chapter 10, the various state governments show marked inconsistency in the level of support they provide to their public and private institutions. Indeed, federal and state entities have not focused their efforts on the health of AMCs even as it has become increasingly obvious that many AMCs—particularly those with safety net hospitals—are experiencing deep systemic crises.

In recent years, governmental agencies have intervened in selected areas of America's AMCs when there has been a public outcry or a political opportunity. An example of governmental intervention in response to public outcries was the institution of regulations by the state of New York governing resident work hours. These actions came about in large part as a result of public outrage over the death of Libby Zion—the daughter of lawyer, former prosecutor, and journalist Sidney Zion—who was admitted to New York Hospital in Manhattan in March 1984 and died within 24 hours of that admission [2].

The physicians who cared for her believed that she had died of an unidentified infection. However, her father became increasingly convinced that his daughter's death was preventable. He pointed to the fact that the intern assigned to Libby was covering an enormous number of patients that night and that the resident team was fatigued from working too many hours without sleep. He used his influence to get publicity in local and national media, including the *New York Times* [3–6], *Newsweek,* and even TV's *60 Minutes.* Due in large part to the aggressive efforts of Mr. Zion, Manhattan District Attorney Robert Morgenthau brought the case before the grand jury to seek an indictment for murder. The grand jury refused to indict the hospital or the doctors because of insufficient evidence regarding the cause of death, but did issue a report that "determined that woefully inadequate care and repeated mistakes made by unsupervised interns and junior residents at a New York hospital resulted in the death of a young woman there in 1984" [7]. Furthermore, it called for new regulations at teaching hospitals.

In response to this request, New York State Health Commissioner David Axelrod established a blue-ribbon panel headed by Bertrand M. Bell. The Bell Commission recommended that residents' work be limited to 80 hours a week and that so-called night floats—doctors who worked overnight to spell their colleagues—be instituted at all hospitals. In June 1988, the State Hospital Review Planning Council unanimously adopted the proposals of the Bell Commission [8]. Assuming that federal agencies would enact similar nationwide regulations, the American College of Graduate Medical Education (ACGME) codified a mandatory 80-hour work week for the accreditation of residency training programs across the country, resulting in universal alterations in the work hour limitations for all residency training programs; these regulations were not put in place until 2003. Ironically, the decrease in physician work hours has had no effect on mortality, but has stressed the physician workforce at many AMCs as hospitals have had to replace residents with physicians or physicians-extendors: a cost that can not be recouped from third-party payors [9,10].

More recently, public outcries regarding conflicts of interest have led Senator Charles Grassley, ranking member of the Senate Finance Committee, and Senator Herb Kohl, chairman of the Special Committee on Aging, to undertake probes of allegations of conflict of interest against a number of prominent biomedical researchers, including those at Emory University and Stanford University. In an October 2008 letter to Lee Bollinger, the president of Columbia University, the senators cited their "duty to protect the health of Medicare and Medicaid beneficiaries and safeguard taxpayer dollars authorized and appropriated by Congress for those programs." They asked the university to provide information detailing the outside income paid to a group of cardiologists on the Columbia faculty who run a large national "educational and scientific" meeting of interventional cardiologists called TCT.

The funds from the meeting go to a "non-profit" foundation called the Cardiovascular Research Foundation. However, concerns had been raised regarding the distribution of large yearly revenues to the foundation ($47.2 million in 2005), the relationship between the cardiologists and the companies that support and exhibit at the meeting, and the disclosures made to the university regarding how any income paid to the cardiologists was reported, and how the research foundation or the meeting might have influenced patient care at Columbia [11].

These issues are important; however, there has been no systematic or strategic approach on the part of government to resolve the larger issues that confront America's AMCs. For example, governmental agencies have not addressed

the fact that AMCs need to care for an increasingly large number of uninsured patients;

the financial cost of new restrictions on physician work hours;

the healthcare manpower crisis;

the failure of safety net hospitals;

the continuing loss of physician–scientists;

the increasing disparity between the financial underpinnings of the academic "haves" and "have-nots";

the enormous variability from state to state in reimbursement from private healthcare companies; and the negative impact of the current financial crisis on the endowments that support many of the academic enterprises of some of America's largest and most successful AMCs.

In addition, members of Congress and other governmental agencies have not questioned the ethics of "nonprofit" healthcare insurance companies that continue to raise rates for patients and decrease reimbursements to physicians while at the same time building multibillion dollar reserves. These reserves could more appropriately be used to support the teaching missions of AMCs, care for the uninsured, and conduct research that would improve patient care and outcomes while at the same time decreasing healthcare costs.

State and Federal Oversight of Quality of Care

For all practical purposes there is little oversight of AMCs by federal or state regulatory agencies. The oversight of AMCs has been left largely to Medicare, a patchwork of state health departments, and the Joint Commission, a nonprofit group based in Oakbrook Terrace, Illinois, that certifies that hospitals are operating safely [12]. With fewer than 1,000 employees, the Joint Commission oversees quality and safety at more than 17,000 U.S. hospitals, nursing homes, and assisted-living facilities, but it lacks the enforcement powers of a federal regulator. Medicare has made efforts to improve care by denying payments for a handful of "hospital-acquired conditions" and has used payment data to assess quality of care. In addition, it has performed chart audits to address particular questions regarding hospital practices.

However, Medicare's efforts have been focused on process of care rather than on quality of care. That states are unable to regulate healthcare because of inherent conflicts of interest and political influence was demonstrated in a recent investigative report in the *New York Times*. The report detailed evidence suggesting that University Hospital in Syracuse, a State University of New York-owned hospital and teaching hospital of SUNY University Upstate Medical Center at Syracuse, was "not a good hospital" [12]. Indeed, in 2006, patients at University Hospital were three times more likely to develop infections during their hospitalization as were patients at the average New York hospital. In addition, Medicare data suggested that the University Hospital was "among the least safe hospitals in the United States" [12].

In 2006, a commission impaneled by the state legislature recommended that University Hospital be merged with Crouse Hospital—a private, nonprofit hospital in Syracuse that was running at 50% occupancy—and that the total number of beds allocated to the two hospitals be reduced from 942 to 600 [12]. However, the two hospitals disagreed with the committee's report and executives of the Upstate Medical University and Crouse Hospital began to lobby the governor to undo the recommendation.

As the largest employers in Syracuse, the university and the hospital were able to exert significant political influence. In addition, the University Hospital unions, a group with richer contracts than the employees at Crouse Hospital, advertised, lobbied lawmakers, and filed a lawsuit to overturn the recommendations. By the spring of 2007, the state health department had backed off the plan to merge the two hospitals.

Although the expose in the *Times* provided a series of anecdotes suggesting that care at University Hospital had not improved, it is clear that no single body collects or disseminates information that can provide patients or regulators with information that accurately assesses the quality of care at an AMC. Furthermore, the situation in Syracuse further points out the need for federal regulation through the efforts of a national commission in order to avoid the politics that govern state and local decisions.

Failure of the Federal Government and State Agencies to Recognize the AMC's Role and Importance

One would assume that the leaders of our government understand the importance of America's AMCs to the future of healthcare in America. Indeed, when senators and congressmen are sick, they often seek their care at some of America's premier AMCs. For example, when Senator Ted Kennedy was diagnosed with a brain tumor, he called together a team of experts from some of the leading AMCs in the country and eventually pursued surgical therapy at Duke. However, the only objective information available that helps us gauge level of understanding is a 2004 survey that found an appalling lack of knowledge regarding the role of America's AMCs in the country's health among both the general public and our government leaders. The survey found that the term "academic medical center" was not viewed as favorably as "teaching hospitals" or "medical schools" and that academic medical centers received a favorable rating only 40% of the time [13].

More disturbing were findings that

45% of respondents were unaware that teaching hospitals were not for profit
28% were not aware of who provided the bulk of healthcare for low-income individuals, and
23% were not aware that academic medical centers faced funding shortages due to the growing burden of the uninsured patient and cuts in Medicare funding.

Furthermore, 47% of U.S. voters and 35% of congressional staffers thought that most medical research took place at laboratories funded by private companies, and an amazing 29% of congressional staffers thought that the NIH intramural programs performed more medical research than the medical schools or teaching hospitals that they funded [13]. Indeed, 41% of members of Congress did not even know how the NIH budget was used to support medical research and 20% thought that the NIH only supported research in NIH laboratories in Washington, D.C. With this type of information gap, it is no wonder that Congress has allocated so few dollars to support the missions of the AMCs. Furthermore, it raises grave concerns that Washington policy makers will not consider the adverse affects that proposals for healthcare reform might have on America's AMCs.

Advocacy Groups and Gaps in Advocacy Activities

AMCs must be blamed, at least in part, for the failure of government to understand their plight because they have clearly not done a good job of advocacy with the public or on Capitol Hill. AMC faculty are represented by an alphabet soup of organizations focused on advocating for the interests of specific specialties (e.g., cardiologists, surgeons, gastroenterologists, etc.). However, the majority of these organizations represent not only the members of AMCs but also the large number of community doctors and the thousands of community hospitals. Thus, academic medicine gets lost in the larger issues advocated by these large societies.

For example, two of the most influential lobbying groups in Washington are those of the American College of Cardiology and the American Cancer Society. The American College of Cardiology spends most of its lobbying dollars dealing with issues that now face the majority of its 36,000 members: cuts in Medicaid imaging services, Medicare physician payment rates, criteria for nuclear cardiology, medical criteria for evaluating cardiovascular disorders, and cuts in reimbursements for cardiovascular services as were found in the Deficit Reduction Act of 2005 [14]. In the past 3 years the American College of Cardiology did send a letter to the House Appropriations Subcommittee on Labor, Health, and Human Services regarding the fiscal year 2007 funding for cardiovascular research and participated with the National Heart Lung and Blood Institute Constituency Group in sending a letter to Congress in support of increased NIH funding.

However, when the American College of Cardiology lobbied against cuts in Medicare payments to cardiologists, the lobbying efforts were highly organized and consisted of organized visits with members of Congress by cardiologists who belonged to the American College, e-mails to college members that could be electronically sent with little effort, and numerous phone calls to congressional staffers. Thus, medical organizations pay little attention in their lobbying efforts to the plight of their colleagues who work in academia or to the AMCs themselves.

Like the American College of Cardiology, the American Cancer Society also has a very strong advocacy group called the Cancer Action Network [15]. In 2008, 500 cancer patients, survivors, and caregivers went to Capitol Hill to urge Congress to pass laws to help fight cancer, including facilitating drug evaluations at the FDA, passing the Family Smoking Prevention Act, creating a national cancer fund to support cancer research by increasing the federal tobacco tax, and increasing funding to the National Institutes of Health and the National Cancer Institute.

However, nowhere in the American Cancer Society's advocacy program is there a recognition that many of the new agents for treating human disease come out of translational science laboratories at AMCs that are part of collaborative efforts of scientists focused on the treatment of many different diseases; that the early phase I evaluations of new anticancer therapies, as well as many of the phase II and phase III studies of new anticancer agents, take place at America's AMCs; or that the majority of new therapeutic interventions are evaluated and tested at AMCs—most commonly at academic centers designated as National Cancer Institute Centers of Excellence. Thus, there is a lack of recognition that, without economically healthy AMCs, it is unlikely that the goals of cancer patients and survivors will be met.

In terms of advocacy, the group that should be leading the charge for the academic medical centers is the Association of American Medical Colleges (AAMC). Steven Moore, the director of government relations for the AAMC, has suggested that "AAMC and our constituents have to do even more advocacy on two levels. We need to work with other groups to make the case for more overall discretionary spending, and then we need to make the case specifically for health programs." He has noted further that "academic medical institutions can help by educating local elected officials on the specific costs and benefits of certain programs, and working to encourage political candidates to discuss healthcare more often during campaigning and make it a stronger portion of their platforms" [16].

However, the AAMC needs to become far more effective as an advocacy organization in order to succeed. For example, Darrell Kirch, president of the AAMC, sent a letter to the platform committees of the Democratic and Republican parties in the summer of 2008 prior to each party's nominating conventions [17]. The letter pointed out the role of AMCs in "educating a diverse workforce of future physicians and biomedical scientists; promoting discovery and innovation through biomedical, behavioral, and health services research;

applying new knowledge to alleviate suffering rehabilitate injury, and prevent disease and premature death; and fulfilling this nation's obligation to provide healthcare to its poorest and sickest members." The letter urged the two platform committees to include in their platforms the statement that AMCs "are the places where hopes become realities every day. We [government] will continue to promote policies that strengthen their core missions of medical education, patient care, and medical research" [17].

Both the Democratic and Republican platforms called for increased investment in medical research; the Democratic platform also called for "strengthening of the healthcare workforce through training and reimbursement incentives" and a commitment to ensuring a sufficient number of well-qualified primary care physicians and nurses as well as direct care workers [18,19]. However, neither platform even mentioned America's AMCs, the challenges they face, or the current academic physician workforce crisis. Obviously, it will take far more than just a letter to move Congress to recognize the importance of AMCs to public health.

Perhaps the AAMC is not the right organization to undertake an aggressive lobbying effort on behalf of academic medicine. Begun in 1876 to "consider all matters relating to reform in medical college work," the AAMC has a Washington location but has not demonstrated itself to be an active force in lobbying Congress for change. By its mission statement, the AAMC seeks to carry out four responsibilities: "educating the physician and medical scientist workforce, discovering new medical knowledge, developing innovative technologies for prevention, diagnosis and treatment of disease; and providing healthcare services in academic settings" [17]. In addition, the AAMC mission statement notes that "these issues cannot be resolved simply by setting medical schools and major teaching hospitals apart from the rest of the system to 'protect' them" [17].

The AAMC is also burdened by a governance structure that includes five governing councils, four areas of interest, and 14 "groups"—one of which is composed of the government relations representatives. Within the governing councils, inherent conflicts of interest may abrogate the ability of the AAMC to be a strong spokesperson for AMCs. For example, one of the governing councils is the Council of Teaching Hospitals and Health Systems. Although this group includes the AMC hospitals associated with private or public medical schools, the 400-member group of hospitals also includes many community hospitals that have residency training programs but do not have to support missions of research or undergraduate medical education. Thus, their needs are quite different from those of the AMCs.

The AAMC councils also include one representing residents, one representing students, and one representing nearly 100 different subspecialty societies. Inherent differences in the needs of the various constituencies that make up the

AAMC may impact their ability to lobby aggressively for AMCs or to target a significant amount of their revenues for lobbying efforts.

In the absence of a single voice to represent the 126 AMCs, individual AMCs have in some cases carried on their own lobbying efforts. For example, the University of Pittsburgh Medical Center spends close to $1 million per year on lobbying efforts at both the state and federal levels [20]. By contrast, Pennsylvania's two Blue Cross Blue Shield health insurers spent $2.4 million in 2007 on lobbying state legislatures in order to support the merger of the two "nonprofit" institutions [21]. Each company has billion dollar endowments and little competition in its individual region, so the combination of the two would have resulted in a health insurance monopoly that would not have been in the best interest of the already struggling AMCs in the state.

Unfortunately, few academic medical centers have the resources to fund their own government relations teams; those that can represent the AMC haves rather than the have-nots. This results in Congress having a skewed view of the health of America's AMCs and over-represents the needs of the haves. However, it is the have-nots that care for America's underserved that most need increased state or federal support. The AAMC also seems to have taken a somewhat cynical approach to advocacy. When commenting on the views of Democratic senators regarding proposed cuts in Medicare and Medicaid, David Moore, senior associate vice president for government relations of the AAMC, noted that "it will be politics all the time, probably with no resolution anytime soon" [16]. Therefore, it is imperative that the AAMC step up to the plate and aggressively lobby for AMCs or, alternatively, that another organization fill the advocacy void.

Ensuring Governmental Support and Oversight of Academic Medical Centers

In 1910, Flexner first noted that AMCs needed support from federal or state governments [22]:

> It is universally conceded that medical education cannot be conducted on proper lines at a profit—or even at cost; but it does not follow that it has therefore ceased to "pay."…Our best medical schools are indeed far from self-supporting; they absorb the income of large endowments or burden seriously the general resources of their respective universities.…the state or city can indeed legitimately aid medical education.

Despite Flexner's warnings, some long-standing AMCs have positive margins based on the availability of large endowments, a favorable payer mix among their patients, linkage with large and established university teaching hospitals, favorable geographic locations, and the opportunity to carry out entrepreneurial enterprises. However, as we have seen in the earlier chapters of this book, only one-third of AMCs have positive margins and many do not receive support for their academic mission from their affiliated hospitals. My more conservative colleagues argue that the plight of these poorer AMCs will be controlled by the marketplace. AMCs that cannot remain fiscally sound while fulfilling their societal missions will simply cease to exist or will limit their areas of expertise; those that share in the profit margins of successful hospitals or health systems will grow and prosper.

Indeed, Porter and Teisberg espoused a similar view when they suggested that the only healthcare delivery organizations that will survive in the future healthcare marketplace will be those that focus on providing only services in which they can provide outstanding care and divest themselves of clinical programs in which they cannot excel. I agree with the concept that AMCs must be willing and able to compete in the healthcare marketplace and limit their services to those that they do best. However, I take exception with the notion that we should simply let the market decide which AMCs survive and which AMCs die. Rather, I would suggest that AMCs are a public trust and have a societal responsibility to provide their patients with outstanding care.

This opinion is not new; as Benjamin Disraeli pointed out in a speech in 1877, "The health of the people is really the foundation upon which all their happiness and all their power as a state depend" [23]. As such, the federal government must step in to help control the environmental and political forces that can abrogate the ability of even the best AMC to fulfill this primary mission. The following sections contain recommendations for how federal agencies can intercede on behalf of AMCs and the population of patients that they serve.

The Federal Government Must Establish a National Commission to Oversee AMCs

Academic medical centers are public trusts that fulfill a group of important societal needs, including providing outstanding care for patients independent of race, religion, ethnic origins, or socioeconomic status. Indeed, over 60% of the country's uninsured are cared for at the 126 AMCs in the country. Throughout this book, we have seen how external constraints and internal cultures have often limited the ability of the AMC to fulfill its societal mission. Furthermore, we have seen how state-to-state differences in healthcare financing, the legal and regulatory environments, and funding for education have either positively or negatively affected the AMCs' ability to succeed.

Although it can be argued that the oversight of an AMC should occur at the state level, many examples demonstrate how the provincial politics of state governments too often lead to enormous mistakes in decisions regarding the healthcare industry. For example, in the late 1990s, the legislature of the Commonwealth of Pennsylvania allowed the law governing certificates of needs to "sundown." This law had limited the construction of high-technology facilities such as cardiac catheterization laboratories to regions that had a population large enough to warrant the ready availability of this technology. Within a very short period of time, Pennsylvania had more cardiac catheterization laboratories and open heart surgery programs per capita than virtually any other state in the United States, and the vast majority of the programs did not meet the volume standards mandated by many healthcare organizations, including the Leapfrog Group. The bill was allowed to sundown because legislators who represented rural communities believed that an open-heart surgery program in their community would enhance the prestige of the community.

By contrast, the state of New York has successfully maintained a certificate of need program. Thus, all of the hospitals in the state that perform interventional cardiac procedures, coronary artery bypass surgery, or heart transplantation have high volumes and outstanding results. New York City has also instituted novel policies that improve care of patients having a heart attack. Rather than taking the patient to the closest medical facility or to the hospital of his or her choice, as is done in most cities, paramedics in New York take the patient to the nearest heart center. Each heart center must meet predefined guidelines for patient care, including the ability to transfer the patient to a cardiac catheterization laboratory and perform an interventional procedure to remove the clot or obstruction within 90 minutes of the ambulance arriving at the emergency room door.

Local politics abrogate the ability of many communities to institute these kinds of programs. However, the development of a national commission on academic medical centers would mitigate many local issues. This national commission should be composed of physician and nonphysician leaders from a wide spectrum of AMCs, including those associated with urban or rural safety net hospitals, those associated with old and prestigious research-oriented medical schools, and individuals from state medical schools. Thus, the academic haves and have-nots will be represented. The commission should also include representatives from federal health insurance agencies, the National Institutes of Health, and the Food and Drug Administration, as well as highly placed representatives from the many industries that support the AMC (including leaders of the pharmaceutical and medical device industries) in order to gain their perspective on the healthcare crisis.

The commission must recognize that AMC leaders sometimes lose sight of the problems faced by their managers, their middle managers, and their faculty; therefore, the commission should also include a representative number of department chairs, division chiefs, service line managers, faculty representatives, and even students. Finally, the commission should include scholars from areas as diverse as healthcare economics, biomedical ethics, healthcare delivery, business structure and organization, population dynamics, and epidemiology of disease.

Because of the size and complexity of the commission's tasks, it should be empowered to form task forces to look at specific issues—for example, the Task Force on the Physician Workforce Crisis discussed early in this book—and to seek testimony from individuals who can educate the commission regarding specific areas in which it lacks expertise. Most importantly, the job of the commission should not be to author one report or several reports. Rather, it should serve as an ongoing governmental body that oversees the important missions of America's AMCs, educates the public about the important societal mission of AMCs, and provides ongoing advice to the legislative and executive branches of government.

The Federal Government Must Establish National Guidelines for AMC Financial Reporting

As was pointed out in an earlier chapter, there is no common reporting mechanism regarding the financial health of an individual AMC. Although AMCs provide some financial information in self-disclosures to the AAMC, these data can only be queried in the aggregate and investigators cannot gain access to data from individual institutions. This lack of public reporting is in marked contrast to publicly traded institutions. Thus, scholars who study the business of healthcare know far more about the financial health of publicly traded companies, such as IBM, Pfizer, or General Motors, than they do about the AMC where they work or where they receive their healthcare.

Indeed, better public disclosure of AMCs may have allowed local officials to learn about the business practices at Allegheny Health System prior to its bankruptcy. The ability of academic scholars in the fields of finance, business, and education to identify the financial structures, organizational structures, and strategic initiatives that have led good AMCs to attain greatness will only take place if there is public access to and consistency in AMC financial reports. Finally, it is imperative that the National Commission on Academic Medical Centers also have access to AMC financial reports: It is very difficult to convince a legislative committee that a specific AMC or group of AMCs needs support from its state or the federal government without allowing policy analysts the appropriate level of financial data for their review.

Similarly, the general public sees AMCs as economic giants with little recognition of the fiscal constraints under which the members of the AMC faculty and staff work. Perhaps one of the reasons that AMCs have found it so difficult to convince state and local governments, as well as philanthropic foundations and individuals, of their needs is a complete lack of knowledge on the part of the public regarding the financial plight of many AMCs. This could be rectified by transparency, national guidelines for reporting, and by making data available through the national commission.

Reimbursement for Patient Care from Private Insurance Carriers Must Be Equitable, Reasonable, and Comparable across All State Boundaries

At a recent meeting, I sat with colleagues who were academic leaders at AMCs in St. Louis and Denver. The three of us shared information with each other that, to the best of my knowledge, cannot be found in any book or any report: the reimbursement rate from the three different Blue Cross Blue Shield providers in each of our regions. The variation was striking. The blended average paid to the practice plan in St. Louis was 180% of Medicare; in Denver it was 140% of Medicare and, for institutions in Philadelphia, it ranged from 120–135% of Medicare. Each of these three institutions has similar patient populations, has faculty of a comparable size, and provides similar clinical services. However, the reimbursements each receives are substantially different.

A recent investigative report in the *Boston Globe* showed similar disparities among Boston hospitals [24]. For example, Massachusetts General Hospital received $51,522 for each coronary bypass surgery; Tufts Medical Center received $50,486, and Boston Medical Center (Boston University) received $33,988. Marshall Carter, chairman of Boston Medical Center, wrote [24]:

> The disparities in payments from private insurers to certain favored providers without a clear connection to quality or greater cost efficiency should trouble us all...For large and powerful hospitals that care for patients with higher incomes and the best insurance plans, these subsidies come in the form of higher payments from private insurers.

Indeed, the *Globe*'s investigation showed that "favored" institutions received payments 15–60% higher than those made to their competitors. These disparities cannot be justified in view of the fact that all of these AMCs have the very same societal responsibilities.

Another important issue is the financial structure of private insurance companies that maintain a nonprofit or not-for-profit status. With reserves in the billions of dollars, it should be unacceptable for a Blue Cross Blue Shield carrier to continue to accrue profits when some of the AMCs in the region are struggling. Because these healthcare insurance companies are regulated at the state level, only federal intervention can bring about a fair and equitable change. If Congress were to begin by passing legislation that opens reimbursement data across all states to public scrutiny through reports from the national commission, AMCs would be able to gain public support for greater state and/or governmental control of the healthcare insurance industry. The public would recognize that the rising costs of health insurance were not due to the cost of physician services or drug costs alone.

The Federal Government Must Carefully Evaluate the Plight of Safety Net Hospitals and Develop Mechanisms to Ensure That the Burden of the Uninsured or Underinsured Does Not Collapse the Foundations of Some AMCs

Traditionally, the funding of safety net hospitals has been left in large part to the individual states and communities in which they reside. However, with the current financial crises and the lack of money in many state budgets, it is imperative that the federal government be prepared to step in and support some of our largest safety net hospitals. The need to support these hospitals should be assessed by task forces of the national commission when individual safety net hospitals are faced with bankruptcy or closure. In addition to providing needed care to the public, these hospitals are important training grounds for tomorrow's doctors. Therefore, they must be supported.

The Federal Government Must Work to Ensure That the Country's AMCs Are Not Haves and Have-Nots

This is a complex but important issue. During his 2008 president's address delivered to the Association of American Medical Colleges' 199th meeting in San Antonio, Texas, Darrell Kirch raised a question [25]:

> How much economic inequality are we willing to tolerate in our own professional community? Do we really want a world in which some teaching hospitals and medical specialties are "haves," doing very well, while others are conspicuous "have-nots"? While some teaching

hospitals have solid margins and endowments, many (especially inner-city and rural safety-net hospitals) struggle to stay alive financially.

These differences limit the ability of the economically challenged AMCs to deliver the level of care provided by health systems with solid margins and large endowments. I have suggested that these financially challenged institutions can improve their finances and their level of care by focusing on what they do best and/or partnering with local or national centers of excellence to improve their level of care delivery. However, some safety net hospitals and their affiliated medical schools will not be able to survive without substantive help from the state or federal government.

A second issue of equally great importance is that we must ensure that the educational experience that students receive does not differ from AMC to AMC. Although some experts have proposed that we can increase the capacity to educate physicians by "limiting" the scope of their education and the infrastructure of rural schools, I would argue that this is a great mistake. If we have different tiers of MDs based on the depth and sophistication of their educational experience, we will be doing a great disservice to the society that we serve. Abraham Flexner addressed this issue when he noted that "the small town needs the best and not the worst doctor procurable. For the country doctor has only himself to rely on: he cannot in every pinch hail specialist, expert, and nurse. On his own skill, knowledge, resourcefulness, the welfare of his patient altogether depends" [22].

This is an issue that cannot be solved by state governments, which often make decisions regarding the establishment of new schools based on economics and politics rather than on what is best for society as a whole or for the students who will be educated in these new schools. Thus, the national commission, rather than a local group of businessmen, should be empowered to make decisions regarding the establishment of new private medical schools to ensure that we do not return to the era of proprietary for-profit medical schools that existed before the Flexner report in 1910.

Finally, we cannot allow a system in which some medical schools are available only to the rich. One example of the disparity in financing medical education was the announcement by Harvard Medical School that it would take steps to reduce the cost of a 4-year education by up to $50,000 for families with incomes of $120,000 or less by allocating up to $11 million per year for student scholarships [26]. As noted by Jeffrey Flier, dean of the School of Medicine, "It is important that the School not be out of reach to a broad segment of undergraduate students and their families. It is equally imperative to avoid burdening families with a new round of debt shortly after a child has finished college."

However, it is equally important that Harvard not be the only prestigious American medical school that provides substantive scholarship while other schools are affordable only for the rich. Realistically, these issues will not be addressed by medical schools collectively; therefore, only a federal advisory body can ensure that we have a medical education system in which clinical care, training, and the cost of a medical education across America's AMCs are as equivalent as possible.

Congress Must Support New Research Efforts to Understand Better the Delivery and Economics of Healthcare in the AMC

Academic medical centers and their leaders have vociferously argued that costs associated with care at an academic center are higher because they care for patients with a higher acuity of disease; incorporate students and residents into the care team, thereby lowering efficiency; provide expensive high-technology diagnostics and treatments that are not available elsewhere; and support clinical and basic research activities. However, it would be disingenuous not to point out that some scholars have questioned the validity of these arguments.

A report from the Dartmouth Institute for Health Policy and Clinical Practice looked at a group of the top-ranked academic medical centers to see whether higher spending and greater use of supply-sensitive care are associated with better care in a group of patients with chronic illness in their last 2 years of life. Supply-sensitive care was defined as services where the supply of a specific resource had a major influence on utilization rates. According to Wennberg et al., "Variations in supply-sensitive care are largely due to differences in local capacity and a payment system that ensures current capacity remains fully deployed" [27].

Surprisingly, higher spending and greater use of supply-sensitive care were not associated with improved outcomes from the perspectives of either patients or physicians. Wennberg and his group found that Medicare spent more than $93,000 per patient at UCLA, but little more than half of that at the Mayo Clinic. To manage similar patients, the Mayo Clinic used fewer beds and half the number of physicians as did UCLA [27]:

> [For instance], the Mayo Clinic and the Cleveland Clinic allocate relatively fewer resources per capita and spend less per capita than their peers, while simultaneously receiving high marks on established quality measures. Other academic medical centers use far more resources, deliver far more supply-sensitive care, and cost significantly more per capita, but with no better quality.

These researchers suggest that using fewer hospital beds, less physician labor, and fewer high-tech treatments (such as intensive care beds and expensive imaging devices) could markedly decrease costs. Not surprisingly, they also found that integrated group practices, in which all physicians and the accompanying hospital are integrated into a single practice group and physicians' salaries are based on their areas of specialization, are associated with the use of fewer resources [27].

Although the results of the Dartmouth study are intriguing, they raise as many questions as they answer. For example, how did the small class size of the medical school at the Mayo Clinic, demographics of its patient population, reimbursement structures for physicians, and the local malpractice environment influence physician behavior and resource utilization? The most important message to come from the Dartmouth study was [27]

> The nation needs a crash program to transform the management of chronic illness to a rational system where what happens to patients is based primarily on illness severity, medical evidence, and the patient's wishes, and where resource allocation and Medicare spending can be guided more and more by knowledge of what is needed to produce cost-effective, high-quality care. The support of such research needs to be the responsibility primarily of federal science policy. It makes no sense for the government to invest in biomedical research…without complementary research aimed at determining how new and existing treatments affect the outcomes of care, the lives of patients, and the efficacy of clinical practice.

Thus, government must support new and innovative research studies; in particular, those that do not fall under the traditional portfolio of the National Institutes of Health could be considered under the mandate of clinical and translational research. Lobbying Congress for the support of innovative new research in healthcare policy by collaborative groups of scholars from both business schools and AMCs might be one of the tasks of the national commission.

Building Infrastructure for the AMC

In order to stem the evaporating jobs and deepening recession, President-elect Obama promised to expand the opportunities for Americans to work by undertaking massive public works projects to improve the country's infrastructure. Projects would include repairing or rebuilding aging roads, schools, sewer systems, mass transit facilities, dams, and electrical grids—as well as creating alternative fuels, building windmills and solar panels, and replacing existing environmental systems with fuel-efficient heating or cooling systems.

Investing in the infrastructure of AMCs could also provide broad local and global economic opportunities. Many institutions have had to defer capital improvements to aging research and clinical facilities; others are struggling to support the debt service on buildings planned and built during the NIH "boom years" between 1997 and 2003, when the NIH budget doubled. In addition, individual investigators and collaborative groups have often been forced to make do with old and outdated laboratory equipment because of marked cutbacks in their NIH funding. At many AMCs clinical facilities are also in need of repair and capital is required to replace aging or outdated equipment—infrastructure support that can improve care, lower costs, and support the economic health of the community.

Perhaps the most important research "infrastructure" needed is talented young physicians and physician–scientists. At a time when most medical students graduate with six-figure debt, tuition reimbursement programs for individuals who pursue careers in the clinical and translational sciences would be one means of providing a bulwark against the continuing attrition of talented physicians and physician–scientists.

References

1. Mayo, W. Rush Medical College commencement, June 15, 1910. 2000. *Mayo Clinic Proceedings* 75:553–556.
2. http://en.wikipedia.org/wiki/libby_zion
3. Myers, M. 1987. When hospital doctors labor to exhaustion. *New York Times,* June 12.
4. Colburn, D. 1988. Medical education: Time for reform? After a patient's death, the 36-hour shift gets new scrutiny. *Washington Post,* Mar. 29.
5. Japenga, A. 1988. Endless days and sleepless nights: Do long work schedules help or hinder medical residents? *LA Times,* Mar. 6.
6. Segal, M. M., and Cohen, B. 1987. Hospital's junior doctors need senior backup. *New York Times,* June 8.
7. Sullivan, R. 1987. Grand jury assails hospital in '84 death of 18-year-old. *New York Times,* Jan. 13.
8. Daley, S. 1988. Hospital interns' long hours to be reduced. *New York Times,* June 10.
9. Horwitz, L. I., Kosiborod, M., Lin, Z., and Krumholz, H. M. 2007. Changes in outcomes for internal medicine inpatients after work-hour regulations. *Annals of Internal Medicine* 147 (2): 97–103.

10. Volpp, K. G., Rosen, A. K., Rosenbaum, P. R., Romano, P. S., Even-Shoshan, O., Wang, Y., Bellini, L., Behringer, T., and Silber, J. H. 2007. Mortality among hospitalized Medicare beneficiaries in the first 2 years following ACGME resident duty hour reform. *Journal of the American Medical Association* 298 (9): 975–983.

11. Meier, M. 2008. Senators question financial ties between doctors and steel manufacturers. *New York Times,* Oct. 17.

12. Berenson, A. 2008. Weak oversight lets bad hospitals stay open. *New York Times,* Dec. 8.

13. AAMC. 2004. Project Apacsor—What Americans say about the nation's medical schools and teaching hospitals, 1–36. Public and congressional staff opinion research project.

14. www.acc.org

15. http://action.acscan.org/

16. Fuchs, E. 2008. Budget battles could last into 2009. *AAMC Reporter* 17 (6): 1.

17. www.aamc.org

18. http://www.democrats.org/a/party/platform.html

19. http://www.gop.com/2008Platform/HealthCare.htm

20. Mamula, K. 2008. UPMC outspends all U.S. hospitals on lobbying. *Pittsburgh Business Times,* Aug. 8.

21. Toland, B. 2008. Insurers spending millions on lobbying. *Pittsburgh Post-Gazette,* Sept. 7.

22. Flexner, A. 1973. Medical education in the United States and Canada: A report to the Carnegie Foundation for the Advancement of Teaching, 346. Bulletin no. 4, New York (reprinted by The Heritage Press, Buffalo, NY).

23. Disraeli, B. 1877. Speech, Battersea Park. *London Times,* 10.

24. Krasner, J. 2008. State urged to review fees to elite hospitals. *The Boston Globe,* Nov. 20.

25. Kirch, D. The tough questions (www.aamc.org).

26. Cohen, B. 2008. Harvard Medical School to reduce student debt burden (http://harvardscience.harvard.edu/print/20205).

27. Wennberg, J. E., Fisher, E., Goodman, D. C., and Skinner, J. S. 2008. Tracking the care of patients with severe chronic illness. The Dartmouth Atlas of Healthcare, Dartmouth Institute of Health Policy and Clinical Practice, Lebanon, NH.

Conclusion

As clearly demonstrated in the preceding chapters, there is little doubt that academic medical centers are threatened by a vast combination of factors, including

intense marketplace competition from private hospitals;
decreased reimbursements from third-party payers;
a change in the demographics of the medical student population;
increasing regulation from authoritative bodies governing requirements for
   undergraduate and graduate education programs;
a shift of clinical research opportunities from the pubic to the private sector
   as well as from the United States to Europe, Asia, and South America;
the steadily increasing cost of a medical school education;
draconian cuts in the NIH budget;
the global economic crisis; and
a general malaise among members of the academic faculty.

Although academic medical centers must begin to change in order to meet these many challenges, the philosophic structure around which change should occur has not been addressed since the publication of Flexner's report in 1910. The goal of this book was to bring to public attention the great challenges faced by AMCs in fulfilling their societal responsibilities and to develop a new model that would allow academicians to have an initial construct around which to base their strategic plans.

Before beginning my research for this book, my impressions of what the AMC of the future would look like rested on a group of assumptions that were based largely on my own experiences. For example, I believed that the difference between a good and a great AMC was that the great AMC had a core focus on the "business of medicine" and that this helped to drive decision making as well as investments of time and money. The second assumption was that a medical school that did not have a substantial endowment and did not share positive margins with its affiliated hospital would probably be better off focusing on education and clinical care rather than struggling to support a research program; this was consistent with how businesses commonly focus only on what they do best. I also theorized that the separation of a hospital and its medical school would allow the physicians to leverage their autonomy and independence. Finally, I assumed that individual AMCs would have the best chance of survival if they could compete effectively in their local healthcare markets. Interestingly, my subsequent research led me to the realization that each of these initial assumptions was flawed.

For example, I found that good business practices were a necessary part of a successful AMC but were not sufficient to make the AMC great. Indeed, making decisions based on "business" rather than basing each decision on what would be best for achieving excellence in patient care could lead an institution to renege on its societal responsibility. Without a core focus on providing outstanding patient care, no AMC could effectively compete in the future healthcare market or successfully teach the next generation of clinicians. I also found that research was a critical component of all medical centers, regardless of whether their goal was to train community physicians or clinician scientists. In conversations with residents, postgraduate trainees, and students, I found that those who had participated in research as medical students or between college and medical school were more adept at critically reviewing clinical trials in the literature, better able to think through complex cases, and far more likely to pursue careers in academic medicine. This information not only had an effect on the construction of the model presented in this book but also resulted in our developing a resident research program to improve the educational experiences in our department.

I also found that the most successful AMCs were not composed of economically and administratively separate units but rather were closely linked by an integrated structure. Finally, in contrast with my original belief that AMCs should focus on their regional environments, I found that outstanding AMCs today must develop regional as well as national collaborations and affiliations in order to provide the best possible care for patients. Thus, although each of the elements of structure, research, education, and business was necessary to support the success of an AMC, none was sufficient in and of itself for an institution to achieve greatness. Only when these elements contributed synergistically to create an environment of outstanding patient care did an individual AMC excel.

Each of the four spheres that constitute the supporting structure of this book contains three chapters. These 12 chapters present recommendations for facilitating the ability of an AMC to attain excellence in patient care. They can be summarized as follows.

- *Sphere of Action I: Structure*
    Chapter 1: Integrate the elements of the AMC, including the hospital, the medical school, and the university, in order to align missions and facilitate funds flow.
    Chapter 2: Integrate clinical care delivery systems to ensure seamless communication between caregivers and care integrated across the many specialties that must be brought together in the treatment of a particular disease to provide outstanding patient care.
    Chapter 3: Develop leaders who can utilize lessons learned from industry, who can focus on preparing their successors, who are empowered to effect change, and who have the stability that allows them to make courageous decisions.
- *Sphere of Action II: Research*
    Chapter 4: Recognize that research is necessary for clinical excellence. Develop mechanisms for the health system and the hospital to support the research mission, enhance the development of translational research, allocate funds appropriately to ensure alignment between the clinical and research programs, and provide the necessary infrastructure to facilitate the ability of the AMC to recapture clinical research.
    Chapter 5: Resolve conflicts of interest in order to regain the public trust in AMCs and their faculty by developing rules that are fair, enforceable, and provide the needed level of confidence and trust for the patient.
    Chapter 6: Effectively commercialize research discoveries by providing an infrastructure that supports the ability of investigators to take their discoveries from the bench to the bedside.
- *Sphere of Action III: Education*
    Chapter 7: Resolve the physician workforce crisis by creating a national task force that can provide recommendations and guidance regarding the development of programs in elementary and secondary schools. These programs will encourage students to pursue careers in healthcare, address the serious issues of indebtedness, enhance public awareness of the looming crisis, and ensure that all schools meet the appropriate standards for producing outstanding clinicians.
    Chapter 8: Address the changing demographics of America's doctors by decreasing the debt of academic physicians, making academic medicine more attractive, creating a culture in the AMC that recognizes

the diverse needs and goals of women physicians, and enhancing the diversity of the AMC.

Chapter 9: Teach medical professionalism in the AMC by educating AMC leaders about how to deal with difficult issues of breaches in professionalism, developing metrics to assess the quality of care and professionalism of hospitals and individual caregivers, eliminating the "hidden curriculum" in AMCs by ensuring consistency between what is taught and what is practiced, and developing multidisciplinary teams to evaluate professionalism.

■ *Sphere of Action IV: Business*

Chapter 10: Develop innovative ways to finance the various missions of the AMC, including documenting the ability to deliver outstanding clinical care, developing a rational system for allocating funds, creating a national financial data bank that is available to investigators to facilitate systems analysis, and improving hospital efficiency and capacity.

Chapter 11: Expand the influence of the AMC and create novel new markets by undertaking global initiatives to provide outstanding care to the world's populations, developing novel collaborations in healthcare delivery that cross state boundaries, and establishing partnerships within local markets to improve care.

Chapter 12: Help federal agencies and Congress to recognize the need for AMCs and the federal government to collaborate in improving the health of the population while decreasing costs. This can be accomplished by establishing a national commission to oversee AMCs, establishing national guidelines for AMC financial reporting, developing a reimbursement system that is consistent from state to state, evaluating the plight of "safety-net" hospitals, working together to ensure consistency in medical education and healthcare across all AMCs, and convincing Congress that future improvements in America's healthcare depend on supporting research initiatives to better understand the delivery and economics of healthcare in the AMC.

Each of the chapters of this book presented recommendations that an AMC should consider in developing a mission of providing excellence in patient care. However, it is important for the reader to recognize that not every AMC needs to or can pursue every recommendation. The financial capabilities, geographic locale, and patient demographics will differ for each AMC, as will the level of competition that it faces from other AMCs and from community hospitals. These differences will dictate where an individual AMC will allocate its resources.

For example, some AMCs may already have excellence in each clinical area, a robust endowment, and a substantial hospital margin that allow them to provide free tuition for their students and to focus on global rather than local collaborations. By contrast, other AMCs may simply be unable to support excellence in all of their clinical missions and will need to collaborate actively within their regions to achieve their goals more effectively. However, many of the recommendations are relevant to virtually all AMCs, such as a need to train tomorrow's physicians and physician leaders, integrate care delivery systems, resolve conflicts of interest, address the changing demographics of the AMC workforce, enhance AMC diversity, and lobby governmental agencies for additional research support.

Regardless of size or geography, however, an AMC can only fulfill its societal mission if it focuses on the core mission of pursing excellence in patient care. This core mission can most effectively be attained through the cohesive interaction of the four supporting spheres: an integrated structure, a research enterprise, an educational mission focused on training today's and tomorrow's physicians, and a business-like approach to finance and administration.

Some of the recommendations provided might be viewed as quite radical. For example, moving to a service line environment might be contrary to the culture of many institutions—in particular, where the political and administrative power of department chairs is great. For many hospital administrators and deans, the thought that funds-flow information would be readily available to department chairs and division chiefs might also be unacceptable. Furthermore, the concept that competing AMCs could enhance their ability to fulfill their missions by merging or affiliating might be perceived as radical—particularly because so many high-profile mergers have failed. Indeed, a core focus on outstanding patient care is in and of itself radical because most AMCs still promote their tripartite missions of research, education, and clinical care. However, each of these proposals has been shown to improve the ability of some AMCs to improve patient care.

As importantly, at a time when many AMCs are struggling to compete in the increasingly competitive healthcare marketplace and many are adversely affected by the crisis in America's financial markets, it is time for AMCs to begin to take radical steps. As in a business, each of these steps should not be perceived as final. Rather, it will be important to define metrics that can be utilized to judge the success of each change on an ongoing basis so that AMC leaders can continually reevaluate the outcomes and pursue modifications or changes in the paradigm when the data do not confirm that the change has achieved its goals. Hopefully, these suggestions for change—both radical and obvious—will provide a platform for all members of the AMC to question their approach, discuss the issues, and initiate change when these introspections identify areas in which patient care can be improved.

For some AMCs, change is not easy. In an environment in which "culture eats strategy," the ability to modify or change decades-old paradigms is never easy. Thus, AMC leaders should call on the expertise of professionals in the areas of business, economics, and healthcare finance and change strategies to facilitate achieving the new goals for the institution. AMCs affiliated with schools of business can draw on expertise from individuals and programs located on their campuses. For AMCs that do not have access to a business school, numerous companies and consultants can provide help and training in developing teams, effecting change, analyzing processes, creating metrics, and allocating resources. AMCs should use consultants in two ways: (1) to help in executing change, and (2) to train individual AMC members from all levels of management as agents of change so that future initiatives can be led internally.

Although the stresses placed on today's AMCs by the current healthcare environment are unprecedented in size and scope, AMCs have met great challenges over the past century: the Great Depression of the early 1930's, two World Wars that drew many of the finest physician groups from major AMCs to the battle fronts in Europe and the Pacific, the entrance of managed care three decades ago, and the current catastrophic collapse of the financial market. Nevertheless, AMCs have stepped forward and continued to assure that their patients were cared for, that students and graduates were trained, and that new forms of care continued to be developed.

Clearly, AMCs will respond to the current challenges with the same level of innovation, commitment, and energy with which they solved earlier crises. This text can be helpful in educating physicians, academicians, policy analysts, healthcare economists, and federal and state authorities and regulators regarding the challenges faced by today's AMCs. The fundamental message of the book is that, by pursuing excellence, we can *preserve America's academic medical centers* and see to it that Americans of all ethnic, racial, and socioeconomic backgrounds will be able to count on AMCs to provide them with the best possible care.

Index

The Author

Arthur Feldman received his BA degree from Gettysburg College and MS and PhD degrees from the University of Maryland, following which he served as a postdoctoral fellow in physiology at the Johns Hopkins University School of Medicine. Dr. Feldman earned his medical degree from the Louisiana State University School of Medicine and then returned to Johns Hopkins, where he served as an intern, resident, and cardiology fellow. After joining the faculty in 1985, he was named the director of the Belfer Laboratory for Molecular Biology of Heart Failure and director of the Heart Failure Research Program at the Johns Hopkins University School of Medicine.

In 1994, Dr. Feldman joined the faculty at the University of Pittsburgh School of Medicine as the Harry S. Tack Professor of Medicine, chief of the Division of Cardiology, and director of the Cardiovascular Institute of the UPMC Health System. In 2002, he was named the Magee Professor of Medicine and chairman of the Department of Medicine at Jefferson Medical College. He is a past president of the Heart Failure Society of America and of the Association of Professors of Cardiology. He was recently named the editor-in-chief of *Clinical and Translational Science.*

Dr. Feldman has received numerous honors, including election to Alpha Omega Alpha, the Association of University Cardiologists, the American Society for Clinical Investigation, and the Association of American Physicians. He has chaired numerous multicenter clinical trials and his research in the molecular biology of heart failure has been published in over 200 peer-reviewed articles. In addition, he is the cofounder and a member of the board of directors of Cardiokine, Inc. Dr. Feldman lives in Wynnewood, Pennsylvania, with his wife, Susan, and two daughters, Emily Kate and Elizabeth Willa.

For Product Safety Concerns and Information please contact our EU
representative GPSR@taylorandfrancis.com
Taylor & Francis Verlag GmbH, Kaufingerstraße 24, 80331 München, Germany

www.ingramcontent.com/pod-product-compliance
Ingram Content Group UK Ltd.
Pitfield, Milton Keynes, MK11 3LW, UK
UKHW021056080625
459435UK00003B/24